THE CHILDREN'S
BIBLE

Stories retold by
Sally Tagholm

Reference spreads by
Peter Chrisp

THE CHILDREN'S
BIBLE

LONDON, NEW YORK,
MELBOURNE, MUNICH, AND DELHI

Senior Art Editor Jacqueline Swan
Project Art Editors Johnny Pau, Sheila Collins
Senior Editor Shaila Brown
Project Editors Victoria Heyworth-Dunne, Andrea Mills

Managing Editor Linda Esposito
Managing Art Editor Diane Thistlethwaite
Publishing Manager Andrew Macintyre
Category Publisher Laura Buller

Senior Jacket and Development Designer Yumiko Tahata
Jacket Editor Mariza O'Keeffe
Design Development Manager Sophia M. Tampakopoulos Turner

Picture Researcher Frances Vargo
DK Picture Library Liz Moore
Senior Production Controller Angela Graef
Production Editor Hitesh Patel
Cartographer David Atkinson

Old Testament Consultant Dr. Jean-Marc Heimerdinger
New Testament Consultant Dr. Steve Motyer
Religious Consultant Dr. Paul D. Murray
Historical Consultant Peter Chrisp

Illustrators
David Callow, Julian De Narvaez, Michelle Dabbs and Peter Mays, Peter Dennis,
Peter James Field, Yvonne Gilbert, Peter Malone, Nilesh Mistry, Neal Murren, and Steve Noon

First published in the United States in 2008 by
DK Publishing, 375 Hudson Street, New York, New York 10014

A catalog record for this book is available from the Library of Congress.
ISBN 978-0-7566-4019-4
Color reproduction by Media Development Printing Limited, UK
Printed and bound by Hung Hing, China

Bible quotes from the Holy Bible, New International Version

Discover more at
www.dk.com

CONTENTS

Books of the Bible

The Bible is the most important and widely read book in the history of the Western world. Its vision of a single, all-powerful God, concerned with individual human behavior, underlies three world religions: Judaism, Christianity, and Islam. The Bible has been translated into more than 2,000 languages. It is made up of 66 books, divided into two parts.

Link between the Testaments
Christians linked the Old and New Testaments, believing that many of the Jewish writings were really about Jesus Christ. For example, the New Testament describes Christ riding into Jerusalem on a donkey. This was thought to fulfill an Old Testament prophecy: "See, your king comes to you, righteous and having salvation, gentle and riding on a donkey" (Zechariah 9:9).

Two Testaments
The Bible is divided into the Jewish Bible, called the Old Testament by Christians, and the Christian New Testament. The Old Testament has the same 39 books as the Jewish Bible, but they are arranged differently. The Christian version follows the Septuagint (right), a Greek translation of the Jewish texts made in the 3rd century BCE.

St. Jerome
In the 4th century CE, Saint Jerome translated the Bible into Latin, the language used by the Church in western Europe. Jerome's Bible included a number of Jewish books written between Old and New Testament times. These are called the Apocrypha ("hidden books"). Although included in the Septuagint, Jews later excluded them from their Bible. Jerome said they were useful for teaching, but did not carry God's authority.

Dead Sea Scrolls
The Dead Sea Scrolls are a collection of Jewish writings found in pottery jars in Israel, dating from the 1st century BCE. They show that, at that time, there was no fixed "Bible" or agreed upon canon of sacred works. The final version of the Hebrew Bible was agreed on by Jewish rabbis (teachers) some time between 90 and 135 CE.

A book with pages

By 125 CE, Christians had stopped writing on long scrolls and were using the codex. A Roman invention, a codex was a book with pages: sheets of papyrus, written on both sides, which were bound together. Thanks to the codex, different books of the New Testament could be easily joined together. This is the oldest surviving codex of John's Gospel. It dates from the late 2nd century CE.

Shepherd of Hermas

Early Christian leaders disagreed over which books to include in the New Testament. This is a page from the oldest complete New Testament, dating from the 4th century CE. It includes a book called the "Shepherd of Hermas," containing a series of visions of a former slave, written in Rome. Although this was one of the most popular Christian writings of the time, it was later rejected by the Church.

Lindisfarne Gospels

Throughout the Middle Ages, Bibles, lovingly copied by hand and richly decorated, were the most prized possessions of royal courts, monasteries, and churches. This is a beautifully illustrated page from the Lindisfarne Gospels, written in Northumbria, England, in the 8th century CE.

In print

In the 1440s, a German named Johannes Gutenberg invented printing with moveable type. The very first book he printed was a beautiful Latin Bible (above). It was designed to look as if it had been written by hand. Thanks to Gutenberg's invention, the Bible became available to a mass audience for the first time. Since Gutenberg's day, billions of Bibles have been printed, and it remains the best-selling book of all time.

Covenants

The word "covenant" means a formal agreement. The central theme of the Bible is that God has established a series of covenants. The Old Testament describes covenants made between God and the Israelites, his chosen people. In the New Testament, Jesus Christ offers a new covenant to all humanity. Such covenants are always marked with a solemn action, such as sacrifice, setting up a stone, or sharing a sacred meal.

Abraham's covenant
After Noah's flood, God makes a covenant with Abraham, who is childless and landless. God promises him that he will father a great nation, provided that he circumcises himself and his male descendants. Jewish boys are still circumcised today, fulfilling Abraham's covenant.

Noah's rainbow
The first book of the Bible describes a universal flood, sent by God to destroy wicked humanity. He spares only the just Noah and his family. God then makes a covenant with Noah, promising to send no more great floods. As a sign of His promise, God sets a rainbow in the sky.

The Commandments
The most important covenant in the Old Testament is made by God with Moses on Mount Sinai. God says that He has chosen Israel to be a "kingdom of priests and a holy nation" (Exodus 19:6). The Israelites must obey all God's laws, the most important being the Ten Commandments, written on stone tablets.

Stone of Shechem

After conquering the Promised Land, the Israelites, led by Joshua, renew their covenant with God, promising to follow Moses's laws and reject other gods. Joshua sets up a great stone at Shechem, saying that it "will be a witness against you if you are untrue to your God." (Joshua 24:27)

King David

King David is the Biblical hero who transforms the Israelite tribes into a nation. God makes a covenant with David, promising that his "throne will be established forever" (II Samuel 7:16). Here, David brings the Ark of the Covenant, holding the Ten Commandments, into Jerusalem.

Prophet Jeremiah

In the 6th century BCE, David's holy city, Jerusalem, was destroyed by the Babylonians. The prophet Jeremiah (left) explained that God had punished His people for breaking His covenants. However, Jeremiah said that one day God would make a new covenant with Israel, offering forgiveness for sins.

Christ's new covenant

For Christians, Jeremiah's promise of a new covenant was fulfilled by Jesus Christ. Through his death, Christ was thought to offer a new covenant to humanity. Faithful Christians were promised forgiveness for their sins and offered eternal life. Christ marked this covenant at his last supper, when he shared wine with his disciples, saying, "This cup is the new covenant in my blood, which is poured out for you." (Luke 22:20)

Lands of the Bible

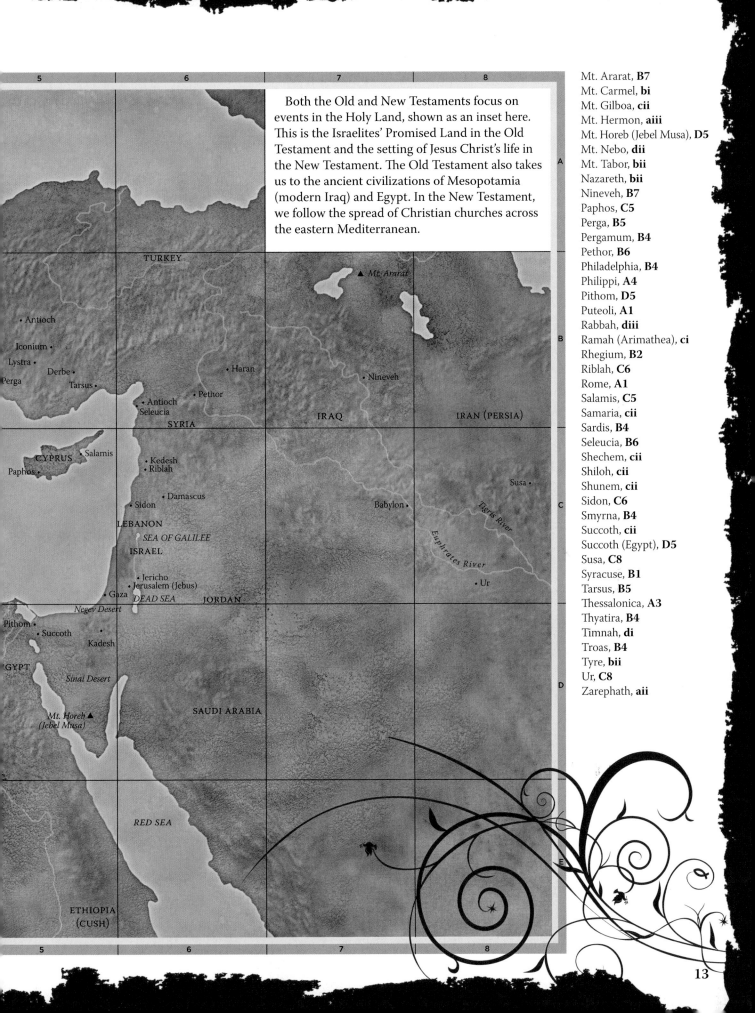

Both the Old and New Testaments focus on events in the Holy Land, shown as an inset here. This is the Israelites' Promised Land in the Old Testament and the setting of Jesus Christ's life in the New Testament. The Old Testament also takes us to the ancient civilizations of Mesopotamia (modern Iraq) and Egypt. In the New Testament, we follow the spread of Christian churches across the eastern Mediterranean.

Mt. Ararat, **B7**
Mt. Carmel, **bi**
Mt. Gilboa, **cii**
Mt. Hermon, **aiii**
Mt. Horeb (Jebel Musa), **D5**
Mt. Nebo, **dii**
Mt. Tabor, **bii**
Nazareth, **bii**
Nineveh, **B7**
Paphos, **C5**
Perga, **B5**
Pergamum, **B4**
Pethor, **B6**
Philadelphia, **B4**
Philippi, **A4**
Pithom, **D5**
Puteoli, **A1**
Rabbah, **diii**
Ramah (Arimathea), **ci**
Rhegium, **B2**
Riblah, **C6**
Rome, **A1**
Salamis, **C5**
Samaria, **cii**
Sardis, **B4**
Seleucia, **B6**
Shechem, **cii**
Shiloh, **cii**
Shunem, **cii**
Sidon, **C6**
Smyrna, **B4**
Succoth, **cii**
Succoth (Egypt), **D5**
Susa, **C8**
Syracuse, **B1**
Tarsus, **B5**
Thessalonica, **A3**
Thyatira, **B4**
Timnah, **di**
Troas, **B4**
Tyre, **bii**
Ur, **C8**
Zarephath, **aii**

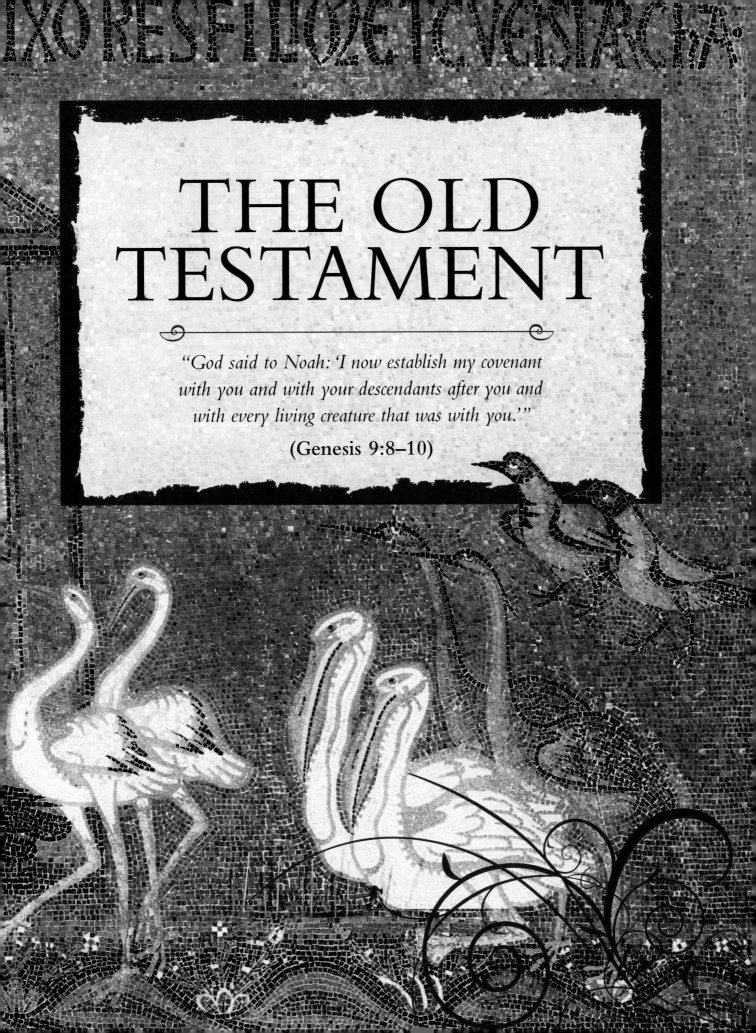

THE OLD TESTAMENT

"God said to Noah: 'I now establish my covenant with you and with your descendants after you and with every living creature that was with you.'"

(Genesis 9:8–10)

Old Testament

The Old Testament is the Christian name for the Tanakh, or Jewish Bible. This is named after the first letters of its three Hebrew sections: Torah, Neviim, and Kethubim. It is a collection of books telling the story of the Israelites, and their dealings with God. The books were mostly written down between the 8th and 3rd centuries BCE, although some of the stories they tell may be much older.

The Torah
The first five books of the Tanakh are called the Torah ("instruction"), also known as the Five Books of Moses or Pentateuch ("five books" in Greek). The Torah tells the story of the Israelites down to their entry into the Promised Land, and records an enormous number of ritual laws. The Torah scroll is the most precious object in every synagogue, where it is kept in a richly decorated case.

Prophets
The Torah is followed by the section called Neviim ("prophets"), eight books recording the words of Israelite prophets. Prophet is a Greek word, meaning "someone who speaks on behalf of a god." Prophets like Ezekiel (right) were ordinary people who felt inspired to voice God's will. They were not fortune-tellers; they were concerned with warning their fellow Israelites about the consequences of disobedience to God.

Writings
The last section of the Tanakh, called Kethubim ("writings"), comprises 11 books, written in a wide variety of styles. These include songs, poems, wise sayings, and short stories. There are also historical works that serve as commentaries on earlier books. Three of the books, called Proverbs, Ecclesiastes, and the Song of Songs, were said to have been written by King Solomon (right), famed for his wisdom.

The name of God

The most sacred word in the Old Testament is the name of God, spelled YHWH, as Hebrew was written without vowels. You can see the Hebrew letters in this Greek Bible text. We do not know how it was pronounced, because it came to be seen as so sacred that it was never spoken aloud, and Jews forgot how to say it.

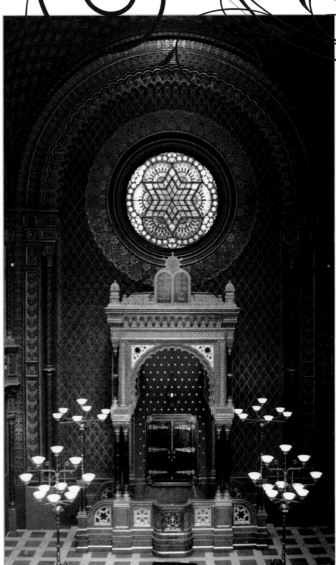

Solomon's Temple

Several books describe worship in the Temple of Jerusalem, where animal sacrifices were offered to God by priests. For example, Leviticus gives detailed instructions for offering sacrifice, and describes the white linen robes of the priests, shown in this painting. Here, King Solomon is bringing the Ark of the Covenant, a sacred shrine, into his Temple.

Synagogue

Following the final destruction of the Temple by the Romans in 70 CE, Jewish religion was reinvented. There were no more priests, and sacrifices could no longer be offered to God. Instead, the synagogue, or assembly place, became the focus of prayer and study, under teachers called rabbis. In this ornate synagogue, you can see the wooden chest where the precious Torah scroll is kept.

The Creation

*I*n the beginning, God created the heavens and the earth. It was a dark and watery place at first, with no form, no shape, no beginning, no end. The entire surface of the earth was covered with deep, black water.

There was no life, but the Spirit of God hovered over the dark face of the waters and He said, "Let there be light." And there was light. He separated the light from the darkness and called the light day and the darkness night. And that was the first day.

On the second day, God said, "Let there be a space above the earth to separate the waters below from the waters above." And He called it sky.

On the third day, God said, "Let the water under the sky be gathered to one place and let dry ground appear." He called the dry ground land and the waters seas. At once, trees, plants, and shoots burst through the ground. And God saw that it was good.

On the fourth day, God said, "Let there be lights in the sky to separate day from night and to mark the seasons and days and years." He made a great shining orb, which He called sun, to light the day. And He made a paler companion, which He called moon, to shine at night. Around the moon He placed the stars like jewels.

On the fifth day, God said, "Let the water teem with living creatures and let birds fly across the sky." And He created all the creatures of the sea and all the feathered birds of the air. And God saw that it was good.

On the sixth day, God said, "Let there be living creatures on the land." And He covered the earth with creatures of all shapes and sizes, from the tiniest flea to the mightiest lion. Then God said, "Let us make man in our image, in our likeness, and let them rule over the fish of the sea and the birds of the air, and over all the creatures that move along the ground." And He made the first man and blessed him, saying, "Be fruitful and increase in number." God looked at everything that He had made in heaven and earth and He was pleased.

On the seventh day, His work was complete, so He rested and He blessed the day and made it holy.

"God looked at everything that He had made in heaven and earth and He was pleased."

*Eve picks a fruit
from the Tree
of Knowledge*

The Garden of Eden

*The Lord God made a beautiful garden in Eden for the
man He had created. It was watered by a sparkling
river and was green and shady—an earthly paradise.*

There were trees heavy with fruit so that the man would never go hungry, and in the
middle of the garden stood the Tree of Life and the Tree of Knowledge of Good and
Evil. And the Lord God named the man Adam and took him to his new home. He told
him that he must take care of it. "You are free to eat from any tree in the garden, but
you must not eat from the Tree of Knowledge of Good and Evil, for when you eat of it,
you will surely die." He brought the beasts of the field and the birds of the air to Adam
and asked him to give them names. But, although God was very pleased with His work
so far, there was one thing that still worried Him. Adam was on his own in the world.

One day, God made Adam fall into a deep sleep and, while he was dreaming, cut open his side and took out one of his ribs. Then, He closed him up again and made a woman out of the bone. The man and the woman stood there happily together in the Garden of Eden.

Now, of all the animals that God had created, the craftiest was the snake. As soon as he spotted the woman in the Garden of Eden, he slithered down the tree and hissed at her, "Did God really say that you must not eat from any tree in the garden?" The woman told him what God had said to Adam about the Tree of Knowledge. "How ridiculous!" spat the snake. "You won't die! When you eat from the Tree of Knowledge, you will become wise and you will be like God! You will know good and evil."

Tempted by the fruit that would make her wise, the woman picked one and sank her teeth into its juicy flesh. Then she gave it to Adam and he ate it all. At once, their eyes were opened and they realized that they were naked. Full of shame, they found some fig leaves that they sewed together to hide their nakedness. They were so ashamed that they ran and hid in the trees when they heard the Lord God walking in the garden in the cool of the day. "Where are you?" called God.

"you must not eat from the Tree of Knowledge of Good and Evil"

"I heard you and I hid," admitted Adam. "I was afraid because I was naked." And when God asked him who had told him he was naked, Adam replied, "The woman you put here with me—she gave me some fruit from the Tree of Knowledge and I ate it."

"The snake tricked me and I ate from the Tree!" cried the woman. Then, the Lord God cursed the snake and banished him from the Garden of Eden.

To the woman He said, "With pain you will give birth to children." And, turning to Adam, He said, "Through painful toil you will eat of the ground all the days of your life. Dust you are and to dust you will return."

The Lord God made clothes for Adam and his wife, whom He named Eve because she would become the mother of all the men and women. And He said to them, "You now know good and evil. Whatever happens you must not eat from the Tree of Life or you would live forever." And He banished the pair from the paradise garden. At the gates of the Garden of Eden, God put winged cherubim and a fiery, ever-turning sword to guard the way to the Tree of Life. Adam and Eve could never return.

Adam and Eve are banished from the Garden of Eden

Cain and Abel

After Adam and Eve had been banished from the Garden of Eden, their first son, Cain, was born. Time went by and Eve gave birth to another boy. They named him Abel.

As the two brothers grew toward manhood, Cain worked in the fields, taking care of the crops, while Abel roamed the hills looking after the sheep and lambs. They both made offerings to the Lord, Cain bringing the fruits of his crops and Abel bringing the finest meat from his lambs. The Lord was greatly pleased with Abel's offerings, but not with his brother's. Cain could not believe it! He was filled with anger—against God, against his brother, and against the unfairness of life.

"Why are you so angry?" God asked. "Do what is right and all will be well. But if not, sin is lurking at your door, ready to devour you. Watch out!"

But Cain was possessed with murderous thoughts and lured his brother to a field far from home. There he attacked and killed him. The Lord asked where his brother was and Cain replied, "I don't know. Am I my brother's keeper?"

> "Do what is right and all will be well."

God, who sees everything, said, "Cain, what have you done? Your brother's blood cries out to me from the ground where it was spilled. You are cursed—as long as you live. You are an outcast from man and from God, condemned to wander the world for the rest of your days."

"My punishment is more than I can bear," wailed Cain. "I have lost everything, driven from the land and from God. I am homeless and will spend my life on the road, at the mercy of murderers."

But the Lord reassured him that anyone who killed him would suffer the most terrible vengeance—seven times greater even than his own punishment. He put a special mark on Cain to keep him safe. Cain went on his way to the land of Nod, east of Eden.

In a fit of jealousy, Cain kills his brother

Noah and the Flood

Adam's descendants increased and multiplied, and so did their wickedness and corruption.

The Lord saw it all and said, "I will wipe humankind, whom I have created, from the face of the Earth for I am grieved that I have made them."

But Noah was different. He alone was righteous. The Lord spoke to him telling him that there would be a great flood. He instructed him to make a huge ark out of cypress wood and to cover it with tar, inside and out, to make it seaworthy. Noah and his wife, and their three sons and their wives, must go into the ark and they would be saved. With them, they must take two of every kind of bird or creature—one male and one female—that walked or creeped or slithered across the Earth and plenty of food to go around.

> "Noah listened and did exactly what the Lord God had commanded him."

Noah listened and did exactly what the Lord God had commanded him. With the help of his three sons, Shem, Ham, and Japheth, he worked patiently, day and night. Bit by bit the great ship took shape as they skillfully sawed and smoothed and planed the cypress lumber, then hammered and coated the ark with pitch. At last it was finished.

And God said to Noah, "Seven days from now I will send rain on the Earth for forty days and forty nights, and I will wipe from the face of the Earth every living creature that I have made." Noah quickly set to work to find the creatures that God had told him he must save and lead them into the safety of the ark. And when the very last pair had scurried in, Noah and his wife followed them. And, just at that moment, the clouds gathered and the heavens opened.

It rained and it rained and it rained, and steadily the waters crept over the face of the Earth. Almost every living thing perished except for Noah and the animals on the wooden ark. Then, after many days, God sent a strong wind that raced and whistled around the world, drying up the water. Slowly but surely, the levels began to drop.

Just as God had instructed, Noah and his sons build an ark

One day, the ark shuddered to a halt. It had run aground on the top of Mount Ararat, surrounded by a vast expanse of sea. Noah wondered whether there might be any dry land over the horizon. So he chose a raven and launched the bird into the air to search for land. But it flew back. Noah tried again, this time choosing a dove. But she returned to the ark, too. Seven days later, he sent her out again and she flew back, triumphant, with an olive leaf.

When the Earth had emerged once more, God spoke to Noah. "Come out of the ark, you and your wife and your sons and their wives. Bring out every kind of living creature that is with you so they can multiply on the Earth."

So they all came out of the ark for the first time in many months. Noah built an altar to the Lord and made sacrifices on it. The Lord was pleased and said, "Never again will I curse the ground because of humankind, even though their heart is inclined toward evil from childhood. And never again will I destroy all living creatures, as I have done."

A beautiful rainbow appeared as He made a covenant with them that life on Earth would never again be destroyed by flood. And He said, "I have set my rainbow in the clouds, and it will be the sign of the covenant between me and the Earth. Whenever the rainbow appears in the clouds, I will see it and remember the everlasting covenant."

The Tower of Babel

*A*fter the great flood, centuries passed and Noah's descendants gradually peopled the earth. Generation followed generation, and the clans of his sons, Shem, Ham, and Japheth, flourished and prospered.

They spread in every direction, all speaking one common language so that, wherever they went, they could understand each other. And in the east they found a wide and fertile plain in Shinar, which became known as Babylonia. They settled there, and life was pleasant. "Come, let us build a city, with a tower that reaches to the heavens, so that we may make a name for ourselves and not be scattered over the face of the earth," the people said to one another. After all their wanderings, this seemed a good idea. It would be the first city to be built since the flood, and the tower would be its crowning glory, admired by the whole world. It would be made of bricks instead of stone, and it would climb up to the stars.

They mixed mud and straw to make the bricks, baking them in the sun, and stirred vats of bitumen, like molasses, to use as mortar. Teams of builders set to work and, slowly, the city began to take shape.

"But the Lord was not pleased with the vanity and pride that He saw."

And the tower rose steadily from the ground, climbing higher and higher into the sky, as if it wanted to reach heaven itself. The finest craftsmen decorated the tower with precious stones. Steep flights of steps zigzagged breathtakingly up and up, through the clouds to the very top. The people marveled at their great achievement and congratulated each other. Even the eagles, flying above, looked down in astonishment.

But the Lord was not pleased with the vanity and pride that He saw. "After this, nothing will be impossible for these people. They are reaching too high! I will bring them down to earth and confuse them so that they no longer speak the same language," He said. And suddenly, the air was filled with a terrifying noise. It was the deafening babble of thousands of voices, each speaking a different language. Nobody could understand what anyone else was saying. Panic-stricken, people shouted and screamed, trying to make themselves understood, but the words that came out made no sense. It was a hideous chorus that shook the city to its foundations and gave it the name of Babel.

Confused and unable to communicate with each other, the people were not able to go on building their city. Instead, they were scattered over the face of the earth, speaking their different languages.

No matter how much they yelled or shouted, the people could not understand each other

Mesopotamia

This map shows the world's very first cities, which were built in Mesopotamia (shaded orange).

Mesopotamia (now modern Iraq) means "the land between the rivers." It was beside these rivers, the Tigris and the Euphrates, that the world's first civilization developed, after 3500 BCE. The Sumerians, who lived in southern Mesopotamia, built the first cities, and invented writing, kingship, law codes, and organized religion, with priests and temples. Their civilization influenced the earliest stories in the Bible.

Floods

The Tigris and the Euphrates were unpredictable rivers, which flooded the flat plains every year. Civilization developed when people learned to work together, digging canals and reservoirs to channel and store the water. The story of a great flood was first told in Mesopotamia.

TIMELINE

c. 3500–2800 BCE
The Sumerians of southern Mesopotamia build the world's first cities.

c. 2330 BCE
King Sargon of Akkad, in central Mesopotamia, conquers Sumer.

c. 2200 BCE
The Gutians from the eastern mountains conquer Akkad and Sumer.

c. 2113–2096 BCE
Reign of King Ur-Nammu of Ur, who drives out the Gutians.

c. 1900 BCE
The Amorites, from the west, conquer much of Mesopotamia, ruling from Babylon.

1792–1750 BCE
Reign of King Hammurabi of Babylon, who rules over Akkad and Sumer, a region now called Babylonia.

c. 1600 BCE
The Hittites, from the west, and the Kassites, from the east, invade Mesopotamia.

1595–1185 BCE
The Kassites rule Babylonia from their capital, Babylon, which they rename Karanduniash.

1185–65 BCE
The Kassites are overthrown by the Elamites, who sack Babylon.

911 BCE
The Assyrians, from northern Mesopotamia, begin their rise to power.

Ziggurats

Every city was thought to belong to a god, whose home was a huge stepped temple, called a ziggurat. Shown above is the restored lower level of the ziggurat of Ur. The Tower of Babel in the Bible was probably based on a Mesopotamian ziggurat.

War

From early times, warfare was common in Mesopotamia. Rival cities fought each other, and were attacked by foreign invaders from the east and west. This carving, made about 2450 BCE, shows King Enneatum of Lagash leading his army into war against a neighboring city.

Royal banquet

This mosaic, of blue lapis lazuli, red sandstone, and white shell, was made in Ur, about 2500 BCE. It shows a royal banquet, with the king seated on the left. Beneath, ordinary people lead farm animals and carry goods in a procession to the palace.

Divine laws

On this carving, King Hammurabi of Babylon stands before Shamash, the god of justice. Beneath are written 282 laws, set out like the laws of Moses. One law, echoed in the Bible, says that a person who puts out another's eye would lose their own eye.

Golden goat

A beautiful statuette, from a royal grave in Ur, shows a male goat standing on its hind legs to eat the leaves of a tree. It is made of gold, lapis lazuli, and shell—materials brought to Mesopotamia from other lands.

29

Abram's Journey

*A*bram was seventy-five years old and he lived in Haran not too far from the Euphrates River in Mesopotamia. He was married to Sarai but, to their great sadness, they had no children.

One day, the Lord came to Abram and told him to leave his country and move to the land of Canaan. "I will make you into a great nation and I will bless you," He promised. "I will make your name great and I will bless those who bless you, and whoever curses you, I will curse. And all the peoples on the earth will be blessed through you." So Abram set off, taking with him Sarai, his nephew Lot, and their servants. The camels were laden with all their possessions and their flocks straggled behind. When they arrived in Canaan, they traveled as far as the great tree of Moreh at Shechem.

> "All the land that you see—north, south, east, and west—I will give you and your offspring forever."

There, the Lord appeared to Abram. He promised, "To your offspring I will give this land." And Abram built an altar there and gave thanks. Then he went on toward the hills east of Bethel and built another altar to the Lord. After this, he continued his wandering toward the Negev and beyond.

Finally, Abram came back to the place near Bethel, where he had built the altar. But, by now, after so long traveling, Abram and his nephew, Lot, were not seeing eye to eye. They both had large flocks of sheep and goats and there was never enough good grazing to go around. Their herdsmen were constantly arguing. At last, Abram said to Lot, "Let's not quarrel. There is plenty of land. Let's part company. You go one way and I'll go the other."

Lot agreed and chose to go to the fertile plain of Jordan, where he settled near the city of Sodom, renowned for its wickedness and sin. Abram stayed in Canaan, and the Lord said to him, "All the land that you see—north, south, east, and west—I will give you and your offspring forever."

But Abram replied, "What can you give me since I remain childless?"

The Lord promised him that, one day, he would have a son and heir, and that he would have as many descendants as stars in the sky. Then the Lord sealed His promise to Abram, "Bring a heifer, a goat, and a ram—each three years old—and a dove and a young pigeon." Abram did as he was told, and put them on the altar.

As the sun set, Abram fell asleep and the Lord said, "Know for certain that your descendants will be strangers in a country not their own and they will be enslaved and ill-treated for four hundred years."

When darkness had fallen, a smoking brazier with a blazing torch appeared in front of Abram. And in this way the Lord made a covenant with him and promised, "To your descendants I give this land from the river of Egypt to the great river, the Euphrates."

Abram's Two Sons

Ten years had passed since Abram arrived in the land of Canaan with his wife, Sarai, and still they had no children. They were old now, and perhaps it was impossible.

They had, however, a young Egyptian maidservant named Hagar, and one day Sarai went to her husband with a plan. Abram should take Hagar as his wife and have a child with her. At least they might be able to start a family like that. Abram agreed and, before long, Hagar was pregnant. But as soon as she knew she was going to have a baby, Hagar got ideas above her station and began to be rude toward her mistress.

Sarai complained to Abram, "I put my servant in your arms and now that she knows she is pregnant, she despises me!"

"Do what you think best," replied Abram. So Sarai began to treat her maidservant with such cruelty that Hagar ran away to hide in the desert. An angel found her weeping by the side of a spring, and Hagar told him the whole story. He said that she must go back and that she would have a son named Ishmael. So Hagar returned and gave birth to Abram's son, who was named Ishmael. Abram was eighty-six years old at the time.

> "I will give you the whole of Canaan as an everlasting possession."

Sarah hears the Lord say that she will have a son

Thirteen years later, the Lord appeared to Abram again and made a covenant with him. "You will be the father of many nations. No longer will you be called Abram; your name will be Abraham. I will establish my covenant as an everlasting covenant between me and you and your descendants after you for the generations to come, to be your God and the God of your descendants after you. I will give you the whole of Canaan as an everlasting possession." And He went on to say that, as a sign of the covenant, every male must be circumcised and that, from now on, Sarai must be known as Sarah. "I will bless her and will surely give you a son by her," He added.

"But I am nearly one hundred years old! And Sarah is ninety!" said Abraham.

The Lord replied, "Sarah will indeed give you a son and you will call him Isaac. I will establish my covenant with him as an everlasting covenant for his descendants after him." And He said that He would also bless Ishmael. "He will be the father of a great nation. But my covenant I will establish with Isaac, who will be born next year." And that very day, Abraham and Ishmael—and every male in the household—were circumcised as the Lord had ordered.

Some time later, Abraham was sitting at the entrance to his tent, near the great trees of Mamre, when the Lord paid him a visit. It was the middle of the day and the heat was intense. Abraham noticed three men standing nearby in the full glare of the sun. He went and greeted them, bowing low on the ground, and invited them to rest in the shade of the trees. "I will get water so that you can wash your feet and please let me give you something to eat," he said. He hurried back into the tent and asked Sarah to bake some bread with the finest flour. Then he ordered the servants to kill a tender young calf and prepare it for the strangers, and to bring some curd and milk. They enjoyed their meal in the shade of the trees and asked Abraham, "Where is your wife, Sarah?"

"There, in the tent," he replied.

The Lord said, "I will surely return to you about this time next year and Sarah, your wife, will have a son." From the tent, Sarah heard these words and laughed to herself at the thought.

And the Lord was not pleased and said to Abraham, "Why did Sarah laugh? Nothing is impossible for God." And, sure enough, when it was time, Sarah gave birth to a boy. They named him Isaac and, when he was eight days old, Abraham circumcised him. "God has brought me laughter and everyone who hears about this will laugh with me," rejoiced Sarah.

But one thing spoiled her joy—and that was Ishmael. She did not like the way he taunted Isaac. She asked her husband to get rid of him and his mother, too. Abraham was saddened by this, but the Lord told him not to worry. "Listen to what Sarah says, because it is through Isaac that your line will be continued. I will take care of Ishmael."

So, early next morning, Abraham gave Hagar some food and water and sent her on her way with Ishmael. It was not long before their food ran out and their water skin ran dry, and Hagar knew that they could not last long in the desert of Beersheba. She put her son under a bush and walked away. She could not bear to watch him die. Then she collapsed on the ground, shut her eyes, and wept.

An angel spoke to her from heaven, saying, "Don't be afraid. Go back to the boy and lift him up and take him by the hand. God will not let him die. He will become the leader of a great nation!" At that, Hagar opened her eyes and saw a well full of sparkling water in front of her. She filled her water skin to the brim and took it back to Ishmael. And God looked after him as he grew up in the desert. He was strong and fearless. In time, his mother found a wife for him from Egypt, the land of her birth.

Just as the angel had instructed, Hagar returns to her son

Sodom and Gomorrah

*T*he twin cities of Sodom and Gomorrah, on the fertile plains of
the Jordan River, were awful places. Awash with sin, the people
led wicked lives, satisfying every desire.

The Lord saw it all and made up His mind to destroy the cities and wipe them from the face
of the earth. But Abraham asked Him, "Will you sweep away the righteous with the wicked?
Just suppose that there are fifty God-fearing people who live there?" The Lord agreed and said he
would spare the cities. Apologizing for his boldness, Abraham pressed Him further. Exactly how
many—or how few—righteous people would it take for God to show mercy and to spare the cities?
In the end, the Lord replied, "For the sake of ten, I will not destroy Sodom and Gomorrah."

That evening, two angels disguised as men arrived in Sodom, and Abraham's nephew, Lot, was
sitting by the city gates. He greeted the visitors, bowing low on the ground. "My lords, please do
me the honor of coming to my house. You can wash your feet there and spend the night, then go on
your way in the morning." At first, they refused, wanting to stay in the square, but Lot insisted and,
in the end, they agreed. The angels went home with him, and Lot prepared a splendid meal
for them and baked loaves of special bread without any yeast.

But as darkness fell, a great crowd of thugs surrounded the house, looking for trouble. "Where are those nice young men who have just arrived?" they jeered. "We'll show them a good time!"

Lot bravely went out to confront them. "No, my friends," he said. "I have two beloved daughters. I would rather give them to you than let anything happen to the guests who are staying under my roof."

"You don't belong here, anyway," they shouted. "Just you wait! We'll give you a good seeing to, as well!" They surged forward to grab him, but the angels managed to reach out from the doorway and pull him inside to safety just in time. And then the angels blinded the mob so that suddenly none of them could see. Sightless, they stumbled over each other in the dark, arms outstretched like sleep walkers, trying to find their way home.

The angels said to Lot, "Do you have any other family here? Sons or daughters or sons-in-law? Get them out because we're going to destroy the place!" Immediately, Lot hurried to talk to his sons-in-law and told them that the Lord was going to raze the city to the ground. But they thought he was joking and took no notice.

"There was no sign of the two cities. It was as if they had never existed."

As dawn broke, the angels begged Lot to save himself. "Hurry! Take your wife and your two daughters and leave! Otherwise you will all perish!" But Lot hesitated. Then the two angels took him and his wife and their two daughters, and led them to safety outside the city walls. There they told them that they must run for it. "Don't look back, whatever you do, and don't stop on the plain! Flee to the mountains or there's no hope!"

"No!" said Lot. "You have shown great kindness to me in sparing my life. But I can't flee to the mountains. It is too far. Let me take refuge in that little town over there on the edge of the plain. It's called Zoar." The angels agreed and told him he would be safe there.

By the time that Lot reached Zoar, the Lord had put his plan into action. He began the destruction of Sodom and Gomorrah. It was a terrifying sight as burning sulfur rained down from the heavens on the two cities, turning them into one gigantic inferno. Flames licked high in the air, devouring everything in their path. There was no escape. Everything that lived or breathed there died an agonizing death that day and the surrounding plains were reduced to charred and blackened cinders.

And Lot's wife forgot what the angels had told them and, as she fled from the flames, she turned around for one last look. Immediately, she was rooted to the ground and turned into a pillar of salt, never to move again. The next morning, Abraham got up and looked down. There was no sign of the two cities. It was as if they had never existed.

Genesis 22

The Sacrifice of Isaac

The Lord came to Abraham again and gave him the ultimate test of his faith. "Take your beloved son, Isaac, and go to the mountains of Moriah. Sacrifice him there as a burnt offering. I will show you where."

Early the next morning, Abraham got up, with a heavy heart, and prepared to make the long journey through the desert. He packed food and water, then saddled his donkey and set off from Beersheba with Isaac and two servants. Slowly they traveled through southern Canaan until the mountains loomed before them. It took them three days, but to Abraham it seemed a lifetime.

They stopped in the foothills to cut some firewood from the trees, choosing young branches of chestnut and poplar, which would burn well on the altar. Abraham told the servants to wait. "Stay here with the donkey while the boy and I go up there. We will worship and then we will come back to you."

He gave the bundles of wood to Isaac to carry on his back. It was a heavy load for the young boy, but he did not complain. Abraham took a sharp knife and a blazing torch to light the fire on the altar. Father and son trudged up the steep path, side by side, but Isaac was puzzled. He said to Abraham, "The fire and the wood are here, but where is the lamb that we are going to sacrifice?"

"God himself will provide the lamb for the burnt offering, my son," replied Abraham quietly, avoiding his eyes. They continued up the mountain and when they got to the highest peak, Abraham finally stopped and built an altar out of stone. He took the wood from his son and arranged it on top. Isaac watched him curiously and looked around. There was no sign of a lamb or any other creature that could be offered to God as a sacrifice. Abraham went over to his son and gripped him tightly. He took a length of rope and tied him up so that he could not move. Then he laid the boy on the altar.

> "You have proved your love of God. You were willing to sacrifice your son for Him."

With a breaking heart, Abraham reached for his knife and held it high in the air, ready to plunge it into his son. But just at that moment, the angel of the Lord called out from above, "Abraham! Abraham! Do not lay a hand on the boy. Do not do anything to him. You have proved your love of God. You were willing to sacrifice your son for Him."

Abraham dropped the knife and released his son, embracing him tenderly. Then, he looked around and saw a mountain ram that had got its horns caught in a bush. Abraham went over and untangled the animal, then slit its throat and offered it as a sacrifice on the altar, instead of his son. He set light to the wood under it and the flames charred the carcass.

And the angel of the Lord called to Abraham for a second time. "Because you have done this for the love of God and would have given your beloved son, you are blessed. Your descendants will be as numerous as the stars in the sky and the sand on the seashore. They will gain control of the cities of their enemies and, through your offspring, all nations on earth will be blessed."

Then, Abraham took Isaac back down the steep mountain to rejoin his servants and, together, they made the journey home to Beersheba.

A mountain ram tangled in a bush is sacrificed instead of Isaac

The servant waits by the well as Rebekah arrives

Isaac and Rebekah

*A*braham was a very old man by now and he was blessed in every way. But he knew that he would not live forever and that there was still one thing that he must sort out before he died.

He called his most trusted servant and asked for his help. "Please put your hand on your heart and swear that you will go back to the country where I was born and find a wife for my son Isaac. I do not want him to marry anyone from around here in Canaan."

The servant pointed out that it might not be easy to persuade a young woman to leave her home and family so far behind. "Why don't I take your son with me back to the country you came from?" he asked.

"No," answered Abraham. "Whatever you do, don't take Isaac with you. The Lord, the God of heaven, will send His angel with you to help find a wife for my son."

So Abraham's loyal servant set out on his mission, taking ten of his master's camels, laden with gifts. He headed for the town in northwest Mesopotamia, where Abraham's brother, Nahor, lived.

He arrived just as the young women were coming down to the well with their jars to fetch water. He stopped, and his camels kneeled down on the ground after their long journey.

And Abraham's servant looked at the young women gathering around the well and he prayed, "O Lord, help me! How will I know who is the one? Please give me a sign. Could it be the one who offers me a drink from her jar and offers to water my camels?"

As he was praying, a beautiful girl arrived, carrying her jar gracefully on her shoulder. She knelt down and drew some water from the well, and Abraham's servant hurried up to her and asked for a drink. "Of course. You are welcome, my lord!" she said. "And what about your camels? They must be thirsty, too." After he had drunk, she emptied all her water into the trough and ran back to the well for more so that the camels could have a good drink.

> "Take her and let her become the wife of your master's son, as the Lord has directed."

Abraham's servant was so pleased that he reached into his bag of gifts and gave her a solid gold nose ring and two heavy gold bracelets. "Whose daughter are you?" he asked. "Please tell me, would there be a room in your father's house where I could spend the night?"

She replied that she was called Rebekah and that she was the daughter of Bethuel and the granddaughter of Nahor. She said that he was welcome to stay the night in her father's house and ran back to tell her family. Her brother, Laban, went straight out to meet the stranger. He knew immediately that the stranger was blessed by the Lord and welcomed him into the house, offering him food.

But Abraham's servant would not eat before he explained why he had come. "I am the servant of Abraham. He has one son, Isaac, and I have been sent to find him a wife here, in the country of Abraham's birth. And the Lord has led me to Rebekah, the granddaughter of my master's brother. She has been chosen."

Laban and Bethuel listened, knowing that it was the will of God, and they answered, "Here is Rebekah. Take her and let her become the wife of your master's son, as the Lord has directed." And the servant gave more jewelry to Rebekah—both gold and silver—and beautiful embroidered clothes. He also gave special gifts to her brother and mother. They would have liked Rebekah to stay with them for a few more days to say goodbye, but Abraham's servant was in a hurry to get home.

Rebekah took her maidservants and her old nurse, and together they set off, with Abraham's servant, to start a new life in Canaan. When they eventually arrived it was dusk, and Isaac was praying by himself out in the fields. He opened his eyes as the camel train approached and saw Rebekah for the first time. Soon afterward, Isaac and Rebekah were married, and Isaac loved his wife dearly. And she comforted him greatly after the death of his mother, Sarah.

Esau and Jacob

*I*saac was forty years old when he married Rebekah, but for many years they remained childless.

They prayed to the Lord and, at last, after nearly twenty years, she became pregnant with twins. As they grew inside her, they kicked and jostled, and she asked the Lord why this was happening? He replied, "Two nations are in your womb, and two peoples from within you will be separated. One people will be stronger than the other, and the older will serve the younger."

When the time came, Rebekah did indeed give birth to twin boys. The first was bright red and covered in hair from his head to his toes and they named him Esau. The second was smooth and slippery as an eel and they named him Jacob.

The twins grew up side by side, but Esau became a hunter, skilful with his bow and arrow, while Jacob preferred to stay at home and help his mother. He was her favorite, while Esau was dearer to his father's heart.

One day, Jacob was stirring a lentil stew when Esau rushed in, famished. "Quick! Give me some stew!"

"I will," replied Jacob. "But only if you give up your rights as the firstborn son and give them to me."

"I can't see what good my rights are anyway," retorted Esau. "You can have them, with pleasure." Then Esau ate his bowl of stew.

The years passed and Isaac lost his sight. He called to his son, Esau, and said, "My son, I am an old man and death is approaching. Go and catch some wild game for me. Prepare my favorite dish. Then I will give you my blessing before I die."

Rebekah overheard his words, but she wanted Jacob to receive the blessing instead of Esau and she thought of a plan. She told Jacob to find two young goats and bring them to her. She would prepare a delicious meal. Then Jacob could take it to his father and receive his blessing. But Jacob protested, "Esau is hairy and I am smooth-skinned. What if my father touches me? He would know I was tricking him and would curse me." His mother told him not to worry, saying that any curse would fall on her.

"Your brother came and took your blessing."

So Jacob got the goats and Rebekah prepared the meal. She dressed Jacob in Esau's clothes and disguised his hands and the skin of his neck with hairy goatskins. Then Jacob took the dish to Isaac. But Isaac hesitated, confused. "Come near so I can touch you, my son," he said. "The voice is Jacob's, but the hands are Esau's. Are you really my son Esau?"

"I am," lied Jacob.

So Isaac sat up and ate the food. When he had finished, he put his hand on Jacob's head and gave him his blessing. "May nations serve you and peoples bow down to you. Be lord over your brothers and may the sons of your mother bow down to you."

Jacob received the blessing and ran out of the tent, glad to get away. Soon after, Esau arrived with a plate of food. "Here I am, father. Esau, your firstborn. I've got the food you asked for." Isaac gasped in horror, knowing that he had been tricked by Jacob.

"Your brother came and took your blessing," he cried. "I cannot take it back."

"He has deceived me twice," replied Esau bitterly. "He took my birthright and now he's taken my blessing."

Isaac nodded. "I have made him lord over you and have made all his relatives his servants," he said sadly.

And Esau wept. "Do you only have one blessing, my father? Bless me, too." But Isaac knew that the Lord's word was in the blessing he had given to Jacob and it could not be altered.

From that day on, Esau hated his brother. He planned to kill him as soon as their father was dead and the days of mourning were over. When Rebekah heard about Esau's plot, she went straight to Jacob and warned him. She told him to hide in her brother's house far away in Haran. "Stay there until Esau's fury subsides. I'll send word when it's safe for you to come back." Jacob fled immediately.

Jacob's Ladder

Jacob continued on his journey from Beersheba to Haran and, when the sun dropped low in the sky, he stopped to rest for the night.

He found a smooth stone and put it under his head like a pillow, and lay down under the starry sky. He was tired from traveling and fell into a deep sleep. He dreamed that he saw a magnificent stairway reaching steeply through the clouds to heaven. A procession of angels glided up and down the steps. And at the very top of the stairway stood the Lord, looking down at Jacob.

"I am the Lord, the God of your father Abraham and the God of Isaac," He said. "I will give you and your descendants the land on which you are lying. Your descendants will spread out to the west and to the east, to the north and to the south. All peoples on earth will be blessed through you and your offspring."

"He dreamed that he saw a magnificent stairway reaching steeply through the clouds to heaven."

Jacob woke up early the next morning, refreshed after his sleep, and he remembered his dream. "The Lord is in this place and I didn't know," he said to himself, shivering with fear. "This is the House of God and that is the gate to heaven." To mark the site of his sacred vision, Jacob took the stone that he had used as a pillow and made a memorial stone. Then, he poured some oil over it and named the place "Bethel," which means "House of God."

And he made a vow, saying, "If God watches over me on this journey so that I return safely to my father's house, then the Lord will be my God and this stone that I have set up will be God's house."

Jacob and Rachel

Jacob left Bethel, where God had appeared to him in a dream, and continued on his way. It was a long journey across the Jordan River to Haran in northwest Mesopotamia, where his mother's brother, Laban, lived.

When at last he arrived, he saw a well in the middle of a field, covered by a large stone. Around it, a few flocks of sheep lay sleeping in the sun. The shepherds watched over them, chatting to each other. Each day, toward sunset, when all the flocks had gathered, the shepherds would roll the stone away from the mouth of the well to reveal the cool water that lay deep below. Then they would set to work, drawing the water up and filling the troughs so that there was plenty for all the thirsty sheep.

Jacob greeted the shepherds and asked them if they knew Laban. "We do indeed," they replied. "And here comes his daughter Rachel with the sheep."

But Jacob could not understand why the shepherds were hanging around, doing nothing. "Look," he said, "the sun is still high in the sky and the rest of the flocks won't be gathered for hours. Why don't you water your sheep now and then you'll be able to take them back to pasture?"

"No, we can't water them until all the flocks are gathered," they replied. "Only then will we roll the stone away."

Jacob turned and saw Rachel, the beautiful young shepherdess, walking toward the well, guiding her flock before her. His heart leapt at the sight of his lovely cousin. He went straight over to her, bowing low, and introduced himself, saying that he was the son of Rebekah and the nephew of her father, Laban. He embraced her warmly and kissed her. And, despite what the shepherds had told him, he immediately rolled the heavy stone from the mouth of the well and drew water for her sheep.

> "He would also be near Rachel with whom he had fallen in love."

Rachel ran home to tell her father and her older sister, Leah, about the visitor, who had arrived so unexpectedly. They were curious to see him as soon as possible, and Laban rushed out of the house to find him. He threw his arms around his nephew and welcomed him warmly, overjoyed to meet him for the first time. Together, they went back to the house and Jacob explained why he had come all the way from Beersheba and told him the whole story about his twin brother, Esau.

"You are my own flesh and blood," said Laban. "You must stay with us here." Jacob agreed, happy to remain in his uncle's house and to help him in any way he could. He would also be near Rachel with whom he had fallen in love. He worked hard from morning until night, helping with the livestock and tending the crops in the fields.

Laban rushes out to meet his nephew

Jacob's Wedding

After a month, Laban came to Jacob, his nephew, and said, "You have been working hard for several weeks now. But, just because you are my own flesh and blood, you should not work for nothing. How can I pay you?"

Jacob replied, "I'll work for you for seven years in return for your youngest daughter, Rachel."

Laban looked at him and thought for a moment. Then he said, "It is better that I give her to you than to a stranger. Stay here with me."

Jacob worked hard for the next seven years but, because of his deep love for Rachel, the time slipped by so quickly that it seemed more like seven days. At the end of this time, Jacob went to Laban and said, "Uncle, give me my wife. I have worked for you for seven years, as promised, and I want to marry her now."

Laban agreed and started to plan a splendid wedding feast, with the best dishes and the finest wines. The celebrations would go on for a week, with music and singing and dancing. Everybody would be invited.

When the great day came, Jacob watched proudly as his bride took her place by his side. She was dressed in the most beautiful embroidered robes and wore a heavy jeweled veil, which concealed her face completely. He took her hand.

That night, as darkness fell, they retired early to bed, leaving Laban and their guests to carry on feasting and drinking. But the next morning, when Jacob opened his eyes and turned over to kiss his new wife, he could not believe his eyes. He saw with horror that it was not Rachel, but her older sister Leah, lying by his side.

Jacob marries Laban's daughter

He rushed to find Laban, shouting, "What have you done? You tricked me! You deceived me! I worked for seven whole years for Rachel and you have given me ugly old Leah."

Laban replied, "It is not our custom here to give the younger daughter in marriage before the older one. We will finish celebrating your marriage to Leah and then, at the end of the week, you can also have Rachel as your wife. But only if you promise to work for another seven years."

And so, a week later, Rachel became Jacob's wife. He loved her from the bottom of his heart and he worked happily for another seven years.

Although Jacob was not in love with his first wife, Leah, she quickly became pregnant and gave birth to their first son, who was named Reuben. And, before long, she went on to have three more sons—Simeon, Levi, and Judah. It was hard for Rachel, who was still not pregnant, and she watched her sister with increasing jealousy. "Give me children or I will die!" she implored Jacob.

Rachel gives birth to Joseph

"Do you think I am God?" he replied angrily.

In desperation, Rachel took her maidservant, Bilhah, and gave her to Jacob as a wife. "Marry her so that she can bear children for me so that, through her, I too can build a family."

> "I'll work for you for seven years in return for your youngest daughter, Rachel."

Bilhah had no difficulty in conceiving and, nine months later, gave birth to a son named Dan. And the next year she had another son named Naphtali. Jacob also fathered two more sons with Leah's servant, Zilpah, and they were named Gad and Asher. And Leah herself bore him two more sons, Issachar and Zebulon, and finally a daughter named Dinah.

All these years Rachel had waited, grieving deeply that she had not been able to give her husband a son. Finally, to her great joy, she found she was pregnant and she gave birth to a son who was named Joseph.

Jacob's Return

*I*n time, Jacob wanted to go home to Canaan, but his uncle, Laban, persuaded him to stay in Haran. Over the years, he had come to rely on his nephew.

But Laban was not always honest with Jacob and sometimes tried to cheat him. Despite this, Jacob had built up large flocks and herds of his own and was now wealthy in his own right. Laban's sons watched Jacob jealously and talked about him behind his back. "Jacob has taken everything our father owned and has gained all his wealth through him," they muttered sourly to each other. And even Laban himself began to give Jacob the cold shoulder.

Then the Lord came to Jacob and said, "Go back to the land of your fathers and to your relatives. I will be with you."

Jacob immediately sent for his wives, Rachel and Leah. "You know that I have worked for your father with all my strength, yet he has cheated me out of my wages. However, God has not allowed him to harm me. And God has told me to leave and go back to my native land."

Rachel and Leah listened and prepared to leave with their children and all their worldly possessions. Then, without a word, they left, driving their flocks and herds ahead of them across the Euphrates to the mountains of Gilead.

When Laban discovered that they had gone, he chased after them and finally caught up with them seven days later. "Why did you deceive me and run off like that?" he asked Jacob. "You didn't even let me kiss my grandchildren and daughters goodbye!"

Jacob takes his family to Canaan

The two men talked and argued long into the night, but eventually they settled their differences, calling God to bear witness. Early the next morning, Laban kissed his grandchildren and daughters goodbye and blessed them. Then he set off and returned home.

Jacob took his family and continued the long journey to Canaan. When they drew near he sent a message to his brother Esau, whom he had fled from so many years before. Soon, news came back that Esau was coming to meet him with a force of four hundred men.

"O God of my father Abraham, God of my father Isaac," Jacob prayed, "I am unworthy of all the kindness and faithfulness you have shown me. Save me, I pray, from the hand of my brother Esau!"

> "Your name will no longer be Jacob, but Israel, because you have struggled with God and with man and have overcome."

Jacob chose his finest animals and sent them ahead with his servants, as a gift to Esau. Then he took his wives and children and all their possessions across the Jabbok River and told them to wait for him there. He spent the night alone, and as he sat, deep in thought, a man suddenly appeared out of the night and lunged at him, gripping him by the throat. Jacob gasped and fought back, pinning him to the ground. They wrestled, on and on, grappling with each other like silent shadows, evenly matched. At last, the sun's rays started to creep over the horizon and the man said, "Let me go, for it is daybreak. What is your name?"

Jacob told him his name and the man replied, "Your name will no longer be Jacob, but Israel, because you have struggled with God and with man and have overcome." With these words He blessed Jacob and disappeared into thin air.

Israel means "he struggles with God" and Jacob realized that he had seen God face to face and that his life had been spared. He went right away to rejoin his family—just in time to see Esau approaching with all his men. Telling his wives and children to stay behind, Jacob went to meet his brother, bowing low before him seven times. Without hesitation, Esau threw his arms around his neck and kissed him warmly, saying that he did not need the animals that Jacob had sent him.

"No, please, if I have found favor in your eyes, accept this gift from me," Jacob replied. "For to see your face is like seeing the face of God, now that you have received me favorably. Please accept the present that was brought to you, for God has been gracious to me and I have all I need."

A stranger appears at night and wrestles with Jacob

Joseph's Dreams

Joseph lived with his father, Jacob, and his brothers in the land of Canaan. Jacob loved all his sons, but Joseph was his favorite.

His father had given Joseph a beautiful coat, intricately woven with the colors of the rainbow. Joseph wore it all the time. Everybody knew that he was the apple of his father's eye and Joseph's brothers hated him for it.

One night, Joseph had a dream and he told his brothers about it. "We were binding sheaves of corn out in the field when suddenly my sheaf rose and stood upright. Your sheaves gathered around mine and bowed down to it." His brothers were incensed. "So you want to rule us, do you?" they jeered.

A few nights later, Joseph had another dream and he foolishly told his brothers about it. "This time the sun and the moon and eleven stars were bowing down to me."

He also told his father, who was not pleased. "What is this dream? Do you think the whole family will actually come and bow down to you?"

Joseph's brothers went to take care of their father's sheep and goats in the north of the country. After some days, Jacob asked Joseph to go and see that all was well. When the brothers saw Joseph approaching, they saw their chance. "Here comes that little dreamer," they said. "Let's kill him and hide him in one of these pits. We'll say a wild animal attacked him."

But Reuben, who was a kind man and liked his brother, pleaded with the others, "By all means, throw him into the pit, but don't kill him." When Joseph finally reached his brothers, they pounced on him and ripped off his coat. They put him in the pit without any food or water.

The brothers sat down to eat their meal that evening, unsure of what to do. And then they saw a caravan of Ishmaelite merchants on the horizon. One of the brothers, who was named Judah, said, "Do we really want to kill Joseph? He is our own flesh and blood. Why don't we sell him? Then we'll be rid of him, without laying a hand on him." His brothers agreed.

> "Do we really want to kill Joseph?"

So, they pulled Joseph out of the pit and offered him to the merchants. A price was agreed, and he was sold and hoisted on to a camel, bound for Egypt.

The brothers slaughtered one of the goats and smeared the blood on Joseph's tattered coat before going home. They showed the coat to their father saying, "We found this. Do you think it could belong to Joseph?"

Jacob recognized the blood-stained bundle and cried, "It is my son's coat! An animal has devoured him." And he mourned for his beloved son. Meanwhile, Joseph had reached Egypt. He was sold by the merchants to Potiphar, who was one of Pharaoh's most important officials.

Joseph the Slave

Joseph, who had been taken to Egypt from Canaan and sold as a slave, worked hard for his new master, Potiphar.

The Lord was always by Joseph's side, and Joseph was good at whatever he did. His master, who was captain of Pharaoh's guard and a man of great standing, was impressed. Before long, he made Joseph his own personal attendant and put him in charge of the whole household.

Now, Joseph was a very handsome man, and Potiphar's wife took a shine to him. Eventually, her passion running high, she tried to seduce him. Joseph spurned her advances. "My master trusts me. How could I betray him? How could I sin against God?"

But Potiphar's wife would not take no for an answer, believing herself to be irresistible. Day after day she pursued him, and day after day he refused her.

At last, in desperation, she cornered him and tore at his cloak. Terrified, Joseph turned and fled, leaving his cloak in her hands. Scorned and rejected, Potiphar's wife called the servants and told them that Joseph had tried to ravish her. "Look! When I screamed, he left his cloak behind and ran!" Then she rushed to tell her husband the story. Potiphar was horrified and ordered Joseph to be thrown into prison.

But the Lord watched over Joseph. The prison warder liked the new inmate. Soon, Joseph was put in charge of all the other prisoners and, before long, he was running the place.

There were two very special prisoners—the royal baker and Pharaoh's chief cupbearer. Before they were criminals, they had specific duties. The cupbearer had to taste Pharaoh's food and drink in case it was poisoned, and the baker made the household's finest sweetmeats.

One morning, while doing his rounds, Joseph saw the two of them sitting in their cells with long faces. He asked what was the matter. "We both had really odd dreams last night," they answered, "but there is nobody who can interpret them."

"Tell me your dreams," said Joseph.

The chief cupbearer began with his. "I saw a vine with three branches. As it budded, it blossomed and its clusters ripened into grapes. Pharaoh's cup was in my hand, and I took the grapes and squeezed them into the cup for him."

The chief cupbearer's dream

"How could I sin against God?"

Joseph explained the dream. "The three branches are three days. Within three days, Pharaoh will restore you to your position and you will put his cup in his hand, just as you used to do." And he added, "Please, when you are back in favor, remember me and mention me to Pharaoh. Try to get me out of prison. I have done nothing to deserve it." The cupbearer agreed.

Then the baker described his dream. "On my head were three baskets of bread. In the top basket were baked goods for Pharaoh, but the birds kept flying down to eat them."

Joseph interpreted the dream. "The three baskets are three days. Within three days, Pharaoh will hang you on a tree, and the birds will eat away your flesh." The baker looked at him, doubtfully.

Now, Pharaoh's birthday was in three days time and he gave a feast for all his officials. He ordered the release of the chief cupbearer and the royal baker from prison. Then he summoned them to court and gave the cupbearer back his old job, but told the baker that he would be hanged, just as Joseph had said. Sadly, the cupbearer was so happy to be restored to his position that he forgot to tell Pharaoh about Joseph's plight.

The baker's dream

Egypt

Ancient Egypt was the world's first state, ruled by a divine king, called the pharaoh. Egypt plays a major role in the Bible, as the setting for the stories of Joseph and Moses. According to the Book of Exodus, the Israelites spent 430 years in Egypt before being led out by Moses to the Promised Land. There is no mention of Israelites in Egypt in any Egyptian writings. Even so, wall paintings show that nomads from Asia, like the Israelites, did visit the country.

Egyptian settlements (shown in orange), developed along the green banks of the Nile River. The deserts on either side protected Egypt from foreign invaders.

KEY EVENTS

c. 3300 BCE
Egyptians invent the world's first writing system, called hieroglyphs.

c. 3000 BCE
Egypt is united under the rule of the first pharaoh.

2686–2181 BCE
The Old Kingdom period, when pharaohs rule from Memphis and are buried in pyramids.

1650–1550 BCE
The Hyksos, an Asian people, take control of northern Egypt.

1550 BCE
Pharaoh Ahmose drives out the Hyksos and founds the New Kingdom. Pharaohs now rule from Thebes and are buried in hidden tombs.

1456 BCE
Pharaoh Thutmose III conquers Canaan to the north.

1207 BCE
Pharaoh Merneptah has an inscription carved, boasting that "Israel is laid waste."

1150–1050 BCE
The Egyptians lose control of Canaan, where the Philistines and Israelites now rule.

Pharaoh

This is a statue of Pharaoh Menkaure (ruled 2532–2503 BCE). He wears a false beard and a royal headcloth, which were worn by Egyptian kings for almost 3,000 years. The hawk is Horus, the sky god, the special protector of the pharaoh.

Nile River

The Nile's annual flooding watered the fields of Egypt and made them fertile. Unlike Mesopotamian rivers, the Nile flooded at the right time to plant crops, and the floods did not cause disaster on the land. Egyptians had a strong sense that their world had been well-ordered by the gods.

Temple of Amun
Egyptian temples were the homes of gods, whose statues lived in a central shrine. Only the priests could enter the temples. To ordinary people, temples must have seemed mysterious and awe-inspiring. This is the entrance of the Temple of Amun, at Thebes, protected by rows of ram-headed sphinxes.

Stele of Merneptah
The earliest mention of Israel outside the Bible appears on this stone tablet, which Pharaoh Merneptah had carved about 1210 BCE. Here he boasts of having invaded Canaan, and says "Israel is laid waste."

Foreigners
Egypt often welcomed nomads from Asia, like the Israelites, who appear in tomb paintings. The figures at the bottom, dressed in white, are Egyptians. The Asiatic foreigners above have paler skin and wear colorful robes.

Pharaoh's Dreams

*T*wo long years had passed and Joseph was still in prison. The chief cupbearer had forgotten about him completely and, far from home, there was no one else to spare Joseph a thought.

One night, in the royal palace, Pharaoh had a strange dream. He was on the banks of the Nile and seven sleek, well-fed cows waded out of the water and began to graze among the bulrushes. Then seven more cows followed them out of the water—but these poor creatures were gaunt and their ribs stuck out pitifully from their hides. They opened their starving mouths and ate all seven of the sleek, fat cows.

That same night, Pharaoh had another dream. Seven ears of plump, healthy corn were growing on a single stalk. Then another seven ears of corn sprouted, but these were scorched and shriveled and they devoured the seven healthy ears of corn.

Pharaoh was troubled. He could not understand what his dreams meant, but knew that they were important. He sent for the royal dream interpreter, who was much revered and practiced in such matters, but even he was baffled. Then Pharaoh issued a decree, summoning all the wise men in Egypt. They came from far and wide and listened to Pharaoh's dreams, but they too were perplexed.

> "Since God has made all this known to you, there is no one more discerning or wise than you."

Then, the chief cupbearer suddenly remembered the young Joseph, who had interpreted his dream so perfectly a long time ago in prison. And he felt bad that he had forgotten Joseph for so long. He told Pharaoh, and Joseph was released from prison and summoned to court.

Joseph bowed down before Pharaoh, who said, "I had a dream and no one can explain it. But I have heard it said that when you hear a dream, you can interpret it."

"I cannot do it," replied Joseph, "but God will give Pharaoh the answer he desires."

So Pharaoh told Joseph about his dreams, and Joseph explained that they were the same dream. They had been sent by God in two different forms because the message they contained was so important. "The seven good cows are seven years and the seven good ears of corn are the same seven years. The seven thin cows that came up afterward and the seven worthless ears of corn are the next seven years."

Joseph said that seven years of great plenty would come to Egypt, but then seven years of famine would follow. And he warned Pharaoh, "The abundance in the land will not be remembered, because the famine that follows will be so severe." And he went on to advise Pharaoh that he should find a wise man and put him in charge to make sure that, during the good years, one fifth of the harvest was saved and stored so that there would be enough food when the famine came.

Pharaoh was impressed by Joseph's words. "Can we find anyone like this man?" he asked. "Someone with the Spirit of God? Since God has made all this known to you, there is no one more discerning or wise than you. You shall be in charge of my palace, and all my people are to submit to your orders. You will be my second-in-command. I hereby put you in charge of the whole of Egypt."

With that, Pharaoh took off his signet ring and put it on Joseph's finger. He dressed him in fine robes and placed a gold chain around his neck. And together, they rode in a magnificent chariot, Joseph by Pharaoh's side, for all to see.

Just as Joseph had predicted, seven years of plenty followed, and the fertile land, watered by the Nile, produced food in abundance. The fields were full of wheat and barley, the fruit trees groaned with figs and pomegranates, and the vines were heavy with the sweetest grapes. Joseph traveled all over the country, making sure that a good proportion was stockpiled and saved for the bad years that he knew lay ahead. Huge quantities of grain were stored in granaries in every town and city.

Then, after seven years, the Nile dried up, the land shriveled and shrank back into itself, and the relentless famine began. But, although the crops failed year after year, there was food for everybody in Egypt and, thanks to Joseph, no one went hungry.

THE PHARAOH
The Bible gives no clues to the identity of the pharaoh in the story of Joseph. The most famous pharaoh was Rameses II (ruled 1279–1213 BCE), who erected more statues of himself than any other king.

So Pharaoh said to Joseph, "I hereby put you in charge of the whole land of Egypt." Then Pharaoh took his signet ring from his finger and put it on Joseph's finger. He dressed him in robes of fine linen and put a gold chain around his neck. He had him ride in a chariot as his second-in-command, and men shouted before him, "Make way!"

Genesis 41:41–43

Joseph the Governor

Famine gripped the land, spreading from country to country. Soon, it arrived in Canaan, which Joseph had left so many years before.

His aged father, Jacob, had heard the rumor that there were great mountains of grain far away in Egypt. So ten of Joseph's brothers made the long journey to Egypt, but the youngest, who was named Benjamin, stayed at home with his father.

Now, although they did not know it, their brother Joseph was the most important governor in all Egypt and was in charge of selling grain. When the brothers arrived, Joseph recognized them. He did not let on, however, and asked them where they came from.

"From the land of Canaan," they replied nervously, not recognizing him.

"You are spies!" Joseph accused them. "You have come to snoop and pry!"

"No, my lord," they protested. "We were twelve brothers, all the sons of one father who lives in Canaan. The youngest is now with our father and one brother is no more."

"I don't believe you! I think you're spies!" retorted Joseph. "But I will test whether you are lying or not. You will not leave unless your youngest brother comes here. One of you must go and get him. The rest of you will stay here in prison. Then we will see if you're telling the truth!" But, for the time being, he put them all in prison.

Joseph was now the powerful governor of Egypt

After three days, Joseph went to them, relenting slightly. "If you really are honest, as you say, one of you can stay here and the rest can go back home and take grain to your starving household. But then you must bring back your youngest brother to prove that you are telling the truth."

The brothers looked at each other, bewildered. "This must be some kind of punishment for what we did to our brother so long ago," they said. Reuben, the kindest of the brothers, who had pleaded with the others to spare Joseph's life, said, "Didn't I tell you not to sin against that boy?"

"Didn't I tell you not to sin against that boy?"

Deeply moved, Joseph turned away from them to hide his tears. When he had composed himself, he turned back and chose Simeon to be held in prison. Then he gave orders for their bags to be filled with grain and for the silver they had brought with them to be hidden among it. He also arranged for food to be given to them for their journey. The brothers loaded up their donkeys and set off for Canaan.

When they stopped to rest that night, one brother opened his sack to give his donkey a few handfuls of grain and he found the piece of silver buried there. He showed it to the others in amazement and they looked at each other uncertainly, and said, "What does this mean?"

They continued their journey and at last arrived in Canaan. As they were emptying their bags, they found the silver hidden in each one and they shivered with fear, not knowing what was going on. They told their father, Jacob, the whole story and begged him to let them take their youngest brother, Benjamin, back to Egypt. But Jacob, distraught at the thought of losing him, refused.

Joseph orders Simeon to be taken to prison

The Silver Cup

The famine continued and, in time, the grain that Jacob's sons had brought from Egypt had run out.

Jacob wanted his sons to go back again to buy more, but Judah reminded him that, this time, they would have to take their youngest brother, Benjamin. They had made a promise to Joseph, the governor of Egypt. "Why did you tell him that you had a young brother in the first place?" grumbled Jacob, who was very fond of his young son.

"He asked all about us and our family," his sons protested. "He wanted to know if our father was still alive and if we had another brother. How were we to know he would insist we brought our brother to him?"

> "If any one of us is found to have it, he will die."

Then Judah spoke to his father, "I myself will guarantee Benjamin's safety. If I don't bring him back, I will bear the blame all my life."

Reluctantly, his father agreed. "So be it. But you must keep on the right side of this governor. Take gifts with you and take twice as much silver this time, for you must return the silver you found in your sacks. And take your brother. May God Almighty grant you mercy."

When the brothers arrived in Egypt, they presented themselves to Joseph. As soon as Joseph saw Benjamin, he said to his chief steward, "Take these men to my house, slaughter an animal, and prepare a feast. They will eat with me at noon."

The brothers could not understand why they were being treated with such favor. Perhaps it was a trick and they were going to end up as slaves? And then, the steward brought in Simeon, who had been left behind in prison, and the brothers threw their arms around him, relieved that he was safe.

Joseph arrived and, bowing low, the brothers gave him the gifts from Canaan. He received them graciously, but could not take his eyes off Benjamin. Unlike the others, Benjamin and he shared the same mother and they were real brothers. Tears welled in Joseph's eyes at the sight of him, but he pulled himself together and ordered the food to be served. It was a feast, but the brothers were astonished as Benjamin was given five times as much as anybody else.

Afterward, Joseph gave instructions for their sacks to be filled with food and grain and for their pieces of silver to be hidden among it. And then he ordered that his own special silver cup should be put in Benjamin's sack.

The brothers headed home, but had not gone far before Joseph's chief steward caught up with them, accusing them of stealing his master's silver cup. The brothers protested their innocence. "Why would we steal silver or gold from your master's house? If any one of us is found to have it, he will die. And the rest of us will become your lord's slaves." Gladly, they opened their sacks and the steward peered inside them. When he saw the silver cup in Benjamin's sack, he pulled it out and brandished it high in the air.

The brothers looked at Benjamin in disbelief. They returned to Joseph's house. "How can we prove our innocence?" asked Judah, sadly. "We are all your slaves."

"No!" answered Joseph. "Only the man who had the cup will be my slave. The rest of you must return to your father."

Judah pleaded with him, explaining how precious Benjamin was to their father. "Please let me stay here as your slave in place of Benjamin. How can I go back to my father if he is not with me?"

At this, Joseph broke down. He sobbed, "I am Joseph! Your brother Joseph! The one you sold into Egypt. But don't be angry with yourselves. It was to save lives that God sent me ahead of you. It was not you who sent me here, but God." And he gave them a message for their father, "God has made me lord of all Egypt. Come here to me. You shall live in the region of Goshen—you, your children, and grandchildren, your flocks and herds, and all you have. I will provide for you because five years of famine are still to come."

When Jacob heard the news he could not believe that his beloved son, Joseph, was still alive. And he was now the governor of Egypt and was offering the family refuge. He exclaimed, "My son Joseph is alive! I will go and see him before I die!"

The silver cup is found hidden in Benjamin's sack

Moses in the Bulrushes

Since the time of Joseph, the children of Israel had thrived and prospered in the land of Egypt. Generations came and went and they multiplied, spreading far and wide throughout the fertile country.

But one day, a new Pharaoh, who had never heard of the Israelites' famous ancestor, Joseph, came to the throne and was consumed with fear. "Look," he said to his counselors, "the Israelites are everywhere. There are far too many of them. If war breaks out, they will side with our enemies."

He ordered that the Israelites be forced to labor, building stone cities with their bare hands. But the more cruelly the Israelites were treated, the quicker they multiplied. Then Pharaoh had a better idea. He ordered that all male children born to Israelite women should be put to death at birth. But the midwives took no notice. "Why have you let the boys live?" thundered Pharaoh.

"Israelite women aren't like Egyptian women," the midwives said. "They are healthy and give birth before the midwives arrive."

At his wits' end, Pharaoh declared, "Every boy that is born must be thrown into the Nile, but let every girl live!"

Now, there was a couple who belonged to the tribe of Levi and the wife had just given birth to a son. She could not bring herself to comply with Pharaoh's cold-blooded order and, for three months, she hid her baby son at home. But as the infant grew bigger and noisier it became impossible. So she fetched a basket and made it watertight. Then she laid her baby in it and took it to the banks of the Nile, hiding it in the bulrushes. Her young daughter went with her to keep watch.

Soon, Pharaoh's daughter came to bathe in the river and caught sight of the basket. She sent a maid to fetch it and, as she lifted the cover, the baby whimpered sweetly and her heart melted. "It must be one of those poor Israelite babies," she said.

"Every boy that is born must be thrown into the Nile"

At that moment, the baby's sister asked innocently, "Shall I get one of the Israelite women to nurse the baby for you?" Pharaoh's daughter agreed. So the baby was brought up by his real mother, and when he grew older Pharaoh's daughter adopted him as her own. She named him Moses, which means "to draw out," because she had drawn him out of the water.

Moses is Called by God

Moses grew up in Pharaoh's palace and was treated as if he were the son of the princess. But he was a thoughtful young man, who never forgot that his birth parents belonged to the Levite tribe of Israel.

One day, he went out and saw the Israelite slave gangs dragging huge slabs of stone out of the quarry. From morning until night they worked in the scorching sun. Suddenly, one of the slaves collapsed on the ground. The Egyptian slave driver went over and kicked him. When the poor man still did not get up, the slave driver gave him a savage beating. Moses, unable to bear it, rushed over and, glancing around to make sure that no one saw, killed the cruel slave driver. Then, filled with horror at what he had done, he dug a large hole in the sand and buried the body.

The next morning, Moses went back and saw two Israelites arguing. One of them grabbed the other by the throat. Moses went up and separated them, asking them why they were fighting.

"Who are you to judge us?" one replied. "Are you going to kill me, just as you murdered that Egyptian yesterday?"

Moses was filled with terror. Word would soon spread and everybody would know about his crime. And when the news reached Pharaoh, Moses knew that his own life would be in danger. He gathered a few belongings and left Egypt, fleeing across the Sinai Desert until he reached the land of Midian. He settled there, far from danger.

> "I am sending you to Pharaoh to bring my people, the Israelites, out of Egypt."

One day, Moses was sitting by a well when seven young women came to draw water for their flocks. The local shepherds tried to stop them, but Moses came to their rescue and helped them get water. They were grateful and took him to meet their father, who was a priest named Jethro. He welcomed Moses and asked him to stay. In time, Jethro gave his daughter, Zipporah, to Moses in marriage.

Moses helped his father-in-law to look after the sheep. One day, he took the flocks across the desert to graze by the sacred mountain of Sinai. He sat down to rest and started to sleep. Suddenly, he sat bolt upright and saw a blazing bush in front of him. Although the flames crackled through the branches, they did not even singe them.

Moses crept nearer and then he heard the Lord's voice coming from the middle of the burning bush. "I am the God of your father, the God of Abraham, the God of Isaac, and the God of Jacob. I have seen the misery of my people in Egypt and am concerned about their suffering. So I have come down to rescue them from the hands of the Egyptians and bring them to a land of their own, flowing with milk and honey. I am sending you to Pharaoh to bring my people, the Israelites, out of Egypt."

Moses was amazed and filled with terror. "But how can I do that?" he asked. "Who am I that I should go to Pharaoh and bring the Israelites out of Egypt?"

"I will be with you," God reassured him. "Say that the God of their fathers has sent you and that His name is 'I AM.' "

And God said Moses must tell Pharaoh that Egypt would be cursed, and plagues would sweep the land, if he did not let the Israelites go.

"But what if he doesn't believe me?" protested Moses.

God told Moses to throw his staff on the ground, which he did at once. Immediately, it turned into a snake, writhing and hissing in the dust. "Pick it up by the tail now," said God. Moses lifted it up at arm's length, and the serpent turned back into a wooden staff.

"Now go," God told him. "Take your brother, Aaron, with you. He is coming to meet you. I will tell you both what to say. And take your wooden staff—it will help you to perform miraculous feats."

God speaks to Moses from within a burning bush

Moses Warns Pharaoh

*A*fter so long in the land of Midian, Moses said goodbye to his father-in-law, Jethro, and set off for Egypt, just as God had told him. He took his wife and sons.

The landscape was bleak and barren and the sun beat down relentlessly. Moses carried the wooden staff that God had given him. As they approached the great holy mountain of Sinai, they could see Moses's brother, Aaron, coming to meet them. They greeted each other warmly and Moses told his brother that God had spoken to him, and had sent him back to Egypt to lead the Israelites out of slavery.

As soon as they got back to Egypt, Moses and Aaron called the elders of the Israelites together and said that the Lord had sent them to rescue their people. When they heard this, and that the Lord was concerned about their misery, the elders bowed down to worship. Then Moses and Aaron went to Pharaoh in his splendid court. "The Lord, the God of the Israelites, has spoken to us," they said. "He told us to take His people into the desert to offer sacrifices to Him. If we do not do this, He may strike you all with plagues or with the sword."

Pharaoh was angry. "Who is this Lord that I should obey and let the Israelites go?" he shouted. "Why are you keeping them from their work?" Incensed, he summoned his chief slave drivers and ordered them to make the Israelites work even harder. From now on they were not to be given straw to make the bricks. And so the slaves were forced to scavenge in the fields for any stubble they could find.

Moses and Aaron ask Pharaoh to free the Israelites

Moses and Aaron were worried. But God reassured Moses and gave him a message for the Israelites. "I am the Lord and I will bring you out from under the yoke of the Egyptians. I will free you from slavery. And I will bring you to the land I swore with uplifted hand to give to Abraham, to Isaac, and to Jacob." The Israelites listened in disbelief.

God told Moses to go back to Pharaoh. "Say everything I command you, and your brother Aaron is to tell Pharaoh to let the Israelites go out of his country."

> "He may strike you all with plagues or with the sword."

And Moses and Aaron did as the Lord had told them. But, still, Pharaoh would not listen. So then Moses told Aaron to throw down his wooden staff. As it touched the ground, it became a serpent. Not to be outdone, Pharaoh called his wise men and told them to throw down their staffs, too. At once, they turned into a mass of serpents. But Aaron's snake opened his mouth and swallowed the other snakes with relish. Pharaoh watched but was not impressed.

Then God said to Moses, "Go to the Nile tomorrow and wait for Pharaoh. Strike the water with the staff and the water will turn to blood." Moses and Aaron did as the Lord had said and the Nile became a river of blood. It was a terrible sight. But it was not just the Nile that turned red. Blood filled the streams, the ponds, and the reservoirs. Pharaoh watched, unmoved. He returned to his palace without a backward glance.

Pharaoh's wise men turn their staffs into serpents

The Plagues of Egypt

*S*even days passed and still Pharaoh would not release the Israelites. Moses and Aaron, after speaking with the Lord again, pleaded with Pharaoh, telling him that the Lord would send a plague of frogs if he did not let the slaves go.

But Pharaoh did not listen. So, the next day, Aaron held his wooden staff over the Nile, as God had commanded, and suddenly a great croaking sound came from the river. An army of frogs emerged from the waters, hopping out in their thousands, up the banks and over the land, covering it like a shiny green carpet. They swarmed everywhere—even into Pharaoh's palace, as the guards watched in horror. They jumped by Pharaoh's feet and on his throne.

This was too much, and Pharaoh called Moses and Aaron, saying, "Pray to the Lord to take the frogs away from me and my people. I will let your people go to offer sacrifices to the Lord." The Lord heard and the frogs died instantly. They were swept up and piled into heaps that rotted in the sun. But Pharaoh broke his word and did not release the Israelites.

So Aaron struck his staff on the ground once more, as God had told him. The dust turned into millions of gnats, which took off in a cloud, biting any Egyptian man, woman, or child they could find.

Pharaoh's magicians went to him, swiping the dreadful insects away, and said, "This is the finger of God." But, although he had been bitten very badly himself, Pharaoh would not release the Israelites.

Then Moses went to Pharaoh again, telling him that the Lord would send a swarm of flies next. They would plague the Egyptians and their animals, but would not bother the Israelites. And the next day a dense black cloud of flies appeared, blotting out the light. At this, Pharaoh relented and said to Moses and Aaron, "Go, sacrifice to your God here in this land."

But Moses replied, "No, the sacrifices we offer to the Lord, our God, would be detestable to the Egyptians. We must make a three-day journey into the desert to offer our sacrifices there." Pharaoh agreed, and the flies died immediately.

Again, Pharaoh went back on his word, and so the Lord sent a terrible disease that killed all the Egyptians' livestock. But Pharaoh would not let the Israelites go.

Then the Lord said to Moses and Aaron, "Take handfuls of soot and toss them high in the air, in front of Pharaoh. It will drop as fine dust all over Egypt and give everyone terrible boils." The brothers did as He said and everyone, except for the Israelites, broke out in boils. Even Pharaoh himself was covered in boils, but still he would not relent.

"Again Pharaoh said he would let the Israelites go, but again he broke his promise."

Next, the Lord sent a violent storm, with hailstones as big as rocks, and after that a plague of locusts that devastated the country, gobbling up the crops and stripping the leaves from the trees. Again Pharaoh said he would let the Israelites go, but again he broke his promise.

And then the Lord said to Moses, "Stretch out your hand toward the sky so that darkness will be spread all over Egypt." Moses did as he was told and the sun went out, blanketing the whole of the country, except for the area where the Israelites lived.

Pharaoh summoned Moses and Aaron again. When they finally found him in the pitch black, Pharaoh said, "Go, worship the Lord. Even your women and children may go with you. But leave your flocks and your herds behind." Moses protested at this, saying they needed to take their animals with them to be used as sacrifices. Infuriated, Pharaoh changed his mind, shouting, "Get out of my sight! If I ever see you again, I will kill you!"

The Tenth Plague

*T*he Lord told Moses that he would bring one last plague to Egypt. It would be so terrible that Pharaoh would go down on his knees and beg the Israelites to leave.

At midnight, each firstborn son in Egypt would die. Even the livestock would not be spared—the firstborn cattle and sheep would also die. But the Israelites would not suffer and not one of their children would be harmed. Moses approached Pharaoh yet again, as he had done so many times before, to plead for the Israelites' freedom and to give him God's chilling message. But Pharaoh did not believe him, and Moses came away seething with rage.

Then the Lord told Moses and his brother, Aaron, that from now on this would be the beginning of the Israelites' year, instead of the first month of harvest. It was early spring and that night there was a new Moon. On the tenth day of the first month each Israelite household must choose the best firstborn lamb and prepare it for slaughter. It should be a one-year-old. Four days later, at dusk, the lamb must have its throat slit and its blood was to be used to mark the door of the house. That night there should be a feast, with the meat roasted over the fire and eaten with bitter herbs and special bread, made without yeast.

"It will be known as the Passover sacrifice to the Lord"

God said that this would be the very night when He would pass through Egypt and all the firstborn sons, cattle, and sheep would die. But He would see the bloody marks on the Israelites' doors and they would be safe.

Moses listened and then summoned all the elders of the Israelites to him. He told them what was going to happen in two weeks time and told them what they must do. "It will be known as the Passover sacrifice to the Lord, because He will pass over the houses of the Israelites in Egypt and spare our homes when He strikes down the Egyptians," he said. "And from that time on the Passover feast must be celebrated for all times."

So, two weeks later, the Israelites slaughtered their lambs and roasted them over the fire. They smeared their doors with blood, then tightly closed them against the night, uncertain of what was to come. They feasted on the roasted meat with bitter herbs—wild lettuce, endive, and nettle—and unleavened bread.

At midnight, when the Moon hung heavy in the sky, the Lord passed silently over Egypt, just as He had promised, and killed all the firstborn sons as they lay sleeping. And He wiped out all the firstborn cattle and sheep, too. After He came and went, the dead lay in their beds and in their cots and in their fields.

Howls of grief were heard as the people discovered their lifeless sons. Soon, a wailing filled the air as the scale of the horror was revealed. Sorrow and terror swept the country. Not one Egyptian household had escaped the massacre— not even Pharaoh's. Beating his breast, he summoned Moses and Aaron and sobbed, "Leave my people, you and the Israelites! Go, worship the Lord as you have requested. Take your flocks and your herds and go! Have pity on me!"

The Israelites left immediately, asking the Egyptians for silver and gold and clothing, as Moses told them to do. They had lived in Egypt for four hundred and thirty years and, at last, they had been released from their slavery. Six hundred thousand men, women, and children set off on foot, with their flocks and herds, at the start of their long journey.

Just as God had instructed them, the Israelites marked their doors with blood

The Crossing of the Red Sea

So the Lord led His people out of Egypt and through the desert, on their way to the land of Canaan. It was a huge group, with all the different tribes and clans of Israel.

The Israelites took what few cattle and sheep they had with them, and their donkeys were piled high. They were careful to avoid the land of their enemy, the Philistines, and went the long way around, toward the land that God had promised their forefathers. They took with them, too, the bones of Joseph, which had been carefully preserved. An oath had been sworn, long ago, that the bones would be taken back to Canaan to be buried by the side of his father, Jacob.

The Israelites traveled eastward, a vast human river creeping through the harsh desert landscape. Then they turned southward toward the Red Sea. And the Lord was with them and He guided them during the day with a pillar of cloud. By night, He led them with a pillar of fire, like a beacon, so they could see the path.

In Egypt, Pharaoh had a sudden change of heart. "What have we done?" he asked. "We have let the Israelites go and lost our slaves. Prepare the chariots!" At once, the army was assembled and Pharaoh set off in pursuit of the Israelites, with six hundred of his finest chariots and the fastest horses. They pounded through the desert in a cloud of dust, with thundering hooves and cracking whips.

The Israelites, camping on the shores of the Red Sea, felt the earth tremble and looked at each other in fear. Then they saw the Egyptians charging toward them, their armor glinting in the sun.

The Lord said to Moses, "Tell the Israelites to move on. Raise your staff and stretch out your hand over the sea to divide the water. The Israelites will be able to go through the sea on dry ground." And the great pillar of cloud and fire, which had guided the Israelites on their journey, moved behind them, protecting them from their pursuers.

As Moses stretched out his hand over the Red Sea, a strong east wind whipped up out of nowhere and the waters parted to reveal a path that stretched all the way across to the other side. The Israelites hurried along the muddy track as fast as they could. Huge walls of water towered above them, to their right and to their left. They crossed in their thousands and arrived on the other shore.

The Egyptians followed, driving their chariots toward the sea. But the wheels got stuck in the mud of the seabed. They could not move.

Then the Lord said to Moses, "Stretch out your hand over the sea so that the waters may flow back over the Egyptians and their chariots." Moses obeyed, and the walls of water crashed together, meeting in a sea of boiling foam. The path across the Red Sea vanished, as the waters swallowed the entire Egyptian army.

The Israelites, watching from the other side, embraced and gave thanks. And Moses's sister, Miriam, took her tambourine and led the women in singing and dancing. "Sing to the Lord for He is highly exalted. The horse and its rider He has hurled in the sea!"

"Raise your staff and stretch out your hand over the sea to divide the water. The Israelites will be able to go through the sea on dry ground."

God Watches Over the Israelites

*A*fter the Israelites had crossed the Red Sea, Moses and Aaron led them up into the Desert of Shur.

For three days they walked under the scorching Sun, and, by the time they reached the spring at Marah, their throats were parched and dry. They rushed to the water, but it was foul and undrinkable and they looked at Moses. "What are we meant to drink?" they asked him.

The Lord showed Moses a special tree. He snapped off a piece of wood and threw it into the spring. Immediately, the water became sweet and pure. The Israelites tried it again and this time drank gladly and quenched their thirst. Refreshed, they continued on their way to Elim, where there were twelve springs and seventy shady palm trees. They slept well that night under a clear, starry sky.

Then Moses and Aaron led them on their way through the dry and stony wilderness. The landscape was so different from the green valley of the Nile River, which they had fled. There, although their lives as slaves were hard, at least the food was plentiful. Here, there was nothing, and their supplies had run out. "If only we had died by the Lord's hand in Egypt," they grumbled at Moses. "There we ate all the food we wanted. You have taken us to a desert to starve."

Then the Lord spoke to Moses and Aaron again and said, "I will rain down food from heaven for you. The people are to go out and gather it each day. At twilight they will eat meat and in the morning they will have as much bread as they want." Moses and Aaron repeated God's words, saying, "In the evening you will know that it was the Lord who brought you out of Egypt and in the morning you will see the glory of the Lord, because He has heard you grumbling against Him. Who are we? You are not grumbling against us, but against the Lord."

That same evening, as the Sun began to set, a huge flock of quails appeared in the distance on their long migration across the desert. They flew toward the Israelites' camp, swooping lower and lower on tired wings, and finally dropped to the ground, exhausted by their journey. The plump little bodies rained down in their thousands, the soft brown feathers matching the sand where they fell. They lay there motionless, waiting to be caught. The Israelites lit their fires and prepared the birds, roasting them over the flames. The flesh was succulent and, after so long without food, the Israelites feasted to their hearts' content.

The next day, the Israelites woke up to find that the ground was covered with strange white flakes that looked like thick frost. They were puzzled, and Moses told them, "It is the bread the Lord has given you to eat, and you are to gather it each morning. Take just as much as you need for that day—no more."

> "How long will you refuse to keep my commands and instructions?"

It was the color of coriander seed and tasted delicious, like the sweetest honey. The Israelites had never seen anything like it and they called it manna. But some people were greedy and ignored the instructions. They grabbed as much as they could and stuffed it in their bags. After a few hours the smell was terrible and the manna was alive with white maggots.

On the sixth day, Moses told them they could take enough manna to last them two days. "Tomorrow is to be a day of rest, a holy Sabbath to the Lord. Six days you are to gather but not on the seventh."

Nevertheless, a few people disobeyed and went out at dawn the next day to look for manna. But the manna had vanished into thin air. And the Lord said to Moses, "How long will you refuse to keep my commands and instructions?"

Then the Israelites traveled on farther through the desert under a burning Sun, and they camped at Rephidim that night. They were tired and thirsty and went to Moses to complain again. "Why did you bring us out of Egypt to make us die of thirst?" they moaned.

Moses did not know what to do. He appealed to the Lord again. "What am I to do with these people?" he asked. "They are almost ready to stone me."

The Lord told him to walk ahead, taking with him his wooden staff. "I will stand there before you by the rock at Horeb," the Lord said. "Strike the rock and water will come out of it for the people to drink." Moses went on and found the spot. He hit the sheer rock face and immediately a stream of crystal-clear water gushed out, sparkling in the sun.

Moses Receives God's Laws

*T*hree months after the Israelites had left Egypt, they came to the sacred mountain of Sinai, where the Lord had appeared to Moses in a burning bush many years before.

And the Lord called to him now, from the top of the mountain, and Moses went up to meet Him. The Lord gave Moses a message saying, "You have seen what I did in Egypt and how I carried you here on eagles' wings. If you obey me fully and keep my covenant, then, out of all the nations, you will be my treasured possession. Although the whole earth is mine, you will be for me a kingdom of priests and a holy nation."

Moses went down and summoned the elders, telling them what God had said. Then the Lord called Moses to Him again and said that, in three days time, He would come down from the heavens in a thick cloud and speak to him in front of all the Israelites.

Three days later, the sky suddenly darkened. Peals of thunder crashed high above and lightning flashed from the heavens. A deafening trumpet blast ripped through the air.

The people huddled together in terror, but Moses went to them and led them to the bottom of the mountain. From the middle of the cloud of smoke the Lord spoke to Moses, and told him to come up with his brother, Aaron. Before he went, Moses said to the Israelites, "Do not be afraid. God has come to test you so that the fear of God will be with you to keep you from sinning." Then the two brothers climbed higher and higher into the thick cloud, where God was waiting. He said to them:

"I am the Lord your God and these are my commandments:
You shall have no other gods before me.
You shall not bow down to idols or worship them.
You shall not misuse the name of the Lord your God.
Remember the Sabbath day by keeping it holy.
Honor your father and your mother.
You shall not murder.
You shall not commit adultery.
You shall not steal.
You shall not give false testimony against your neighbor.
You shall not covet your neighbor's house or his wife or his belongings."

"I am the Lord your God and these are my commandments"

When he had finished, the Lord told them to go down and to make an altar at the bottom of the mountain. He went on to give them some more laws and said that an angel would go with the Israelites on their journey to the Promised Land. Moses and Aaron went back down to their people, who had been waiting and repeated the Lord's words. "Everything that the Lord has said, we will do," said the people. So Moses wrote all the Lord's words down in the Book of the Covenant.

They built an altar with twelve stone pillars, one for each of the twelve tribes of Israel, and they made burnt offerings to God. The best young bulls were sacrificed, and Moses sprinkled some of the blood on the altar and some over the people, saying, "This is the blood of the covenant that the Lord has made with you in accordance with all His words."

Moses holds the stone tablets given to him by God

Then Moses and Aaron went up the mountain again. This time they took with them Aaron's two sons, Nadab and Abihu, and seventy of the Israelite elders. When they reached the top, God was waiting for them, standing on a beautiful sapphire floor. And God said to Moses, "Come here and I will give you tablets of stone with the laws and commands I have given you written on them." And Moses went into the cloud and stayed on the mountain for forty days and forty nights.

The Golden Calf

With Moses staying on the mountain for such a long time, the Israelites thought he was never coming back.

They went to his brother, Aaron, and said, "Please make us a god. We need someone to worship! Moses brought us out of Egypt, but we don't know what has happened to him. He has deserted us!"

Aaron listened and thought for a little while. Then he told them to bring whatever gold jewelry they had to him. Obediently, they took off their necklaces, slipped off their bracelets and their rings, and unclipped their earrings. They even searched in their bags for any gold trinkets that they might have hidden at the beginning of their journey. They gave it all to Aaron.

The pile of gold grew, glittering in the sun, and Aaron took it and poured it into a great vat. It looked like an enormous treasure chest. He placed it over the fire, melting the gold into a thick paste. Then he let it cool slightly and molded it into the shape of a young calf. When he had finished, it bore a passing resemblance to the Egyptian bull god Apis. The Israelites watched, impressed by his skill.

Then Aaron built an altar for the golden calf, and the next day the people worshipped their new idol. They made sacrifices to it and put burnt offerings on the altar. And they feasted and drank and danced through the night.

Moses had been on the mountain for forty days, and the Lord told him that he must go down to his people again. "They have been quick to turn away from what I commanded and have made themselves an idol cast in the shape of a calf. Now, leave me alone so that my anger may burn against them and destroy them," He said.

The people persuade Aaron to make a golden calf to represent the image of God

But Moses pleaded with the Lord to spare the Israelites. He reminded Him of His promise to make their descendants as numerous as the stars in the sky in the land of Canaan. The Lord listened carefully and relented.

"They had made themselves a god of gold. But, now, please forgive their sin!"

Moses left Him and went back down the mountain, taking with him the two stone tablets that the Lord had given him, inscribed with the Lord's own writing. He had engraved the Ten Commandments on both sides. As Moses got to the bottom of the mountain, he could hear music and singing. It got louder and louder and, when he neared the camp, he saw, with horror, the shiny golden calf standing by the altar and the Israelites drinking and reveling around it. In anger, Moses threw the stone tablets to the ground, smashing them into pieces.

The Israelites looked at him in stunned silence. Then, Moses went straight over to the golden calf and hurled it into the fire. It melted in the heat, the body writhing and bubbling in the flames. When it had cooled, he took the golden cinders and pounded them into a fine powder, which he mixed with water and made the Israelites drink.

Then, he confronted his brother, Aaron. "What were you thinking of?" he shouted furiously. "How could you allow them to do this?" Moses could see that the Israelites were out of control. They were a danger to themselves and had become a laughing stock to their enemies.

Moses went to the entrance of the camp and summoned the people to him. "Whoever is on the side of the Lord, come to me!" he shouted. And the people of the Levite tribe were the only ones who came to his side. Everyone else stood back and looked the other way. He told the Levites that they must take their swords and teach the rest of the Israelites a lesson. There was a terrible massacre that day as the Levites killed at least three thousand of their kinsmen.

Afterward, Moses congratulated the Levites and said to them, "You have been set apart today and the Lord has blessed you." Then he went back up the mountain to speak to the Lord and to ask for His forgiveness. "Oh what a great sin these people have committed," he said. "They had made themselves a god of gold. But, now, please forgive their sin!"

"Go, lead the people to the Promised Land and my angel will go with you," replied the Lord. "However, they have sinned and I will punish them when the time is right!" And He told Moses to write the Ten Commandments on two new tablets of stone to replace the ones that had been broken.

Balaam's Donkey

After many years, the tribes of Israel were finally allowed to go to the Promised Land of Canaan.

They arrived on the plains of Moab, fresh with victory over the neighboring Amorites, and camped in the thousands along the Jordan River, across from Jericho. Balak, who ruled Moab, was horrified at the sight of them. He sent his envoys with a message and a fee to the famous soothsayer Balaam, who lived on the banks of the Euphrates. "A people has come out of Egypt; they cover the face of the land and have settled next to me. Come and put a curse on them because they are too powerful. Then I can defeat them and drive them from my country."

Balaam received the message and slept on it. In the night, the Lord came to him and said, "Do not go with these men. You must not put a curse on the tribes of Israel because they are blessed and are the chosen people." So Balaam told the envoys that he could not help them and they returned, unsuccessful, to Balak.

But the King refused to give up and sent the most distinguished princes in the land to Balaam. They offered Balaam great riches, but he replied, "Even if Balak gave me his palace filled with silver and gold, still I could not go against the word of the Lord my God. Stay here tonight and I will find out what the Lord says."

That night, God spoke to Balaam to see what was in his heart. "Go with these men, but you must obey me and do only as I say," He told him. So, the next morning, Balaam saddled his favorite donkey and set off with the princes back to the land of Moab. But God was not pleased that Balaam had gone.

Suddenly, as they plodded along the dusty road, the angel of the Lord appeared, sword in hand, to stop Balaam. The little donkey saw him and shied off the road. But, full of his own self-importance, Balaam was blind to the apparition. He cursed and beat the donkey to get her back onto the road.

Then the angel appeared again, blocking a narrow path that snaked between two vineyards, with walls on each side. Again, the donkey saw the angel and squeezed against the wall to avoid him, crushing Balaam's foot in the process. As before, Balaam did not even glimpse the angel and beat the donkey.

For the third time, the angel appeared, standing in the middle of the path. It was impossible to get past. The little donkey's legs folded under her and she collapsed to the ground. Balaam could not see the apparition and he beat the donkey to within an inch of her life. At this point, the donkey opened her mouth and asked, "What have I done to make you beat me?"

"You have made a fool of me!" he shouted. "If only I had a sword, I would kill you now."

"You must not put a curse on the tribes of Israel because they are blessed and are the chosen people."

Then suddenly, the Lord removed the veil from Balaam's eyes and he saw the angel, gleaming sword in hand. Terrified, Balaam fell to the ground.

"Why have you beaten your donkey?" asked the angel. "I would have killed you, if she had not saved you. But I would have spared her." Balaam begged forgiveness and the angel told him to continue with the princes to Balak in the land of Moab. "Go with these men, but speak only what I tell you," he said.

When Balaam arrived, he was met by the King. "I have come here as asked," the soothsayer said, "but I can speak only the words that God puts in my mouth." Together, they went up to the mountains where they could see the tribes of Israel below. There, they built seven great altars and put a bull and a ram on each one as offerings. Then Balaam left Balak and his princes with the sacrifices and climbed higher to the most solitary peak to meet the Lord. When he came down again, the charred offerings were still smouldering and Balaam delivered God's message, blessing the people of Israel instead of cursing them.

THE PROMISED LAND
Towering 4,058 ft (1,237 m) over the Dead
Sea, Mount Nebo provides a panoramic view
of the Promised Land. According to the Bible,
God would not let Moses enter this land,
as punishment for an earlier disobedience.

Then Moses climbed Mount Nebo from the plains of Moab to the top of Pisgah, across from Jericho. There the Lord showed him the whole land—from Gilead to Dan…. Then the Lord said to him, "This is the land I promised on oath to Abraham, Isaac, and Jacob when I said, 'I will give it to your descendants.' I have let you see it with your eyes, but you will not cross over into it."

Deuteronomy 34:1–4

The Promised Land

*T*he Israelites were camped in the Paran Desert, near Canaan, and the Lord told Moses to send some scouts ahead. Moses picked twelve men, one from each of the tribes of Israel, and sent them on their way.

"Go through the Negev and into Canaan," Moses said to them. "Check out the lie of the land and see what the people are like."

The twelve men set off, traveling through the arid landscape until they got to Canaan. They reached Hebron and the Valley of Eschol, which was fertile and green. The trees were heavy with fruit. They cut a gigantic bunch of sweet grapes from the vines, so heavy that it took two men to carry it. They also took juicy pomegranates and luscious figs. Altogether, they spent forty days exploring Canaan, before returning to Moses and the Israelites.

When they got back, the scouts reported that Canaan was a beautiful country that did, indeed, flow with milk and honey. But ten of them, who liked to stir up trouble, made up a story that Canaan was full of giants who lived in walled cities. "We can't attack them—we wouldn't stand a chance!" they said. "They are much stronger than us. Beside them, we look like grasshoppers!"

Two of the scouts, named Caleb and Joshua, remained silent. The rest of the Israelites looked at each other grimly. "If only we had died in Egypt," they sighed, looking at Moses and Aaron. "Or in this desert. Why did the Lord bring us to the Promised Land if we are going to be killed? Why don't we go back to Egypt?"

Caleb and Joshua then told their story. They said that the inhabitants of Canaan were not giants and that it would be an excellent place to live. "Do not rebel against the Lord," they pleaded. "And don't be afraid of the people who live in Canaan. We will easily get the better of them. The Lord is with us." But no one believed them and some talked about stoning them to death.

The Lord heard the tribes of Israel complaining yet again and was saddened and angry. "How long will these people treat me with contempt?" He asked Moses. "How long will they refuse to believe in me, in spite of the miraculous signs I have shown them?" He said that, as a result of their sins, they would be condemned to wander in the desert for forty years before being allowed to enter the Promised Land of Canaan. "In this desert you will die, every one of you who has complained so much. Not one of you will enter the land I swore to make your home—except Caleb, son of Jephunneh, and Joshua, son of Nun. But your children will reach Canaan and will enjoy the land that their parents will never reach."

The years went by and the tribes of Israel wandered in the bleak and inhospitable wilderness. Moses grew old and he realized that, after all this time, he would not live to cross the Jordan River and get to Canaan. He summoned Joshua and, in front of everyone, said to him, "Be strong and courageous, for you are the one who must lead the people into the Promised Land. And you must divide it between them. Do not be afraid, the Lord will be with you."

Moses told the Israelite people to follow God's Law, the Ten Commandments, which were written down on two tablets of stone and kept in the Ark of the Covenant—a magnificent golden chest, guarded by two cherubim with outstretched wings. The Israelites carried the Ark with them wherever they went on their wanderings. When they stopped to set up camp, the Ark was put in the most sacred place, deep within the holy tabernacle—the brightly colored tent that was set up for worship.

The Lord shows Moses the Promised Land

The same day, Moses went to Mount Nebo in Moab, just across from the city of Jericho. Although he was very old, his body was still strong and his eyes were keen. He climbed slowly up the high mountain and the Lord showed him the land of Canaan, which had taken so many years and such hardships to reach. He stood at the top and saw the Promised Land, at last. It stretched across the Jordan River and the Salt Sea all the way to the waters of the Great Sea in the west. And the Lord said to him, "This is the land I promised on oath to Abraham, Isaac, and Jacob. You have now seen it with your own eyes, but you will never reach it."

"How long will they refuse to believe in me, in spite of the miraculous signs I have shown them?"

And Moses died that day in Moab, one hundred and twenty years after he had been found as a tiny baby, hidden in the thick bulrushes of the Nile River in Egypt. The Israelite people grieved for thirty days, weeping and mourning. They knew that there would never be another prophet like him in the history of Israel.

Canaanites

During the 3rd millennium BCE, the land later settled by the Israelites was called Canaan. The Canaanites lived in many small city-states, ruled by kings. Finds of pottery from Greece and ivory from Egypt show that the Canaanites were great traders. Their need to keep records led to their invention of an alphabet, in about 1700 BCE, which later developed into the Hebrew script.

The most important Canaanite city-states are shown on this map. From about 1550 BCE, these city-states came under the control of Egypt.

King of Megiddo
An ivory plaque from Megiddo shows a king seated on a throne, entertained by a harp player. On the right, he returns from battle with two prisoners of war.

Mound of Megiddo

Over many generations, layers of debris from Canaanite cities built up, forming mounds called "tells." This aerial photograph shows the mound of Megiddo, where archeologists uncovered 25 layers of occupation.

GODS

Asherah

The mother goddess Asherah was the wife of the creator god, El. She was worshiped in the form of a wooden pole. In the Bible the Hebrews are told to "cut down their Asherah poles" (Exodus 34:13).

Astarte

A goddess of war, storms, and love, Astarte was linked with the planet Venus. She was also worshiped in Mesopotamia, where she was called Ishtar. In the Bible she is called "Ashtoreth, the vile goddess of the Sidonians" (II Kings 23:13).

Baal

The storm god, Baal, brought the rain that made the crops grow. "Baal" means lord, and was a title used as a sign of respect. Only his priests were allowed to say his real name, which was Hadod.

Dagon

The father of Baal, Dagon was a god of farming and grain. He was adopted as a chief god by the Philistines, who later settled on the coast. After capturing the Israelite hero Samson, "the rulers of the Philistines assembled to offer a great sacrifice to Dagon their god and to celebrate" (Judges 16:23).

El

El was the supreme creator, who made all the other gods. In Canaanite texts, the gods are called "elohim," meaning the family of El. The Bible uses "Elohim" as a name for God, or to mean "heavenly beings."

Goddess

This pottery figurine shows a Canaanite goddess, perhaps Asherah. The Canaanites worshiped their gods at open-air shrines, called "high places," often on hilltops. In the Bible, God tells Moses to "demolish all their high places" (Numbers 33:52).

Mycenaean flask

This flask, with its circular decoration, is evidence of Canaanite trade. Although it was found in a Canaanite tomb, it was made across the sea in Greece by a Mycenaean potter. It would have held perfumed oil.

Bronze

The Canaanites lived during the Bronze Age, when bronze was the hardest available metal. Bronze is made of copper and tin, both rare metals. The copper used to make this Canaanite wine pitcher and strainer came from Egyptian mines in Sinai.

Rahab and the Spies

*A*fter the death of Moses, the Lord told Joshua
that the Israelites should get ready to cross the
River Jordan and enter the land of Canaan.

"It will all be yours—from the desert to the Lebanon and from the Euphrates
River to the Great Sea in the west," He said. "No- one will be able to stand up to
you. As I was with Moses, so I will be with you. I will never leave you or forsake
you. But always be careful to obey the laws that my servant Moses gave you!"

Joshua told his people the Lord's message but, first, he sent two spies ahead
to Jericho on the west bank of the Jordan. Jericho was the most important city
in the whole of Canaan. The two men set off through the desert, at dead of
night. Guided by the Moon and the stars, they crossed the river and drew near
to the city. The great stone walls of the city loomed darkly over them, with their
lookout towers and fortresses. The two spies hid among the palm trees until the
Sun began to rise. Then they slipped quietly through the city gates, just as they
opened, mingling with the noisy traders
and merchants. Like shadows, they flitted
through the narrow streets and past the
temple, hearing fearful talk about the
Israelites on every corner.

> "I will never leave you or
> forsake you. But always be
> careful to obey the laws that
> my servant Moses gave you!"

But the spies needed somewhere to lie
low. They found a little house in the city
walls that was perfect. It belonged to a
woman named Rahab. She invited them in and told them to make themselves
comfortable, offering them food and water. And soon, she agreed to help them.

By now, the ruler of Jericho had heard a rumor that some spies might have
gotten into the city and he was worried. He knew what a danger the Israelites
were. They had wreaked death and destruction on the neighboring Amorites,
and everybody had heard how the Lord had parted the waters of the Red Sea for
them. He sent his henchmen to search every house in Jericho from top to bottom.

Rahab had taken the two spies up to the roof of her house and had hidden
them under some flax that she was drying in the sun. The henchmen arrived
and asked her if she had seen the men. "They did come here," replied Rahab,
smiling sweetly at them, "but I didn't know who they were. If only I'd known!"
They searched her house anyway and climbed the steep steps up to the roof.
All they saw were large bundles of plants laid out to dry. The men left to
search the house next door.

*With the help of Rahab, the
spies escape from Jericho*

When they had gone, Rahab climbed up to the roof and gave the two spies the all clear. They emerged cautiously from the piles of flax and dusted themselves off. Rahab looked at them and said, "I know that the Lord has given this land to the Israelites. We have all heard about you. We are frightened! Please be kind to me and my family. Haven't I been kind to you? I beg you to spare my father and mother, my brothers and sisters."

The men smiled at each other and nodded. "A life for a life!" they replied. "Help us to escape and we will help to save you when we attack Jericho." They told her to tie a scarlet ribbon in her window when she heard that the Israelites were advancing. It would be a sign, and she and her family would be spared. But she must swear that she would not betray them. She agreed, thankfully, and went to find a thick rope.

They waited till the middle of the night when all was quiet and still in the city. Then they tiptoed to the window. They could see the guard dozing off. They waited patiently, listening to the distant snuffling of boars and the screeching of an owl, until at last the guard fell fast asleep. Rahab took the rope and dropped it silently out of the window, tying it firmly to a thick beam inside. Then, one after the other, the men climbed down and landed outside the city walls. "Go to the hills and hide!" Rahab whispered. "They'll never find you there!" The spies stayed hidden for three days in the hills. Then they returned to Joshua and told him what had happened.

The Battle of Jericho

*T*he two spies got back from Canaan, and they told
Joshua that the country was gripped by fear.

So the Israelites moved forward and made their camp by the side of the
Jordan River. Joshua spoke to the assembled group. "The Ark of the Covenant
will go first, carried by the Levite priests. You must follow it—but at a distance. As
soon as the priests set foot in the river, the waters will stop flowing. There will be
a path of dry land to the other side, and you will all be able to cross safely."

Three days later, the priests led the way, carrying the Ark, which contained the
two stone tablets with the Ten Commandments written on them. Sure enough,
as soon as they stepped in the water, the river stopped flowing and they walked
to the middle. They waited there with the golden Ark glinting in the sun, and
the Israelites started to walk across.

Joshua chose twelve men, one from each tribe. He told them to stop in the middle of the dry path, where the priests stood, and to pick up a stone. They did this, and carried the stones to the other side. When all the Israelites had crossed, the priests came with the Ark. As they stepped onto the bank, the river began flowing again.

They set up camp at Gilgal on the plains of Jericho. Joshua took the twelve stones and set them in the earth as a memorial to the people of Israel. Now the forty thousand Israelite soldiers were gathering. It was a fearsome sight. The King of Jericho ordered the city gates to be shut tight and bolted.

Then the Lord said to Joshua, "Go to Jericho with your soldiers and march round the city once. Take the Ark with you. Seven priests must walk in front of it, sounding their trumpets. Do the same for six days. Then, on the seventh day, march around the city like this seven times. At the end, the priests must sound a long trumpet blast and everyone must shout together, as loud as they can."

"Go to Jericho with your soldiers and march round the city once. Take the Ark with you."

And so, the soldiers advanced on Jericho and marched round the city walls. The priests sounded their trumpets in front of the Ark. The walls shook, and inside the people watched in terror. For six days, the Israelites marched. On the seventh day, they marched round the city seven times and the priests raised their trumpets. A long, mournful blast filled the air. At this, Joshua gave the signal and the Israelites shouted at the tops of their voices.

But as the chorus faded away, another sound could be heard. A rumble came from the city walls and it grew louder. Suddenly, cracks appeared in the stone and bricks. The Israelites watched as the walls collapsed, crashing to the ground.

Without its great wall, Jericho was at the mercy of the Israelite soldiers. They rushed in and killed every living thing. The soldiers knew where Rahab lived, because of the scarlet ribbon in her window, so she and her family were spared.

The Call of Gideon

For seven years, the tribes of Israel suffered at the hands of their neighbors, the Midianites. The Lord told the Israelites that they were being punished because they had been worshipping false gods.

One day, a young Israelite named Gideon was busy at work, threshing wheat. From the shade of a great oak tree, a tall figure approached him. He greeted Gideon courteously and said, "The Lord is with you, mighty warrior!"

"But, sir, if the Lord is with us why does He allow our enemies, the Midianites, to overrun our country?" Gideon asked. "The Lord has abandoned us!"

The stranger smiled and said, "The Lord has chosen you. You are to save Israel from the Midianites. The Lord will be with you!" Gideon shook his head in disbelief.

He went to get some food for the stranger. The man had sat down to rest under the oak tree and, when Gideon approached, he asked him to put the dishes on a rock just by him. He then tapped the food with the tip of his wooden staff and a bright flame shot out of the rock and the food disappeared. And then the stranger vanished into thin air himself. As Gideon stood staring in wonder, it slowly dawned on him that he had seen an angel.

That night, Gideon smashed the altar that his father had made to the god Baal. He also cut down the wooden Asherah pole, which was sacred to the goddess Asherah. Then, with the help of his servants, he made a new altar to the Lord and sacrificed a fully grown bull on it.

In the morning, when the people saw that Baal's altar had been destroyed and that the Asherah pole had vanished, they were angry. They discovered that Gideon was the culprit and called for his blood. But his father, Joash, replied, "If Baal really is a god, he can defend himself when someone destroys his altar!" The people listened and agreed.

The Midianites and their allies from the east had now joined forces. They were camping in the Valley of Jezreel. Gideon knew the moment had come, and he took his trumpet and blew it loud and clear, calling the Israelites to arms.

Thousands of men came to join him. Next morning, he led them all to the Spring of Harod at the foot of Mount Gilboa, and they made their camp. To the north, the Midianites were gathered in the valley near the hill of Moreh.

Gideon smashes the altar to Baal and cuts down the Asherah pole

The Israelite soldiers smash their jars and blow their trumpets

But now the Lord said to Gideon, "You have too many men. I do not want my people to forget me and to think that it is their strength alone that will bring victory over the enemy. If some of your men are having second thoughts, let them go." And twenty-two thousand of Gideon's men turned around and left. There were still ten thousand soldiers, but the Lord said again, "There are too many! Take them down to the water and see who drinks using their cupped hands. They shall stay with you. But those who drink kneeling down shall be sent away." After this, Gideon was left with only three hundred men.

Later, at dead of night, he crept toward the Midian camp. From inside a tent, Gideon could hear a man talking. "I had a dream last night," he said. "A round loaf of barley bread came tumbling into our camp. It hit the tent with such force that it collapsed."

> "The Lord has chosen you. You are to save Israel from the Midianites."

And another voice replied, "That must be Gideon, the son of Joash, the Israelite. We've heard about him! God has promised him victory!"

Gideon rushed back to his men. "Get up!" he shouted. "I know the Lord is with us! He will destroy the Midianites for us!" He gave them all trumpets, jars, and torches, and silently they approached the enemy camp. On Gideon's order, they blew their trumpets and smashed their jars. Then they held their torches high in the air, lighting the darkness, and shouted loudly into the night. The Midianites woke up, confused and terrified. They did not know what the noise was or what the strange lights were. In panic, they drew their swords and turned on each other, and then fled into the night.

Jephthah's Daughter

Jephthah lived in Gilead and was a brave young warrior. But his brothers did not like him because he had a different mother from them.

When their father died, they ganged up against Jephthah and drove him away from home. "You're not going to inherit anything," they jeered. "You're the son of that other woman. Our father never even married her."

Jephthah left, knowing that there was no place for him there. He went south to the land of Tob, not far from the Sea of Galilee. It was a wild and lawless place, and he lived there for many years. He gathered a band of men, drifters from far and wide. He taught them to be fearless fighters, who joined battles wherever they could.

"If you give the Ammonites into my hands, I will sacrifice the first thing I set eyes on when I get home."

The years passed and the Ammonites attacked the Israelites in Gilead. There was terrible bloodshed and the elders of Gilead remembered a brave young soldier named Jephthah who had disappeared long ago. They tracked him down in Tob and begged him to return. "Come," they pleaded. "Be our commander so we have a chance against the Ammonites."

But Jephthah's heart was steely. "I was hated in Gilead and driven from my father's house. No one helped me. Why should I help you now?"

"Come back with us and fight the Ammonites, and we will put you in charge of all the soldiers. The Lord is our witness," they said.

At last, Jephthah was persuaded and he said goodbye to his men and went back with the elders to Gilead. He was appointed commander-in-chief of the army and was regarded with great respect.

Jephthah sent a message to the Ammonite King to ask him why he had invaded Gilead. A message came back from the King. "When the tribes of Israel came out of Egypt, they took my land from the Arnon River to the Jabbok River, all the way to the Jordan. We want it back."

Jephthah replied that the Israelites had won the land fairly and squarely, long before the Ammonites were there. He responded, "Now, since the God of Israel drove the Ammonites out of the land and gave it to the Israelites, what right have you to take it over? I have not wronged you, but you are doing me wrong by waging war against me. Let the Lord, the Judge, decide the dispute this day."

As the troops assembled under their new commander, Jephthah made a vow to the Lord. He was desperate for victory. "If you give the Ammonites into my hands, I will sacrifice the first thing I set eyes on when I get home," he promised. The battle was long and bloody, but Jephthah's soldiers swept all before them, devastating twenty towns that belonged to the Ammonites.

Jephthah returned home in triumph. The door of his house was open and his daughter skipped straight out to meet him. She was playing her tambourine and singing to welcome him home. As soon as he set eyes on her, he screamed in horror, screwing up his eyes to blot out the sight of her, but it was too late. He cried, "Oh my precious child—my blessing and my curse! I made a vow to the Lord and I cannot break it. What hollow victory!"

She said sadly, "Father, I know you have given your word to the Lord. He has given you victory and you must keep your promise. But, please give me time to say goodbye to my dear friends." Jephthah nodded, unable to speak.

And she went away with her friends for two months to weep. They mourned for the life that would be taken from her. Then, she came back and presented herself to her father. True to his word, he killed his only daughter and sacrificed her on the altar as an offering to the Lord.

Jephthah's daughter runs out to greet her father

The Philistines

From the end of the 13th century BCE, Egypt came under attack by fleets of invaders from the Aegean Sea. Although the Egyptians fought off the "Sea Peoples," as they called the invaders, they lost control of Canaan. Here one of the Sea Peoples, the Philistines, settled on the southern coastal plain. The Philistines then moved into the hill country to the east, which was the homeland of the Israelite tribes.

Pottery coffin
Until recently, human-shaped pottery coffins, like the one shown here, were thought to be Philistine. The headdress on this coffin seems to match Egyptian carvings of Philistines. Such coffins are now thought to date back to the earlier Egyptians stationed in Canaan.

This map shows Philistine territory at its greatest size, around 1050 BCE. There were five main Philistine cities, shown here.

Philistine prisoners
Philistine warriors wore unusual feathered or spiked headdresses, shown on this Egyptian relief. It was set up by Pharaoh Rameses III to celebrate his defeat of the Sea Peoples. These are Philistine prisoners of war who have been tied together.

TIMELINE

1184–1153 BCE
Reign of Egyptian Pharaoh Rameses III, who defeats an invasion by Sea Peoples, including the "Peleset," or Philistines. Driven out of Egypt, the Philistines conquer and settle the southern coast of Canaan.

1150–1050 BCE
The Philistines expand their territory inland, seizing territory from the Israelite tribes.

1025 BCE
The Israelite tribes are united under Saul, their first king.

1005 BCE
Saul is killed in battle, fighting the Philistines.

1005–965 BCE
Reign of King David, whose armies drive the Philistines back to the coastal strip.

Chariots

Unlike the Israelites, the Philistines went to battle in horse-drawn chariots. According to the Bible, the Philistine army included 3,000 chariots and soldiers "as numerous as the sand on the seashore" (1 Samuel 13:5).

Iron weapons

The Philistines knew how to work iron, which is harder than bronze and more readily available. Iron weapons, such as this dagger, gave Philistine armies an advantage over the Israelites. In time, the Israelites also learned to use iron.

Philistine pottery

Our idea of the Philistines comes from the writings of their enemies, the Israelites. So "Philistine" became a term of abuse for someone uncultured. Yet this Philistine strainer, decorated with a face, is finer than any Israelite pottery of the time.

Samson and the Lion

The Philistines swept through the south of Canaan, where the tribes of Dan and Judah lived. They brought their gods and they set up altars to them.

Although the Israelites feared the invaders, they began to worship their gods. So the Lord decided to punish them by allowing the Philistines to stay for forty years.

Manoah belonged to the tribe of Dan and he lived in the village of Zorah. He was faithful to the Lord but, to his great sadness, he had no children. One day, his wife was working in the fields when a stranger suddenly appeared. He told her that he had come from God and announced that she was going to have a son. "The boy is to be a Nazarite and his hair must never be cut," he said. "He will be set apart from other children and will dedicate his life to God. He will be the one who will start to save Israel from the Philistines."

> "The boy is to be a Nazarite and his hair must never be cut."

Manoah's wife listened in amazement and rushed to find her husband. She told him the joyful news, and Manoah wanted to hear it for himself. He prayed to the Lord, and the messenger came back and repeated his words. Then Manoah invited him to stay for something to eat. He also asked him his name.

"Why do you ask my name?" the man asked. "It is beyond understanding. I am happy to stay, but do not give me food. Make an offering to the Lord, instead."

So Manoah took a young goat and sacrificed it on the altar, with an offering of grain. The divine messenger rose to the heavens in the smoke and disappeared. Manoah realized that their visitor had been the angel of the Lord.

In time, their baby boy was born and they named him Samson. He was blessed and, from the very first moment, his life was dedicated to God. As the years went by, Samson grew tall and strong and his hair grew longer and longer. But he fell in love with a beautiful young Philistine woman who lived in the fortress town of Timnah in the Sorek Valley. His parents were not pleased.

One day, Samson was on his way to Timnah when a young lion jumped out from the undergrowth in front of him. Samson felt an incredible strength surge through him. He knew it came from God. He grabbed the animal's throat and killed it with his bare hands. He left it lying there and carried on his way.

Days later, when he was coming back along the path, he saw the lion's carcass still lying there. He could hear a loud buzzing. He bent down and saw that, inside the ribcage, there was a bees' nest oozing with honey. He broke off a chunk of the honeycomb and ate most of it on his way home. There was just a small corner left to give to his parents, although he did not tell them where it came from.

*Samson kills the lion
with his bare hands*

Still his parents would not agree to their son marrying a Philistine, and Samson knew he would have to go ahead without them. He arranged the wedding feast, which would be held at his bride's house in Timnah. Her kinsmen and friends were invited, and thirty young Philistine men. The feast lasted seven days, with singing, dancing, and games from morning until night.

But, although Samson loved his bride, he felt alone among the Philistines. He knew that some of the men mocked him. He wanted to outwit them and made up a riddle. "If you give me the answer by the end of the celebrations, I will give you each a set of the finest clothes," he told them. "If you fail, you have to give me thirty sets of the finest clothes—one from each of you." And then he gave them the riddle: "Out of the eater comes forth meat; out of the strong comes something sweet."

For three days, his guests scratched their heads. Defeated, they asked the new bride to coax the answer from her husband. They even threatened to burn her house down. She went to her husband and sobbed, "You don't really love me at all, do you? If you did, you'd tell me the answer to that stupid riddle."

Samson finally relented. She told her friends and, that evening, when Samson put the riddle to them again, one of them stood up with the answer, "What is sweeter than honey? What is stronger than a lion?"

When Samson heard this, he knew he had been cheated by the Philistines and tricked by his wife. In a rage, he headed for the walled city of Askelon. Mad with fury, he ambushed thirty Philistines and slit their throats. He stripped off their clothes and took them as payment for the wager he had been cheated out of by his wife and her friends. He returned to his father's house, and his wife was given to one of his friends.

On his wedding day, Samson poses a riddle to the Philistines

Samson and Delilah

Mighty Samson was feared and hated by the Philistines. He had harassed them for years, killing thousands of them and ravaging their crops.

When he fell in love again with another Philistine beauty, Delilah, his enemies saw their chance. The five most powerful lords sidled up to her with words of temptation. "We will each give you eleven hundred pieces of silver if you can find the secret of Samson's strength."

Now, Delilah's love for Samson was great, but her greed and her fear of the scheming lords were even greater. When Samson came to see her, she flattered him, "You are afraid of nothing, my love, and your strength is legendary. What is your secret, my sweet?"

Samson smiled gently to himself. "If I was tied up with seven new bowstrings, all my strength would disappear and vanish into thin air."

Delilah persuaded him to try it out for fun. What Samson didn't know was that the Philistines were waiting next door. He went along with the game pretending to lose his strength and turn to jelly. Then, to test him, Delilah warned, "The Philistines are coming!"

Samson leapt up, snapping the knotted bowstrings as if they were the flimsiest of fairy cobwebs. "Why did you lie to me?" shouted Delilah. Samson laughed. The truth was, he said, that he had to be tied up with thick ropes that had never been used before. Again, Delilah persuaded him to play the game with brand new ropes. But as she was tying the last knot, she screamed, "The Philistines are coming!" Samson broke free immediately.

Desperate with rage, Delilah asked him again. Samson told her that if she wove his long hair into her loom he would lose his strength. The next evening, when he had fallen asleep near her loom, she set to work, weaving his hair. Then she cried, "The Philistines are coming!" Samson woke and tore free of the loom.

*Delilah weaves
Samson's long hair*

Delilah still would not give up. "How can you say you love me when you tell me nothing but lies?" she sobbed.

At last, Samson relented and told her his deepest secret. "I am a Nazarite and my life is devoted to the service of the God of Israel. As a token of obedience, I took a vow that my hair must never be cut. If I were robbed of my hair, I would lose all my strength."

> "How can you say you love me when you tell me nothing but lies?"

The next evening, after dinner, Samson fell asleep contentedly on Delilah's lap. Suddenly, one of the Philistines crept in and cut off all his long, braided hair. Staring in horror at his shaven head, Delilah screamed again, "The Philistines are coming!"

And this time they did come, and Samson woke up, helpless and weak as a kitten, unable to defend himself. The Philistines dragged him away and blinded him with burning spikes and threw him into prison in shackles. Day in and day out, he was put to work grinding corn, but day in and day out his hair began to grow back.

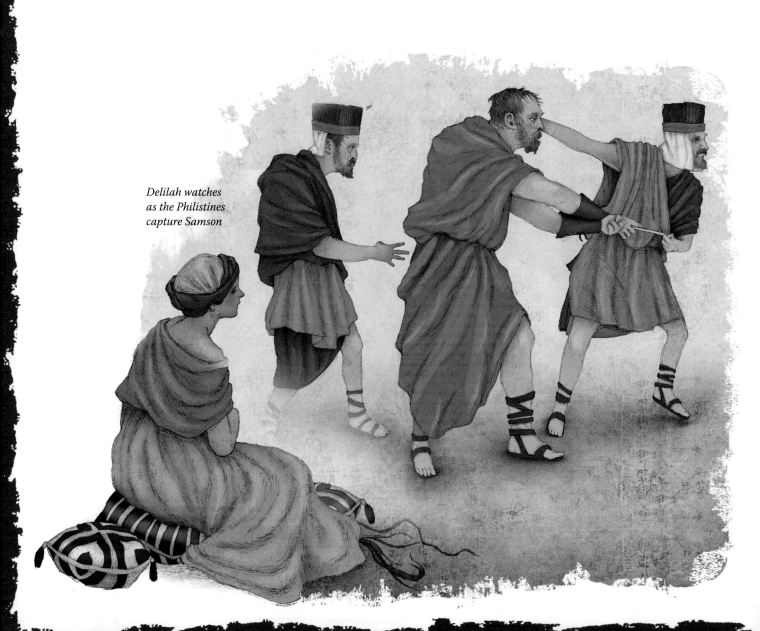

Delilah watches as the Philistines capture Samson

Samson in the Temple

*T*he Philistine lords assembled in the great temple to give thanks to Dagon, the fish god, for delivering Samson into their hands.*

They gathered, with the priests and dignitaries, to celebrate and to offer a sacrifice. And they called for Samson to be brought up from the dungeons to be paraded in front of them in his chains. It was a sweet victory for the Philistines to have at last captured their greatest foe. Three thousand people packed into the temple when they heard that they might get a glimpse of Samson. When it was full to bursting point, they poured up onto the flat roof above.

And then there was a great clanking sound, and Samson was led out of prison by his jailer. He shuffled into the temple, with blinded eyes and manacled hands and feet. Everybody craned their necks to see him. They jeered, then started to prod and beat him. And the great warrior was forced to dance on his toes to the sound of his own chains. It was a pitiful spectacle. Gasping, Samson asked his jailer to take him to rest against the temple pillars.

Then he prayed to the Lord, "O Sovereign Lord, remember me. O God, please strengthen me just once more. Let me get revenge on the Philistines for my two eyes."

Samson was standing between the two great central columns, which supported the whole of the temple. Then, he braced himself, arms outstretched between the columns, and cried, "Let me die with the Philistines!"

Samson pushed with all his might and the two pillars trembled, bringing the roof down with a crash. Soon, the other pillars gave way like a pack of cards. Everyone in the temple and on the roof—who had taunted Samson just a few moments before—was crushed to death.

When Samson's kinsmen heard the news they searched for his broken body among the ruins, then took him home. They buried him in a tomb next to his father, Manoah. With his death, Samson had killed more Philistines than he had during the whole of his lifetime.

"O God, please strengthen me just once more. Let me get revenge on the Philistines for my two eyes."

Ruth and Naomi

There was a famine in Judah, and Elimelech took his family from their home in Bethlehem to live in the land of Moab, beyond the Salt Sea.

He grew old and died there, leaving his wife Naomi with two sons. Both sons married Moabite women—one was named Orpah and the other was named Ruth. Then, sadly, both her sons died and Naomi lived with her daughters-in-law.

> "Where you go, I will go and where you stay, I will stay."

In time, Naomi heard that the famine had passed in Judah and she decided to go back, with both of her daughters-in-law. All three of them set off, but Naomi suddenly had second thoughts. How could she take the young women away from their own people? "Go back, both of you! May the Lord show kindness to you, as you have shown kindness to your dead and to me!" she said.

They both protested and wept, but Naomi would have none of it. She had made up her mind. Orpah turned around, kissing her mother-in-law goodbye, but Ruth still clung to Naomi and insisted on going with her. "Where you go, I will go and where you stay, I will stay. Your people will be my people and your God, my God," she said. So the two women traveled on together and they arrived in Bethlehem just as the harvest was beginning. Naomi's relatives welcomed her home with open arms.

Ruth joined the workers in the fields and picked up any grain that was scattered behind the harvesters. She gathered as much of the leftover grain as she could, working hard from morning till night. And Boaz, who was a relative of Elimelech, came back from town and saw the young girl working in his field. He asked his foreman who she was, then went over to talk to her. "You are welcome to collect any grain you can find," he said. "I will tell my men to look after you. Help yourself to water from the jars whenever you feel like it. It's hot work!"

Ruth bowed down low on the ground. "How kind you are. Why have I found such favor in your eyes?" she asked. "I am a foreigner!" Boaz replied that he had heard about her kindness to her mother-in-law, Naomi. He invited her to sit down and eat with the harvesters.

That evening, Ruth took the grain she had gathered back to Naomi, along with some food that had been left over from the meal. She told her mother-in-law how kind Boaz had been to her. "The Lord bless him!" said Naomi. "He is one of the very best!" And each day, Ruth went back to the same fields and worked there until the harvest was finished.

Naomi knew that Boaz admired Ruth and she decided that he would make a good husband for her. "Wash and perfume yourself and put on your best clothes," Naomi told Ruth. "Go and lie at his feet tonight after he has finished threshing and wait until he is asleep."

Ruth did as she had been told and lay down beside Boaz. In the middle of the night, Boaz woke up and was startled to find a woman lying at his feet. "Who are you?" he asked.

"I am Ruth. I have come to ask for your protection."

Boaz was delighted, and said, "The Lord bless you! Everyone knows you are a woman of noble character. You have not run after younger men, whether rich or poor. And now, don't be afraid. I will take care of you." Before long they were married and Ruth gave birth to a son, who was named Obed.

Everybody was pleased for Naomi, who had no grandchildren of her own. "Praise be to the Lord!" they said. "May this baby become famous throughout Israel. He will sustain you in old age. Your daughter-in-law loves you and is better to you than seven sons!"

Boaz sees Ruth working in one of his fields, gathering the leftover grain

Samuel is Called to Serve God

*E*lkenah had two wives, Peninnah and Hannah. Each year they all went to Shiloh to make a sacrifice and to worship in the tabernacle, with its great pillars.

Hannah was beautiful, the apple of her husband's eye, although she had not given him any children. She sat by his side at the feast and he gave her all the choicest meat. Peninnah watched, green with envy. She had given her husband children, so why was she not his favorite? She went to Hannah, taunting her cruelly, "You'll never have a baby, will you? What kind of wife are you?"

Hannah was reduced to tears. She fled to the tabernacle where Eli, the high priest, was sitting on a chair. He watched her. "O Lord! Remember me!" she prayed. "Please give me a son! I will give him to the Lord for all the days of his life, and his life will be dedicated to you." She was in such a state that Eli got up from his chair and went to her. He asked her if she was drunk? "Not so, my lord," Hannah replied, sadly. "I am a woman who is deeply troubled. I was pouring out my soul to the Lord."

Eli smiled at her and said, "Go in peace. May the God of Israel grant you what you have asked Him." Before long, Hannah discovered that her prayer had been answered and she was going to have a baby. In time, she gave birth to a son and she named him Samuel, which means "Asked of the Lord."

The time came for Hannah to take Samuel to Shiloh. When they got there, she approached Eli in the tabernacle. "I am the woman who stood here beside you praying to the Lord. Do you remember? I prayed for this child and the Lord has granted me what I asked of Him," she said. "So now I give him to the Lord. His whole life shall be dedicated to the Lord." Hannah kissed her son goodbye and handed him to Eli. From that day on, Samuel helped the high priest with his duties. Samuel wore a special linen tunic, with an embroidered belt, just like the other priests.

Each year, when Hannah came back with her husband to Shiloh, she brought a coat she had made for Samuel to wear. And Eli blessed her, saying, "May the Lord give you children to take the place of the one you prayed for and gave to the Lord!" And the Lord blessed Hannah with more children.

Samuel respected the Lord and worked hard, helping Eli as he grew older. But Eli's own sons, who were priests, were dishonest and stole offerings that were meant for the altar. Their father begged them to mend their ways, but they took no notice.

Eli watches Hannah pray in the tabernacle

One day, Eli had a visitor with a message from God, "I chose your ancestors out of all the tribes of Israel to be my priests. Why do you honor your sons more than me? Why do you allow them to grow fat on offerings that belong to me? They have brought shame and disgrace on the name of the Lord!" Eli listened, but did nothing.

> "His whole life shall be dedicated to the Lord."

In the middle of the night, Samuel heard his name being called. He ran to Eli who said, "I didn't call you! Go back to sleep!"

Samuel jumped back into bed and was just drifting off to sleep when he heard the voice again. "Samuel! Samuel!" it called.

He ran back to Eli, who said, "You must be dreaming. Go back to bed, my child!" Obediently, Samuel did as he was told and had just fallen into a deep sleep when he heard the mysterious voice again, calling "Samuel! Samuel!" Frightened, he ran to Eli again. The old man sat up and knew that it must be the Lord. He told Samuel to listen to the voice if he heard it again.

Samuel obeyed and, when he heard his name being called again, he said, "Speak, Lord, for your servant is listening."

"You must tell Eli that he and his bloodline are doomed! His sons are sinful, and he failed to stop them."

The next morning, Samuel told Eli what God had said. Eli replied sadly, "He is the Lord. He knows best!" And, as Samuel grew to manhood, the Lord was with him, and all the tribes of Israel knew that he was the prophet of the Lord.

Samuel is woken by a voice calling his name

The Ark is Captured

*T*he Philistines and the Israelites fought a battle on the Plain of Sharon. At least four thousand Israelites died, and the survivors asked, "Why did the Lord bring defeat upon us today at the hands of the Philistines?"

That night, the elders talked together, knowing that the Lord had deserted them. They decided, as a last resort, to bring the Ark of the Covenant from the tabernacle in Shiloh. They believed it would save them from their enemies.

They sent a messenger to Shiloh and, before long, the golden Ark arrived in their camp. It was brought by the high priest's two sons, Hophni and Phinehas, and was a magnificent sight. The soldiers stared in amazement and a great cheer filled the air. The ground shook. The Philistines heard the cheer from the other side of the plain and they wondered what was going on. When they found out that the Israelites had the famous Ark of the Covenant by their side, they were filled with terror. "A god has come into their camp!" they said. "We must attack!"

They advanced on the Israelites again and a battle was fought at Ebenezer. The slaughter was terrible and the Ark did not help the Israelites. Thirty thousand of them died on the battlefield, including Hophni and Phinehas. The Ark was captured by the Philistines.

> "They have sent us the Ark of the God of Israel to kill us!"

Eli, the high priest, who was ninety-eight years old, was saddened by the news of his sons. But when he was told that the Ark had been captured, he fell off his chair and broke his neck. And so the Israelites lost the high priest, as well as the Ark.

The Philistines took the Ark to the town of Ashdod and put it in the temple beside their great god, Dagon. In the morning, when they went there to pray, they saw with horror that the statue of Dagon had fallen to the ground in front of the Ark. Dagon's head and hands lay smashed on the threshold of the temple. The Lord then sent a plague of boils and a plague of rats to torment the people of Ashdod. These brought terrible disease and death.

The Philistines knew that it was all the fault of the Ark. "What shall we do with it?" they asked each other. They persuaded the neighboring town of Gath to give the Ark a home. As soon as it arrived there, plague and pestilence hit the town, and the people could not wait to get rid of the Ark. They sent it on to Ekron but, as it was carried through the town, the people shouted, "They have sent us the Ark of the God of Israel to kill us!"

The Philistine lords called an emergency meeting. The Ark had been with them for seven months now and had brought nothing but death and destruction. "How can we send the terrible thing back?" they asked each other.

The lords conferred, then told the people, "Do not send it back empty. Send a guilt offering to the God of Israel. That will do the trick." They told the people to make five gold boils and five gold rats, and put them in a chest beside the Ark, on a cart pulled by two cows. If the cart went, of its own accord, toward Beth Shemesh, where the tribe of Dan lived, then the Lord of Israel had brought the plagues. If it went the other way, the plagues had happened by chance.

Before long, a cart carrying the Ark and a chest of gold boils and gold rats set off. The cows headed straight for Beth Shemesh. The Israelites could not believe their eyes when they saw the cart. It stopped right by them and they placed the Ark on a rock, with the chest containing the gold boils and gold rats by its side. They sacrificed the two cows as offerings to the Lord.

From there, the Ark of the Covenant was taken to Kiriath Jearim in Judah, which was to become its home for the next twenty years. A shrine was made for it and a man called Eleazar, from the tribe of Levi, was consecrated to guard it.

The Ark of the Covenant is taken back to Judah

Saul, King of the Israelites

Times were hard for the tribes of Israel and they quarreled with each other all the time. There was discontent and powerful enemies on every side.

The elders gathered and came to their prophet Samuel at his home in Ramah. "You are getting old and we do not think that your sons can carry on in your footsteps," they said. "We need a king, not a prophet, to lead us."

Samuel did not like the idea of a king at all and he prayed to the Lord. "Listen to them," replied the Lord. "It is not you they have rejected but me. Just as they have rejected me from the moment that I brought them out of Egypt. They have forsaken me and worshiped other gods. But warn them what kings are like."

Samuel repeated God's words to the elders, but they took no notice. "We want to be like other nations, with a king to lead us and fight our battles."

The Lord told Samuel to do as the people asked. He said that He had chosen a young man named Saul, from the tribe of Benjamin, to be the first king of Israel. "I have decided to give my people a king. Anoint Saul as leader of all my people. He will deliver them from the hands of the Philistines."

The next day was much like any other for Saul. He had no idea what was in store. Some of his father's donkeys had wandered off and he was searching for them in the hills. When he came to the town of Zuph and heard that a seer had just arrived to bless the sacrifice, his ears pricked up. He thought that the seer might be able to use his special powers to help him find the donkeys. As Saul went into the town, he saw an old man walking slowly up the hill. He asked him where he could find the seer. The man replied, "I am the seer." And, as if he could read Saul's mind, he went on, "Do not worry about your donkeys—they have been found. Come with me to the holy place where I am going to bless the sacrifice. You have been chosen to be the first king of Israel."

Saul listened in amazement. "But I am a Benjamite from the smallest tribe of Israel. And my clan is the smallest clan of the tribe of Benjamin. Why me?" Samuel smiled but did not answer the question. He just led him up to the holy place at the top of the hill.

After the sacrifice had been made, there was a splendid feast. Saul sat in the place of honor at the head of the table and was given a special piece of meat by Samuel that had been set aside for the prophet himself.

The next day, Samuel took a large horn that was filled with oil, perfumed with spices and myrrh. He poured it slowly over Saul's head, saying, "The Lord has anointed you king of Israel, leader of all His people." And then he went on, "Now you must go home. You will meet two men who will tell you that your donkeys are found, but that your father is worrying about you. Then, by the great tree at Tabor, you will see three men with three goats, three loaves of bread, and a skin of wine. They will give you two of the loaves. Then you will go on and meet some prophets, chanting to the sound of lyres, tambourines, flutes, and harps. Join them and you too will prophesy. The Spirit of God will come upon you."

Samuel said goodbye to Saul and blessed him, telling him that he would meet him in seven days time. Saul went on his way and, sure enough, all the things that Samuel had predicted came true.

> "Anoint Saul as leader of all my people. He will deliver them from the hands of the Philistines."

Samuel summoned all the people to Mizpah to make the great announcement that a king had been chosen. But as they assembled in their thousands, Saul was nowhere to be seen. Eventually, he was found hiding behind some bags, pale with fear and apprehension. Reluctantly, he came out and stood by Samuel, head and shoulders above the rest of the crowd. "This is your king!" the prophet declared. "He has been chosen by the Lord."

Everybody cheered and shouted, "Long live the King!" But some people looked doubtful and shook their heads. Then Samuel explained the rules of kingship and wrote them down on a scroll that he dedicated to the Lord.

People had come from all over the country to see their new king, to swear allegiance, and to bring him gifts. But some of the Israelites were not happy with their new king. "How can he save us? We've never even heard of him," they hissed. "And he's a Benjamite, of all things. He was so frightened he went and hid when he was proclaimed king!"

Saul is anointed king of the Israelites

Saul's Downfall

Soon after Saul had been proclaimed king, the Ammonites besieged the great walled town of Jabesh, a few miles east of the Jordan River in Gilead.

The Ammonites besiege the city of Jabesh

It was a rich and fertile part of the world, and Nahash, the Ammonite King, wanted to drive the Israelites from their stronghold. He surrounded the walls with his troops. For weeks, nothing could get in or out of the town, and the food began to run out. The people were starving and their thoughts turned to surrender. Eventually, they sent messengers down to Nahash saying that they would make a treaty. But Nahash replied, "I will only make a treaty with you on the condition that I gouge out the right eye of every single man in the town!"

When the elders of Jabesh received this ghastly message they asked for seven days grace. Then, at dead of night, they sent messengers out of the city to tell their kinsmen of their plight. When the news reached Gibeah, where Saul lived, he was just coming back from the fields with his oxen.

Saul listened in horror and, burning with rage, snatched the messenger's gleaming sword and plunged it deep into the oxen. He sent the scraps of meat, like bleeding messages, all over the country, calling the Israelites to arms. In response, the tribes of Israel flocked to Saul's side. But it took more than five days for them all to arrive and only one day was left before every man in Jabesh would lose an eye.

Saul sent word to the besieged city that help was on its way. When they received the message the people of Jabesh told the Ammonites that they would surrender the next day. Meanwhile, Saul divided his men into three companies and headed toward Jabesh. Then, in the dead of night, they surrounded the Ammonite camp. At daybreak, the Israelites sounded their trumpets and swept in. The Ammonites, sleepy and unprepared, were swiftly defeated.

> "You have not obeyed the Lord. If you had, your kingdom would have lasted forever."

But, despite this triumph over the Ammonites, Saul was king of the Israelites in name only. For years the tribes of Israel had been under the thumb of the rich and powerful Philistines. Saul longed to free his people, but his army was small and his weapons were few compared to the might of the enemy. His son, Jonathan, was one of his most important lieutenants. He was stationed at Gibeah, near a small Philistine outpost that caused him nothing but trouble.

One day, infuriated by the insults of the officer in charge of the enemy outpost, Jonathan attacked it, killing all of the Philistine soldiers there. News of the bloodshed soon spread and, before long, the entire Philistine army was being mobilized against the Israelites.

Saul waited at Gilgal with his men quaking at his side. But he could not give the order to join battle before a sacred offering had been made to the Lord. The prophet Samuel had said that he would be there within a week to make the blessing. As the days went by and the tension rose, some of Saul's men fled in fear. Finally, on the seventh day, unable to wait any longer, Saul made the offering himself. And, just as he finished, Samuel arrived and said, "What have you done?"

"You had not arrived when you said you would, and my men are deserting me," Saul replied.

Samuel looked him straight in the eye and said, "You have not obeyed the Lord. If you had, your kingdom would have lasted forever. The Lord has chosen someone else now and will make him leader of His people." With that, the prophet turned around and left. Saul watched him go, aghast, as the full meaning of his words sank in.

God Chooses David

*S*aul reigned over the Israelites for more than forty years,
but, because he did not always obey God's commands,
God decided to choose a new king for His people.

The prophet Samuel remembered the day, long ago, when he had anointed the young Saul as king. He had not seen him for many years now and was saddened. God said to him, "How long will you mourn for Saul? You know I have rejected him as king of Israel. Fill your horn with oil and be on your way. I am sending you to find a farmer named Jesse in Bethlehem. I have chosen one of his sons to be king." He told Samuel to take a heifer with him and to invite Jesse and his sons to the sacrifice. "I will show you what to do," He said. "I will tell you which one to anoint."

So Samuel traveled to Bethlehem in Judah. When he arrived, the elders greeted him with awe. They did not know why the great prophet had come to their village. "Do you come in peace?" they asked, bowing down before him.

> "I will tell you which one to anoint."

"Yes, I have indeed come in peace," Samuel replied. "I have come to make a sacrifice to the Lord."

They took him to find Jesse, who was a descendant of Boaz and Ruth. Samuel asked Jesse to call his sons together. The humble farmer was amazed, not knowing why he and his sons had been singled out. Samuel invited them all to the sacrifice, but first he consecrated them to God. One by one, the young men stepped forward. The first, who was named Eliab, was tall and handsome and Samuel thought that he must be the one whom God had chosen. But God said, "Do not consider his appearance or his height. This is not the one. Man looks at the outward appearance, but the Lord looks at the heart."

Jesse called his next son, who was named Abinadab, to step forward. He also was a fine young man, but Samuel said, "The Lord has not chosen this one either." Then it was the turn of the third son, named Shammah. But he was not the one, and Samuel shook his head. All seven of Jesse's sons came to Samuel in turn, but none of them were chosen. The great prophet was puzzled and said to Jesse, "Are these really all the sons you have?"

"There is another one," replied Jesse. "He is the youngest—still a child really. He is named David and he is out in the fields looking after the sheep."

Samuel asked him to send for his last and youngest son immediately. He waited calmly, holding the horn of holy oil in his hand. In a little while, the door burst open and a young boy ran in. He was a fine looking child with ruddy cheeks and blue eyes. Samuel looked at him and heard the voice within him saying, "This is the one I have chosen. Anoint him."

So Samuel poured the perfumed oil over David's young head and anointed him in front of his father and his seven brothers. They watched in silence, hardly able to believe their eyes. And from that day on, the Spirit of the Lord was with David wherever he went and whatever he did.

Samuel anoints David as God's chosen king

David and Goliath

*T*he Philistines and the Israelites drew up their battle lines above the Valley of Elah in Judah and faced each other from the peaks of their separate hills.

Out of the Philistine camp emerged a terrifying figure. He was at least nine feet (three meters) tall, with legs like tree trunks and fists like hams. He was called Goliath and he came from Gath. He wore a massive bronze helmet and a heavy suit of armor. A huge javelin was slung on his back, while he clasped an iron-clad spear. He bellowed across the valley, "I defy the ranks of Israel this day! Choose one man to come and fight with me, King Saul. I dare you! If he is able to kill me, the Philistines will become your servants. But if I kill him, then you will become our slaves."

King Saul and the Israelites listened in horror. Who could take on the Philistine giant? For forty days, Goliath appeared each morning and each evening and repeated his challenge.

One morning, David arrived in the Israelites' camp, bringing food for his brothers, who were soldiers with King Saul. He saw Goliath for the first time and heard his words. "Who is this monster who dares to threaten the army of the Lord?" he asked. The Israelite soldiers told him about Goliath. David went to the King and said that he would take up the giant's challenge.

"You can't fight this Philistine brute," smiled King Saul.

"But I am the keeper of my father's sheep and I am used to protecting them," David protested.

Saul reluctantly agreed. "Go and the Lord be with you," he said. He gave David his own tunic, a coat of armor, a bronze helmet, and a sword. David tried on his unfamiliar finery, but then shook his head and took it all off.

He ran down to the valley and chose five smooth stones from the stream. He put them in his leather pouch and moved toward the giant. Goliath could not believe his eyes. "What's this? I ask for a man and they send a shrimp!"

David replied, "You come against me with sword, spear, and javelin, but I come against you in the name of the

"I come against you in the name of the Lord Almighty"

Lord Almighty, the God of the armies of Israel, whom you have defied. I am not scared of you." And with that he fished the largest stone out of his pouch and put it in his sling. He whirled it round and let the stone fly. It sped through the air and reached its target, sinking into Goliath's forehead. The giant screamed and crashed to the ground. David ran to him, took his sword, and cut off his head. Triumphantly, he lifted it high in the air.

The Philistines fled in terror. The Israelites pursued them, hacking them down as they went. Then they returned to plunder the Philistines' camp.

Saul Turns Against David

*A*fter David had killed the Philistine giant, Goliath, he was invited to live with King Saul in Gibeah. It was very different from the life he had been used to as a humble shepherd boy in the fields around Bethlehem.

From the very first day, he and Saul's son, Jonathan, were inseparable. Jonathan loved David and shared everything with him—giving him his finest clothes as well as his sword and bow. And Saul, seeing how close the two young men were, made David an officer in the army, just like Jonathan. He gave him command of more than one thousand men, and David led them on the battlefield with great success. And, in time, Saul's daughter, Michal, fell in love with David and they were married.

David's fame spread throughout Israel and Judah. His triumph over Goliath was the stuff of legends and would never be forgotten. Women sang and danced to the music of their tambourines and lutes and cymbals. "Saul has slain his thousands!" they chanted. "And David has slain his tens of thousands!"

Although Saul had grown fond of David and knew how highly regarded he was, his heart sank and his stomach tied itself in knots when he heard these words. "They say that David has killed tens of thousands, but that I, their king, have only slain thousands!" he said to himself. "That young man will be after my kingdom next!"

And, in his heart, Saul despaired because he knew that the Lord, who had chosen him so long ago, had now deserted him. He did not understand why. All his years as king and all the battles he had fought seemed to stand for nothing. He was afraid of David and knew that the Lord was with him. He kept a jealous and wary eye on his young son-in-law.

In anger, Saul throws a spear at David

One day, David was playing his harp, filling the air with sweet and soothing music. Saul listened, his eyes heavy, almost dropping off to sleep. But suddenly, as if possessed, he leaped to his feet. The hatred that had quietly gnawed away at him for so long erupted like a volcano. He seized a spear and hurled it at David's head. It missed by a hair's breadth and sank deep into the wall. David looked at Saul, stunned and unable to move. Incensed, Saul grabbed another spear and tried again, but this time David was prepared and dodged nimbly aside, then ran away as fast as he could.

> "That young man will be after my kingdom next!"

He reached his house and told his wife, Michal, what had happened. She seized her husband tightly and cried, "You must escape while you can! You must not stay here another moment! They will find you here and you will not stand a chance!" And, when night had fallen, she lowered David out of the window on a rope, and he fled into the darkness. Then, she found a life-sized statue and put it in David's bed. She arranged goats' hair on its head and drew the covers up over it so that it looked just like a man fast asleep.

Saul's men arrived at the crack of dawn the next morning. They hammered on the door, asking for David. Michal let them in and whispered, "He is sick in bed. Please do not disturb him!" They pushed her aside and crept up the stairs, opened the bedroom door and tiptoed silently toward the bed. They pounced, swords drawn, and pulled the covers off, only to discover that they had been tricked by a statue and a handful of goats' hair.

By then, David was far away from Gibeah. He had gone straight to the prophet Samuel at his home in Ramah and told him the whole story.

David the Outlaw

David had fled from King Saul and taken refuge with the prophet Samuel at Ramah. He knew that Saul was determined to kill him and that his life hung by a thread.

One night, he left Samuel and went secretly back to Gibeah to talk to Jonathan, his great friend and the King's son. "What have I done?" he asked. "What is my crime? How have I wronged your father and why does he want to kill me?"

"You are not going to die!" said his friend. "I would know. My father tells me everything."

"Your father knows how close we are. Would he tell you if he was going to kill me?" retorted David.

Jonathan promised to do his best to find out what his father was thinking. He would find David and let him know, with a signal, whether King Saul still wanted to kill him. The two friends said goodbye, and David fled to the fields.

It was the new moon festival the next day and everybody came to the feast with King Saul. But, when they sat down to eat, there was one empty place at the table. Saul looked at Jonathan but said nothing. The following day, when David had still not appeared, Saul asked Jonathan, "Where is David? Why has he not come to eat with us either yesterday or today?"

Jonathan excused his friend, saying that David had gone home to Bethlehem to make a sacrifice with his family. Saul stood up and banged the table in fury. "You are on his side, aren't you? I am ashamed of you!" he shouted. "You must go and find him. Bring him to me! He must die!"

Jonathan felt his blood boil. "Why should he die?" he protested. "What has he done?" And he got up and stormed away from the table.

The next morning, as they had arranged, Jonathan went to the remote field where David was hiding. He fired an arrow high in the air.

To warn David that his life is in danger, Jonathan fires an arrow into the air

It landed far away in the distance—way beyond the place where David had concealed himself. This was the signal. It meant that David's life was still in danger and that he must flee far away.

David came out from his hiding place and, sadly, the two young men embraced and wept. "Go in peace, for we have a sworn friendship with each other in the name of the Lord," said Jonathan. They both knew that they would never see each other again.

> "I know that you will surely be king and that the kingdom of Israel will be yours."

Jonathan turned and went back to Gibeah. David set off in the other direction, heading for the hills far away by the Salt Sea. It was a long and difficult journey by foot through the desert. But, just after he passed the oasis of En Gedi, he saw the perfect place to hide—a cave, tucked neatly into the crags where the wild goats lived. Its entrance was concealed by big boulders and it stretched back into the darkness. As time went by, men came to join David and soon he had a band of four hundred followers.

When Saul heard that David was hiding in the desert of En Gedi with a band of loyal men, he set off to hunt him down. He took three thousand soldiers with him. He was determined not to let David get away again. As they neared the Salt Sea, Saul went inside a cave to shelter from the sun. It was the Cave of Adullam, where David and his men were hiding. They watched Saul from the depths of the cave, where the darkness concealed them completely. David knew that his enemy had been delivered into his hands. He could creep up and kill him just like that.

Instead, he tiptoed up to Saul and cut a corner of his robe. But he immediately felt stricken with guilt and said to his men, "The Lord forbade that I should do such a thing to my master, the Lord's anointed, or lift my hand against him."

When Saul left the cave, David followed him and called out, "My Lord the King!" Saul turned in astonishment and David went to him, bowing low. "See, my Lord," he said. "Look at this! It is a corner of your robe. I just cut it off. I could easily have killed you at the same time, but I could not harm someone who has been anointed by the Lord!"

Saul looked at the scrap of material. He was overcome by shame. "You are more righteous than I am. I have treated you badly. May the Lord reward you well for the way you treated me today. I know that you will surely be king and that the kingdom of Israel will be yours."

David and Abigail

*D*avid and his band of followers moved through the desert and into the foothills near Carmel. It was shearing time, and David protected the shepherds who were working in the fields.

Most of the flocks belonged to a wealthy man named Nabal. When the shearing was done, and it was time to celebrate, David sent some of his men to Nabal with greetings. And, hoping to be invited to the feast, they asked if there was any spare food. Nabal was very rich, but very mean. "Who is this David? Why should I give his men food? I'll look after my own men."

David was angry. "I protected his sheep from harm. What kind of man is he? He has paid me back evil for good." David told his men to get their swords and set off, thirsty for revenge.

Although Nabal was a nasty piece of work, his wife Abigail was kind and beautiful. When she heard how ungrateful her husband had been, she was appalled. In secret, she went to the storehouse and sorted out the best food she could find. With the help of her servants she piled the feast into big baskets and loaded them onto five donkeys. Then she went to find David.

Abigail was riding down a ravine when she saw David approaching. She got off her donkey and bowed to him. "My lord," she said. "I offer my deepest apologies. Pay no attention to my husband. His name, Nabal, means "fool" and that's what he is. Folly goes with him everywhere."

Abigail's servants help to load up the donkeys with the finest food for David

She offered David the food and begged for mercy. "Please forgive him. Do not take revenge."

David listened to her. "Go home in peace," he told her, smiling. "I have heard your words and granted your request."

When Abigail returned home, Nabal was holding a banquet, fit for a king, so she slipped quietly up to bed. The next morning, she went to her husband and told him the whole story about David. Nabal listened, and her words struck like the sharpest daggers into his heart. Soon he could hardly breathe. A deathly chill crept through his veins and he lay there unable to lift a finger. For ten days, he stayed there, like a cold marble statue, and finally he died. Abigail did not leave his side.

"Praise be to the Lord, who stopped me from doing wrong, but brought Nabal's wrongdoing down on his own head!"

When David heard the news of Nabal's death, he rejoiced and gave thanks. "Praise be to the Lord, who stopped me from doing wrong, but brought Nabal's wrongdoing down on his own head!" And he sent word to Abigail, whom he had fallen in love with, asking her to marry him. She went with her maids and all her possessions, and became David's wife.

THE CITY OF DAVID
King David captured Jerusalem from the
Jesubites, and it made a perfect royal capital.
It had a central location, between his
southern homeland and the northern tribes.
The city had a good water supply and was
protected by valleys on three sides.

David then took up residence in the fortress and called it the City of David. He built up the area around it, from the supporting terraces inward. And he became more and more powerful, because the Lord God Almighty was with him.

II Samuel 5:9–10

The Death of Saul

The great prophet Samuel died and was buried at home in Ramah. All of Israel mourned, including King Saul.

He had not seen Samuel for many years but, in the past, the prophet had guided him in everything he did. Now, the Philistines were gathering their forces yet again to take on Israel. When he saw the might of the enemy, Saul was overcome with terror. He could not eat and he prayed to the Lord for guidance. But there was no answer.

In desperation, Saul longed to contact Samuel. But he had banished the people who might have been able to help him. The sorcerers and magicians had been expelled. Saul asked his attendants if anyone had secret powers to summon up the spirit of Samuel. "I think there is still an old witch who lives in Endor—not too far away," one replied.

That night, when everyone was asleep, Saul disguised himself in a cloak of sackcloth. He took two of his men and they set off for Endor. When they found the witch's shack, Saul knocked on the door. There was no reply—except for a sudden scream from a screech owl. They knocked again and waited, chilled to the bone. At last, the door creaked open and an old woman beckoned them in. A fire crackled in the hearth and a black pot bubbled in the flames. Shivering with fear, Saul told her why he had come.

> "Why do you consult me now that the Lord has turned away from you?"

She refused to help. "Surely you know what King Saul has done? He tried to get rid of us. He is scared of our powers. This must be a trap. Do you want to get me killed?"

Saul reassured her, "As surely as the Lord lives, you will not be punished for this."

Reluctantly, the witch agreed to help and asked him who he was trying to get in touch with. Saul replied, "The great prophet Samuel, who died not long ago."

She peered at him in the gloom and let out a piercing scream. "You have tricked me!" she shrieked. "You are Saul, aren't you?"

"Do not be afraid," said Saul. "What do you see?"

She croaked, "I see a spirit coming up out of the ground. It is an old man with a white beard and he is wearing a robe." Immediately, Saul knew that it was Samuel.

"I am in such distress!" he cried. "The Philistines are gathering to fight again and God has deserted me. I beg you to tell me what to do."

Samuel answered, "Why do you consult me now that the Lord has turned away from you? He has given your kingdom to David because you were disobedient. He will hand over both Israel and you to the Philistines. Tomorrow you and your sons will die!"

When he heard these words, Saul collapsed in a heap on the ground, weak with fear. He had not eaten anything all day and all night. The old witch saw what a terrible state he was in. "Let me give you something to eat so that you can get your strength back." When the meal was ready, Saul and his men ate it gratefully. And that same night, before the first light of dawn filled the sky, they set off to rejoin their army in the camp.

The next day, the massed ranks of Philistines attacked the Israelites on Mount Gilboa, above the valley at Jezreel. It was a decisive victory for them and, before long, hundreds of Israelites lay dead. Hundreds more had fled for their lives. Saul's sons, Jonathan, Abinadab, and Malki-Shua, were killed, and Saul himself was mortally wounded. He turned to his armor bearer and asked him to finish him off. "Draw your sword and kill me!" he pleaded. "Do not leave it to those Philistine brutes!" But the armor bearer was terrified and would not do it. So Saul took his own sword and fell on it, dying just as Samuel had prophesied.

After the battle, the Philistines cut off Saul's head and stripped him of his armor. Then they took his body, along with the bodies of his sons, and put them on display on the walls of their great fortress at Beth Shan for all to see.

But, when the people of Jabesh in Gilead heard, they went straight there and took the bodies away. Saul had saved them many years before and this was the least they could do. Respectfully, they carried the bodies back home. They buried their bones under a tamarisk tree and fasted for seven days.

The spirit of Samuel rises up from the ground

Long Live the King

When David heard that Saul and his son Jonathan had died, he was grief-stricken and composed a beautiful lament.

"Your glory, O Israel, lies slain on your heights.
How the mighty have fallen!
Saul and Jonathan—
 In life they were loved and gracious
And in death they were not parted.
They were swifter than eagles,
They were stronger than lions."

After Saul's death, David was anointed king of Judah. Saul's surviving son, Ish-Bosheth, was made king of the tribes of Israel to the north. And so the country was divided—Judah in the south and Israel to the north. They warred constantly, but David and his people grew stronger and stronger. Eventually, Ish-Bosheth was killed and David was made king of all the tribes. He was thirty years old and he had already ruled Judah for more than seven years.

David wanted to establish a new capital, so he took his men and marched from Hebron in Judah to the great walled city of Jerusalem. It was a natural stronghold, sandwiched between Judah and Israel, and surrounded by three valleys. But the Jebusites, the Canaanite tribe who lived there, barred the gates firmly against the intruders.

The Israelites camped out while David devised a strategy. There was a long water shaft that went to the heart of the city—the perfect route. He sent a few of his men and, with the help of their scaling hooks, they climbed the shaft, emerging within the city walls.

The men unlocked the gates and the Israelites poured in and captured the city. David made it the capital of his kingdom and it became known as the City of David. He became more and more powerful because the Lord was always with him. He built a splendid new palace out of cedar wood and stone, with plenty of room for his wives and all their children.

> "I am celebrating before the Lord, who chose me as king of Israel"

With great rejoicing, the Ark of the Covenant was brought to Jerusalem. It was accompanied by a huge procession of people singing and dancing. Joyfully, they played their harps, lyres, tambourines, and cymbals as the Ark was carried through the great walls into the city. David took off his royal finery to join in the celebrations.

But one of his wives, Michal, who was the daughter of Saul, watched from the window and did not like what she saw. "How the King has distinguished himself today!" she shouted at him sarcastically. "Taking off his royal robes in front of those slave girls. How vulgar. Whatever next?"

David looked up at her and said, "I am celebrating before the Lord, who chose me as king of Israel rather than your father or anyone from his house. I will be even more undignified if I want to." And with that he turned away and carried on dancing and praising the Lord.

The Ark was put into the innermost part of the tabernacle, its new home in the middle of the city. And David gave thanks, sacrificing a bull and a fattened calf. He made the offerings to the Lord in front of everyone. Then he blessed the people in the Lord's name and gave each of them a loaf of bread and a little cake made of raisins and dates.

David celebrates in front of the Ark of the Covenant

David and Bathsheba

It was spring and the Israelite troops had won a decisive victory over the Ammonites. They were now besieging the walled town of Ramah under their commander-in-chief, Joab.

David had stayed behind in Jerusalem, not far away. One evening, he was walking on the roof of his palace, deep in thought. Suddenly, he noticed a beautiful woman not far away. She was washing herself and combing her long, dark hair. David gazed at her, entranced. He asked his attendant to find out who she was. "Isn't she Bathsheba, the daughter of Eliam and the wife of Uriah, the Hittite?" he replied.

Although she was the wife of one of his most loyal soldiers, David sent for her and courted her with sweet words. And soon, she told him that she was carrying his child. At once, David sent a messenger to summon Uriah back from the battlefield. He came to the palace and told David what was going on in Ramah. David listened, thanked him, and sent him home for the night. But, the next morning, when he got up, he discovered that Uriah had slept on the floor at the entrance to the palace with the servants.

"I have sinned against the Lord."

When David asked him why, Uriah replied, "My master, Joab, and all his men are in their camp, ready to risk their lives for their country. How could I go home to eat and drink and lie with my wife? I would never do such a thing."

David persuaded Uriah to stay for another day. They drank wine together and talked late into the night. Once again, Uriah slept on the palace floor. But David could not sleep. He got up as soon as the first hint of daylight crept through his window and went up to the roof of the palace. It was his favorite place to think things out. Pacing up and down, he remembered the first time he had seen Bathsheba. And then, he made up his mind. He went down and wrote a letter to Joab, asking him to put Uriah in the front line of battle, where the fighting would be fiercest. David sealed the letter and put it into Uriah's hands, telling him to take it to Joab. Uriah was to deliver his own death warrant.

When Joab received the message, he carried out David's orders. And, when the Israelite troops attacked the city, Uriah died alone in the first moments of battle. Bathsheba heard that her husband had died and she grieved deeply for him. But, after the time of mourning was over, she agreed to marry David and, before long, gave him a baby son. But the Lord had seen all this and was not pleased. He sent the prophet Nathan to David to show him how badly he had behaved. Nathan told David a story:

"Once upon a time there was a rich man and a poor man. The rich man had large flocks of sheep, but the poor man had nothing at all—except for one tiny ewe lamb. He had brought her up from the moment she was born because her mother had died and she was weak and sickly. She shared the poor man's food, drank from his cup, and even slept in his arms. She was like a daughter to him.

"A traveler arrived at the rich man's house, tired and hungry after a long day on the road. But the rich man was so mean that he did not want to slaughter even one of his many, many sheep. Instead, he took the poor man's precious, solitary lamb and slit her throat. Then he prepared a good meal for the traveler."

David was shocked and appalled when he heard this story. "He should die!" he shouted. Nathan looked at him and replied, "You are that man, David. You were anointed king of Israel and given everything. You struck down Uriah the Hittite and took his wife to be your own. Why did you despise the word of the Lord by doing what is evil in his eyes?"

"I have sinned against the Lord," David replied.

"You are not going to die, but the Lord is going to bring calamity out of your own household," answered Nathan.

Soon after, David and Bathsheba's baby was gripped by a terrible fever. David pleaded with the Lord to spare his child. He fasted and prayed. But after a week, the baby died. David finally washed and changed his clothes, and asked for something to eat. And, in time, Bathsheba gave birth to another son. They named him Solomon and he was much loved by God.

Just as David had hoped,
Uriah is killed in battle

Absalom's Rebellion

*K*ing David had several different wives and fathered many children. The eldest son was named Amnon.

When he became a man, Amnon fell in love with his half sister, Tamar. She was young and beautiful and the daughter of Maccach, whom David had married when he was king of Judah. But he knew that his love was hopeless and that, according to the Law of Moses, he could never marry her.

One day, pretending to be sick, Amnon persuaded his father to send Tamar to him in his bedroom. When they were alone, he grabbed her. She struggled and tried to fend him off. Afterward, he sent her away in disgrace. She fled, broken and ashamed, and took refuge in the house of her true brother, Absalom. When David found out what had happened, he was furious, but did nothing to punish his son. But Absalom resolved to avenge his sister's honor. He ordered his men to kill Amnon when he was senseless with drink.

When David heard that his eldest son had been murdered and that another of his sons was responsible, he tore his clothes in grief and wept. He did not know what to do. Absalom fled immediately and went into hiding in the city of Geshur, where his mother came from. He stayed there for three years. David thought about him often and longed to see him, despite everything. Finally, Absalom was allowed to return to Jerusalem.

By now, Absalom was a very handsome young man, with long, dark hair that curled around his shoulders. He was admired wherever he went. But he was also ambitious and cold-hearted. He was determined to take the crown from his father.

Some people were not happy with the way David was running things and Absalom did his best to make things worse. "If only I were in charge," he would say when he heard someone complaining. "Then you could come to me and I would put things right." Gradually, the conspiracy gathered strength, and Absalom decided to go to Hebron, taking two hundred men with him. From there, he secretly sent messengers far and wide, calling the tribes of Israel to his side against David. And then he proclaimed himself king and challenged his father to battle.

David could not believe it. "We must leave the city immediately and prepare for battle," he told his officials. So David left Jerusalem with his entire household and all his men, making their way across the Kidron Valley toward the desert. They crossed the River Jordan and made their camp in Gilead. Absalom followed with his men. That night David talked to the three commanders in charge of his men and said, "Be gentle with Absalom, for my sake."

"We must leave the city immediately and prepare for battle."

The next morning, the battle had begun. The fighting was long and bloody but, finally, Absalom and his army admitted defeat. More than twenty thousand soldiers died and the rebels who survived fled. Some of them were badly injured and did not manage to flee very far. Absalom himself was unhurt and managed to escape on a mule. But, terrified by the noise of the fighting, the mule bolted through the thick oak wood, and Absalom's hair got entangled in some low branches. He was left dangling in midair.

One of David's soldiers saw Absalom swinging helplessly from a tree and he went straight to Joab, the commander-in-chief, to tell him where he was. "What? You saw Absalom? Why didn't you kill him there and then? I would have given you ten shekels and a warrior's belt!"

But the soldier replied, "I would not have lifted a hand against the king's son—even if you gave me one thousand shekels. The king told us to be gentle with Absalom for his sake." So Joab stormed off, taking three javelins with him, and headed straight for the tree where Absalom was hanging. Without hesitating, he plunged all three of the javelins deep into Absalom's heart. Ten of his armor bearers finished him off. They took his body and buried it in a big pit in the middle of the forest and covered it with rocks.

When David heard the news of his son's death, he wept. "Oh my son Absalom!" he cried. "If only I had died instead of you!"

Absalom is killed by Joab when he gets caught in the branches of a tree

King Solomon's Wisdom

*A*fter forty years reigning over Israel, David lay dying. He gave his son Solomon some advice. "Be strong," he told him. "Show yourself to be a man and observe what the Lord requires. Walk in His ways and keep His decrees and commands, His laws and requirements, as written in the Law of Moses."

When the time came and David died, Solomon became king and married the daughter of Pharaoh, the king of Egypt. And the Lord appeared to Solomon one night in a dream and said, "Ask for anything you want. I will give it to you."

Solomon thought long and hard. "You have made me king of your great people, after my father David. Please help me to govern your people and to distinguish between right and wrong. Please, Lord, give me wisdom."

The Lord was pleased with Solomon's answer. He said, "If you walk in my ways and obey my commands as David your father did, then I will give you a wise and discerning heart so that there will never have been anyone like you, nor will there ever be."

Soon after, two women came before Solomon as he sat on his throne. They were in a terrible state as they clutched and fought over a bundle. Arguing and spitting at each other, they appealed to the King for help in settling their dispute. At last they calmed down and managed to tell him their story, bit by bit. They lived together in the same house and had given birth to baby sons within three days of each other. But during the night one of the babies had died in his sleep. Each woman claimed that it was the other one's baby that had died. The two women pointed angrily at each other.

"Don't believe a word she says!" shouted the first woman. "It was her baby that died. Then she crept into my room, stole my baby, and put her dead son in his place."

> "Please help me to govern your people and to distinguish between right and wrong."

"That's not true! What terrible lies! Your baby died and mine is alive. Here he is. You can see he's mine!" sobbed the second woman.

The King asked an attendant to get a sword and ordered, "Cut the infant in two and give one half to the first woman and the other half to the second woman. That should keep them happy."

The first woman shrieked in horror and fell to the floor sobbing. "Please, my Lord! Do not harm the baby. Give him to her. I don't mind. Whatever you do, don't kill him!"

But the second woman snarled, "Go ahead! Cut him in half! Neither one of us shall have him. See if I care."

Then Solomon in his wisdom spoke and gave his ruling. "Do not kill him. Give the baby to the first woman. She is his mother."

When the people of Israel heard of the judgment of Solomon, they were pleased and looked at him with great respect. They knew such wisdom could come only from God.

Solomon's Temple

It was four years since Solomon had succeeded David and become king of Israel. His thoughts started turning toward the temple that his father had longed to build.

The temple would replace the tabernacle as a place of worship and provide a permanent home for the Ark of the Covenant. For years, David had worked on the idea, drawing up detailed plans for its construction in the heart of Jerusalem.

Solomon sent envoys with a message for King Hiram of Tyre. "You know that my father David was never able to build the temple because of the constant demands of war. Now there is peace, and I am going to build a temple in the name of the Lord my God. So please order cedars of Lebanon to be cut for me."

Hiram was pleased, saying, "Praise be to the Lord today for He has given David a wise son to rule over his nation." They made a treaty. Hiram would send cedar, pine, and craftsmen, and in return, Solomon would give him wheat and oil for his household.

Laborers were conscripted from all over Israel. Altogether, more than thirty thousand men were sent off in shifts to help cut down the great cedars of Lebanon and float them on huge rafts across the sea.

Skilled workers cut the stones for the temple

Meanwhile, eighty thousand stonecutters were sent to work in the quarries up in the hills, hewing vast blocks of stone for the foundations and the outer walls of the temple. Another seventy thousand men transported the stone down to Jerusalem, overseen by their foremen. It was very hard work but, finally, in the month of Ziv (the second month of the year), Solomon laid the foundation stone. It took four long years before the foundations were completed and another three years to build the temple.

Gradually, the magnificent building took shape, with Solomon supervising everything. When it was finished it was twice as big as the old tabernacle. The walls inside were lined with fragrant cedar wood and overlaid with gold, while the floor was made of pine. Beautiful cherubim, palm trees, and garlands of flowers decorated the walls and the altar. All the furnishings of the temple were made of gold.

> "Now there is peace, and I am going to build a temple in the name of the Lord my God."

An inner sanctuary, the Most Holy Place, was partitioned off at the rear of the temple for the Ark of the Covenant. Two splendid golden cherubim, carved out of olive wood, spread out their huge wings. They would be the permanent guardians of the Ark. Two huge bronze pillars supported the roof at the entrance of the temple, their capitals festooned with chains and hundreds of bronze pomegranates.

The temple was finished in the eleventh year of Solomon's reign. When all the preparations had been made, the Ark of the Covenant, containing the Ten Commandments, was brought in by the priests, the elders of Israel, and the leaders of all the tribes. The priests entered the Most Holy Place and laid the Ark underneath the outstretched wings of the cherubim.

When they withdrew from the sanctuary, a great cloud suddenly appeared from nowhere, filling the temple from the floor to the ceiling, and the priests could not continue with the service. It was the Glory of God filling the House of God. Afterward, Solomon stood in front of the altar and said a prayer of dedication to God. He blessed all the people of Israel, and they offered sacrifices to the Lord.

The Temple in Jerusalem

In Jerusalem, King Solomon (ruled c. 968–928 BCE) built a great temple to hold the Ark of the Covenant—the portable shrine where God was thought to be powerfully present. By building the Temple, Solomon was giving God a house to live in. The Temple, which stood beside Solomon's palace, brought great prestige to the King and to his royal capital.

Temple plan
Solomon's Temple followed a standard plan, found in earlier Canaanite temples. Two free-standing columns created an impressive entrance. Inside, a porch led to a big hall—the Holy Place—and the small inner shrine room—the Holy of Holies.

Ark of the Covenant
Unlike other ancient temples, Solomon's had no statue of a god. Instead, the Holy of Holies held the Ark, which was made of gilded acacia wood. The Ark contained the stone tablets, inscribed with the Ten Commandments.

Bronze sea
Outside the Temple stood a huge bronze bowl, 14 ft (4 m) wide and 7 ft (2 m) deep, supported by 12 bronze statues of bulls. Called the "Bronze Sea," it stored the water used by the priests for ritual bathing.

Cherubim

Two large statues of cherubim, carved from olive wood and covered with gold, stood on guard inside the Holy of Holies. This Syrian ivory carving shows how they would have appeared, with the bodies of lions, human heads, and wings.

Worship

Music played a big part in worship. Temple musicians sang songs praising God, and played cymbals, drums, pipes, and harps—like those on this Assyrian carving. They played in the Temple courtyard, while animals were sacrificed at a great altar.

The Queen of Sheba

*K*ing Solomon ruled over the people of Israel for *more than forty years. During his reign, people were prosperous and there was plenty to eat.*

Israel was divided into twelve districts, and they each paid King Solomon a tribute. His own tribe, Judah, was exempt from tax. The kingdom stretched from the Euphrates River in the north to Egypt in the south. It was the land that God had promised Abraham many years before.

Solomon was richer and wiser than any other king on Earth. People came from all over the world to seek an audience with him and to hear the wisdom that God had given him. Year after year they came, bringing with them gifts for the king. When the Queen of Sheba heard about the wisdom and the wealth of Solomon, she could not believe it. She decided she must see King Solomon for herself and she must test his wisdom. So she set off from Sheba, on the southwest tip of Arabia, and journeyed through the desert and north along the trade route known as the King's Highway to Jerusalem. She traveled with an enormous caravan of camels, laden with rich and exotic gifts for Solomon.

When the Queen of Sheba arrived in Jerusalem, Solomon greeted her from his magnificent throne. He showed her around his splendid palace and his stables with their thousands of horses and chariots. He took her to see his huge collections of shields, all hammered out of beaten gold. And then they returned to the throne room and he listened to all her questions. He answered them with great wisdom. Nothing was too difficult or too much trouble for him.

The Queen of Sheba was overwhelmed—by his wisdom and by the magnificence of the surroundings. "The report I heard in my own country about your achievements and your wisdom is true. But I did not believe these things until I came and saw with my own eyes. In wisdom and in wealth you have far exceeded the report I heard," she said. "O Praise be to the Lord your God, who has delighted in you and placed you on the throne of Israel!"

> "In wisdom and in wealth you have far exceeded the report I heard."

And she gave him the gifts she had brought with her—one hundred and twenty talents of pure gold and huge quantities of precious stones and spices. And, in turn, Solomon heaped lavish presents on his visitor, to take back with her to Sheba.

THE WILDERNESS OF BEERSHEBA
The wilderness is important throughout
the Bible. Most people feared it as a hostile,
lonely place, inhabited by wild animals and
demons. The wilderness is also a place where
prophets, such as Elijah, had visions.

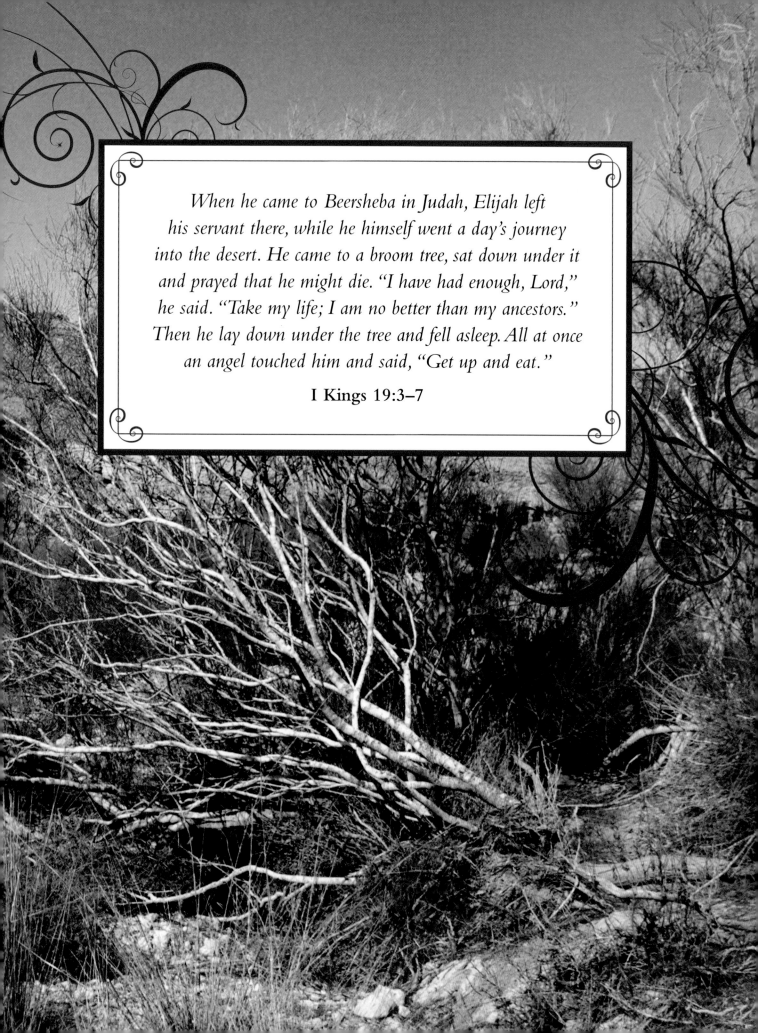

When he came to Beersheba in Judah, Elijah left his servant there, while he himself went a day's journey into the desert. He came to a broom tree, sat down under it and prayed that he might die. "I have had enough, Lord," he said. "Take my life; I am no better than my ancestors." Then he lay down under the tree and fell asleep. All at once an angel touched him and said, "Get up and eat."

I Kings 19:3–7

Elijah in the Wilderness

After the death of Solomon, his son Rehoboam became king of the Israelites. But the tribes of the north had not been happy for a long time.

Under the rule of Solomon they had been subjected to high taxes. They thought that things might get better now, but their hopes were soon dashed. "My father laid on you a heavy yoke. I will make it even heavier," their new king told them with satisfaction. So the tribes rebelled against their new ruler. And soon, the kingdom was split in two once more, with Israel in the north and Judah in the south.

In time, Omri became the king of Israel and he made Samaria the capital. He made an alliance with Phoenicia through the marriage of his son Ahab to Jezebel. She was the daughter of the ruler of Sidon, and she encouraged her new husband to worship her god Baal. When he became king, Ahab built temples and altars to the pagan god.

The prophet Elijah foretold what was in store for the people of Israel, because they had turned away from the Lord. He said that there would be a drought lasting for many years, and, with it, famine. Elijah went to King Ahab in Samaria and warned him, "As the Lord the God of Israel lives, whom I serve, there will be neither dew nor rain in the next few years except at my word," he said.

"Now I know that you are a man of God!"

And God spoke to Elijah. "Leave here, turn eastward, and hide in the Kerith Ravine, east of the Jordan River. You will drink from the brook, and I have ordered the ravens to feed you there!" Elijah did just as God had told him and lived happily by the stream, being fed by the ravens and drinking the water. All around, the crops failed and the people began to starve. But then the stream dried up, and the Lord said to Elijah, "Go at once to Zarephath in Sidon and stay there. I have commanded a widow there to supply you with food."

So Elijah went to Zarephath in Sidon, the land where Queen Jezebel had come from. As he approached the gates of the town, he saw a woman stooping down and gathering sticks. Elijah went up to her and greeted her. "Would you bring me a little water in a jar so that I may have a drink?" he asked her. "And please, if you would be so kind, bring me a piece of bread."

She shook her head. "I don't have any bread," she said. "All I have is a handful of flour in a jar and a little oil in a jug. It is hardly enough for me and my son as it is!"

Elijah drinks from the brook, while food is brought to him by ravens

"Don't be afraid," replied Elijah. "Make a small cake of bread for me and then make something for you and your son. The Lord will make sure that the flour and the oil do not run out until the rain comes." The widow looked at him doubtfully, but did as he said. And, sure enough, her flour and oil did not run out, and there was plenty of food for her and her son and Elijah until the rain came.

But, some time later, her son fell ill and, no matter what the woman did, he got worse and worse. Finally, one night, he stopped breathing completely and she said to Elijah, "What do you have against me? You have let my son die! And you call yourself a man of God!"

Elijah looked at her calmly and told her to give him her son. Gently, he carried the boy upstairs and laid him out on the bed, cold and still. Then he stretched over the little body three times and cried, "O Lord my God, let this boy's life return to him!" And immediately the boy's chest started moving and the color returned to his cheeks. His eyelids fluttered, as if he was waking up from a dream. Finally, he stretched and opened his eyes. Elijah carried him down and gave him to his mother. "Look, your son is alive!" he said.

The widow could not believe it and clutched the boy to her tightly. "Now I know that you are a man of God!" she cried to Elijah.

Elijah builds an altar to God

Elijah and the Prophets of Baal

*T*he drought in Israel had lasted for three years. It was a punishment from the Lord because the Israelites had been worshipping the pagan god Baal.

The prophet Elijah went to see King Ahab in Samaria again. Ahab greeted him rudely, saying, "Is that you, the troublemaker, the thorn in Israel's side?"

"I have not made trouble for Israel," replied Elijah. "But you and your father's family have. You have abandoned the Lord's commands and have followed Baal. Now summon the people from all over Israel to meet me on Mount Carmel. And bring the four hundred and fifty prophets of Baal, who eat at Queen Jezebel's table."

Ahab sent word and summoned the people and the prophets to Mount Carmel. Elijah stood before them all and said, "You cannot worship both God and Baal! How long will you waver between them? If the Lord is God, follow Him. But if Baal is God, follow him." But nobody said anything.

> "O Lord, answer me, so these people will know that you, O lord, are God."

Elijah continued, "I am the only one of the Lord's prophets left, but Baal has four hundred and fifty of them." And, although there were so many of them and only one of him, he challenged them to a contest to see who the true God was. The prophets were to make an altar to Baal. Then they were to place a sacrificial bull on top—but they must not set fire to it. He would do exactly the same, but his altar would be to the Lord. "Then you call on the name of your god and I will call on the name of the Lord, and we will see who wins," he said. "The true God will set the fire on His altar alight."

He let the prophets of Baal go first. They called their God's name from early morning till the middle of the day. And they danced around and around the altar they had made. But there was no response. The wood on the altar remained unkindled, and the calf lay on top of it uncooked.

Elijah could not resist taunting them. "Shout louder! Perhaps he's deep in thought? Or busy doing something else!" So the prophets shouted louder and louder and slashed themselves with their swords and spears until they bled, as was their custom. By evening they were exhausted, and there was still no response. The altar to Baal remained unlit.

Then Elijah called everyone over to his altar, but it was in ruins so he repaired it. He took twelve stones, one for each of the tribes of Israel, and rebuilt the altar. He arranged his wood and cut his calf into pieces and laid them in position. When this was done he asked for several large jars of water to be poured over the altar until it was soaking wet.

He stepped forward and spoke, "O Lord, God of Abraham, Isaac, and Israel, let it be known today that you are God in Israel and that I am your servant. Answer me, O Lord, answer me, so these people will know that you, O Lord, are God." Immediately, the sodden wood on his altar burst into flames, crackling around the sacrifice and leaping high in the air. Everyone gasped in amazement and fell to the ground, crying, "The Lord—He is God! The Lord—He is God!"

Elijah gave orders for the prophets to be rounded up. "Seize the prophets of Baal! Don't let them get away!" he commanded. And the four hundred and fifty prophets of Baal were taken down the mountain and slaughtered in the Kishon Valley.

Meanwhile, Elijah walked up the mountain with his servant, through the olive groves and the oak trees. When they reached the very top, the Great Sea lay like a sheet of silver at their feet. Elijah asked the young man what he could see.

"I can't see anything," replied the servant. "Only a clear sky and a calm sea."

"Look again," said the prophet. But again the servant could see nothing.

Elijah asked him the same question seven times, and it was only then that the servant replied, "A cloud as small as a man's hand is rising from the sea." And immediately, Elijah told him to go to Ahab to say that the rains were coming. As he spoke, the sky grew black and the wind roared wildly, bringing the rain with it. Ahab rode off as fast as he could to his home in Jezreel, but Elijah, filled with the power of the Lord, ran ahead of Ahab.

The Israelites slaughter the prophets of Baal

Elijah runs back to Jezreel ahead of King Ahab

The Assyrians

From the 9th to the 7th centuries BCE, the most powerful state in the Near East was Assyria, in northern Mesopotamia. The Assyrian Empire included the Jewish kingdoms of Judah and Israel. Their kings were allowed to keep their thrones, as long as they sent tribute to Assyria. In both countries, kings made the mistake of rebelling. The northern kingdom, Israel, was destroyed. Judah survived, though many of its cities were sacked.

Israelite tribute

In 841 BCE, King Shalmaneser III of Assyria received tribute from King Jehu of Israel. This carving shows King Jehu, or his ambassador, bowing before the Assyrian king. The tribute was in the form of golden cups, bowls, vases, and a royal scepter.

The fall of Lachish

In 701 BCE, following a rebellion, King Sennacherib of Assyria invaded and captured many cities in Judah. Reliefs from his palace show the fall of the city of Lachish. Here the Assyrians are wheeling battering rams up a ramp against the walls.

Destroyed by fire

Archeologists digging at Lachish found evidence of the fall of the city, including the Assyrian siege ramp, shown at the center right of this picture. There were also pits, where the victors dumped 1,500 bodies. The city was destroyed by fire.

Flayed alive

In this scene two naked men are stretched out by Assyrian soldiers, who are flaying them alive. While other ancient peoples were equally cruel to their enemies, only the Assyrians decorated palace walls with such gruesome scenes.

Taken to Assyria

The people of Lachish who were not killed were taken away into slavery in Assyria. This relief shows an Assyrian soldier with a spear and shield guarding three captive men. In front, a captive woman and child ride on a cart.

King Sennacherib

After capturing Lachish, Sennacherib laid siege to Jerusalem, boasting that he had made King Hezekiah "a prisoner in his royal residence, like a caged bird." Here he wears the Assyrian crown, which was cylindrical and topped by a small cone.

153

Naboth's Vineyard

*T*here was a vineyard next to King Ahab's residence in Jezreel, which belonged to a man named Naboth. Ahab had eyed it enviously for some time.

"Let me have your vineyard to use for a vegetable garden since it is so close to my palace," he said to Naboth. "In exchange, I will give you a better vineyard, or, if you prefer, I will pay you whatever it is worth."

But Naboth refused point-blank. "The Lord forbids that I should give you the inheritance of my fathers," he replied politely. He could not even think about it as, according to the Law of Moses, Israelites were not allowed to sell any of the ancestral lands that had been allotted to them after the conquest of Canaan.

Ahab was furious and headed back to his palace in a rage. He lay on his bed with his face to the wall and would not talk to anyone, sulking like a little boy. His wife, Jezebel, came in and could not understand why her husband was lying there on his bed in the middle of the day. "What's wrong with you?" she asked. "Why won't you eat anything?"

> "And the Lord says that, just as the dogs licked up Naboth's blood from the roadside, so they will lick up yours!"

To begin with, he did not respond, but finally he turned over and told her about the vineyard. Jezebel looked at him in disbelief. "And you call yourself king of Israel! I ask you!" she sneered. "I'll get that vineyard for you!" Ahab turned back to face the wall.

Jezebel knew exactly what to do. Without delay, she sat down and wrote dozens of letters, forging Ahab's signature and stamping them with his own royal seal. She sent them to all the elders and nobles who lived in the city. In them, she said that there would be a day of fasting, which showed that someone had committed a serious crime. Naboth was to be seated in a prominent position among the people, and she told the elders to make sure that two good-for-nothings, who could be bribed to do anything, were seated opposite Naboth. They would set him up, testifying that he had spoken against God. This was a crime that carried the death sentence.

The elders and the nobles did as they were told, thinking that they were carrying out King Ahab's orders. And the two villains, happy to earn their money, sat across from Naboth and brought the charges against him. "That man sitting there has cursed both God and the King!" And Naboth was taken outside the city and stoned to death.

When Jezebel heard that her plan had worked and that Naboth had been killed, she rushed to Ahab to tell him the good news. "Get up! The vineyard that you wanted so much is yours. Naboth is dead!"

Ahab was delighted and went straight to the vineyard to inspect his prized possession. But the Lord had already spoken to the prophet Elijah, and he was there waiting for Ahab.

"You have murdered a man and stolen his property! And the Lord says that, just as the dogs licked up Naboth's blood from the roadside, so they will lick up yours! You have sold your soul and have done evil in the eyes of the Lord, and so disaster will fall on you and your descendants. And dogs will devour Jezebel by the walls of Jezreel!"

When Ahab heard these words, he was appalled and deeply ashamed. He tore his clothes, put on sackcloth, and fasted. God saw that he was truly remorseful and He spoke to Elijah again. "Because Ahab has humbled himself and is truly sorry I will not punish him, but I will bring disaster on his descendants."

To show how sorry he is, King Ahab dresses in sackcloth

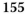

Elijah's Final Journey

*T*he prophet Elijah was walking with his disciple Elisha. He knew that his life was drawing to a close and that the Lord would soon take him up to heaven.

"I have to go to Bethel now, but you stay here," he said to Elisha.

But Elisha protested, "As surely as the Lord lives and as long as you live, I will not leave you." So they went on together and arrived in Bethel. The company of prophets who lived there came out to meet them. They greeted them both and said to Elisha, "Do you know that the Lord is going to take your master from you today?"

"Yes, I know," replied Elisha, "but do not speak of it." Then Elijah told him to stay in Bethel while he went on to Jericho.

Again, Elisha protested, "As surely as the Lord lives and as long as you live, I will not leave you." So they left Bethel together and went to Jericho.

When they arrived in Jericho, the prophets who lived there met them and said to Elisha, "Do you know that the Lord is going to take your master from you today?"

"Yes, I know," replied Elisha, "but I would rather not speak of it." Then Elijah told him to stay in Jericho while he went on to the Jordan River.

Again, Elisha protested, "As surely as the Lord lives and as long as you live, I will not leave you." So they left Jericho together and traveled to the Jordan. When they got there, fifty prophets stood at a respectful distance, watching them.

Elijah is taken up to heaven in a chariot of fire, as Elisha looks on

They stopped by the edge of the river. Elijah took off his cloak and rolled it up. Then he bent down and struck the surface of the water with it. Immediately, the river divided and a path of dry ground stretched in front of them. Elijah and Elisha walked across together until they reached the other side. Then Elijah said to Elisha, "What can I do for you before I am taken from you?"

"What I would like, more than anything in the world, is to follow in your footsteps and be your spiritual heir," Elisha replied.

Elijah listened and was silent for a few moments. Then he said, "You have asked a difficult thing. Yet, if you see me with your own eyes as I am taken from you, you will get what you have asked for. Otherwise, not."

At that moment a chariot of fire appeared between them, pulled by blazing horses. It separated them and Elijah went up to heaven in a whirlwind. Elisha watched him disappear. And that was the last he saw of Elijah.

Elisha wept and tore his clothes in grief. He picked up Elijah's cloak, which had fallen to the ground, and held it closely to him. Then, he went back to the banks of the river and rolled the cloak up tightly, just as the great prophet had done not long before. He struck the water with it and, once again, the river divided and a path of dry ground stretched in front of him. He walked back to the other side. And the company of prophets who were watching said, "The spirit of Elijah is resting in Elisha!" They went to meet him, bowing low on the ground.

> "Do you know that the Lord is going to take your master from you today?"

Elisha and the Woman of Shunem

*E*lisha often visited Shunem in the beautiful Valley of Jezreel. Whenever he was there, he was invited to dinner by a rich woman and her elderly husband.

The woman knew that Elisha was a prophet and a holy man of God. "Let's make a little room on the roof for him," she said to her husband. "We can put a bed and a table in it—and a chair and a lamp. We will make it comfortable for him and he can stay there when he wants to. It will be a home from home."

Elisha accepted their hospitality gratefully. One evening, as he was resting on his bed, he thought how lucky he was. He called his servant Gehazi and said, "How can I repay their kindness?"

"The woman has no son—no children at all," replied Gehazi. "And her husband is an old man—too old to father a child. She would like a son more than anything else in the world." Elisha asked him to fetch the woman immediately, and she came and stood in the doorway.

"About this time next year," Elisha told her, "you will hold your very own son in your arms!" The woman could not believe her ears. But, sure enough, about one year later, she gave birth to a baby boy, just as Elisha had predicted. The woman still could not believe it, and every day she gave thanks to the Lord for blessing her with a son.

The child grew, healthy and strong, and life was good for the family. But, one day, the boy went to find his father who was supervising the harvest in the fields. The boy clutched his hands to his head, howling in pain. "My head! My head! It hurts so much! I can't bear it!" His father ordered one of the servants to carry his son back home as quickly as possible.

By the time they got back to the house, the boy was almost unconscious, and the servant gave him straight to his mother. She tried to revive him, but he lay there as white as a sheet. His breathing became shallower and shallower and finally stopped completely. His mother sat weeping. Then, slowly, she took him upstairs and laid him gently on the bed in Elisha's room.

Forcing back the tears, she went to her husband and said, "Quick! I need a donkey and one of the servants! I am going to fetch Elisha!" Moments later, she set off for Mount Carmel, where she knew she would find the prophet.

When she reached Elisha, she bowed down before him and clutched at his feet, crying. His servant, Gehazi, came over to push her away, but Elsiha rebuked him. The woman told him what had happened and that her son was dead. Elisha listened and said to Gehazi, "Tuck your cloak into your belt, take my staff, and run back to Shunem as fast as you can. If you meet anyone, don't stop, whatever you do! When you get there, lay my staff on the boy's face."

"Take your son. He is alive!"

Gehazi did exactly as his master had told him, while Elisha followed with the distraught woman. But when he laid the staff on the little boy's face, nothing happened. So Gehazi rushed back to tell his master.

When Elisha reached the house, he climbed the stairs and went into his room. The boy lay on the bed. The prophet shut the door and prayed to the Lord. Then he got on the bed and lay on top of the boy. As he stretched himself out, the boy's body gradually started to get warm. Elisha got up and paced back and forth across the room. Then he went back and stretched himself on top of the boy again. At once, the boy sneezed loudly seven times and opened his eyes.

Elisha summoned Gehazi and told him to get the boy's mother. She peeped fearfully around the door and Elisha smiled at her and said, "Take your son. He is alive!" She gasped and rushed in, thanking Elisha from the bottom of her heart. Then she went to her son and put her arms around him.

The little boy is brought back to life by Elisha

Elisha and Naaman

*N*aaman was a commander in the Syrian army. He was a brave soldier and was highly regarded by his troops.

But Naaman suffered from an affliction, which made every inch of his skin white and scaly. It itched and stung, tormenting him from morning till night, and he knew that people avoided him when they could.

Recently, a young girl from Israel had been taken captive by the Syrians and she became the maidservant to Naaman's wife. The girl was horrified when she first saw Naaman and said to her mistress, "If only your husband could see the prophet Elisha in Samaria, he would cure him!" That evening, Naaman's wife encouraged her husband to go to Israel. He agreed and went to the Syrian King and asked him if he might be relieved of his duties for a while. "By all means, go!" said the King. "I will send a letter to the King of Israel, asking him to cure you."

The next day, Naaman left for Israel, taking with him ten talents of silver, six thousand shekels of gold, and ten sets of the finest clothing. He was not sure how much it would cost to cure him, but he was willing to pay anything. When he finally arrived, Naaman gave his letter to the King of Israel. But, as soon as the King had read it, he erupted in fury. "Why does the King of Syria send someone to me to be cured?" he stormed. "He's just trying to pick a quarrel!" Naaman wished he had never come.

But when Elisha heard about this, he sent a message to the King. "Tell the man to come to me and he will know that there is a prophet in Israel."

> "Now I know that there is no God in all the world except in Israel."

Naaman went straight to Elisha's house, but Elisha did not come out to greet him. Instead, he sent a messenger to tell Naaman to wash himself seven times in the Jordan River and he would be cured. But Naaman was not happy. "I thought that he would come and wave his hands over me and call on the name of the Lord, and that I would be cured," he said. "The rivers in Damascus are just as good as the Jordan. I shall go straight home and wash myself in the waters there!"

But his servant stopped him. "Master, if the prophet had told you to do something important and difficult, you would have risen to the occasion, wouldn't you? All he wants you to do is to bathe in the waters of the Jordan and be cleansed!"

Naaman listened and reluctantly agreed. He went down to a deserted part of the river and waded into the water. He submerged himself completely, seven times, and then came out. As he stepped onto the bank, he looked down in amazement. His skin disease had completely disappeared.

Naaman went back to Elisha and said to him, "Now I know that there is no God in all the world except in Israel. Please accept a gift of thanks." But Elisha declined. "In that case, would you give me as much earth as my two mules can carry so that I can take it back with me and worship the God of Israel on Israelite soil?" asked Naaman. And Elisha agreed gladly.

But Gehazi, Elisha's servant, thought that his master should have accepted a gift from Naaman. So, filled with greed, he went back to Naaman and pretended that he came with a message from Elisha. "My master has had a change of heart!" he lied. "He wants me to tell you that there are two young prophets who have just arrived from Ephraim and they would be grateful for anything you could give them. Maybe a talent of silver and a set of clothing each?"

"By all means," said Naaman. He tied up the two talents of silver in two bags and sorted out two fine sets of clothing. And he insisted that his servants carry them back for Gehazi. But, as soon as Naaman was out of sight, Gehazi grabbed the silver and the clothes and sent the servants on their way. He went back to his own room and hid his ill-gotten gains under the bed. Then he went back to Elisha.

But Elisha looked him straight in the eye and said, "Is this the time to take money or accept clothes—or anything else for that matter? The skin disease that used to torment Naaman will now be yours. It will cling to you and your descendants forever!"

Gehazi watched in horror as his hands and arms and toes turned scaly and white. He felt a terrible itch creep up his legs and spread across his back. Naaman's affliction was now his.

After submerging himself seven times in the river, Naaman's skin is totally cleansed

The Prophet Isaiah

O ne day, the prophet Isaiah had a vision in the Temple in Jerusalem. He saw the Lord seated high on His throne, the train of His robe filling the whole of the Temple.

Two beautiful angels, each with six feathery wings, looked down on Isaiah from above. "Holy, holy, holy is the Lord Almighty! The whole earth is full of His glory!" they sang, as the Temple shook and filled with smoke.

Isaiah was overwhelmed by the power and majesty of the Lord, and by His holiness. He fell to his knees and cried, "I am unworthy and I am unclean! My eyes have actually seen the Lord God Almighty himself!"

> "Tell the people that the Lord is coming and that they must prepare the way for Him."

Immediately, one of the angels flew down to the altar and picked up a burning coal with a pair of tongs. He placed it on Isaiah's lips, then swiftly took it away again saying, "This coal that touched your lips has taken away your guilt and made amends for your sin."

Then Isaiah heard the Lord's voice saying, "Spread the word of God. Tell the people that the Lord is coming and that they must prepare the way for Him. At first, they will not listen. There will be destruction and devastation and the land will be laid waste. But eventually, the Glory of God will be revealed. The wilderness will blossom and water will gush forth in the desert. The weak will become strong, the blind will see, and those who follow the Lord will be given strength. The Lord Himself will come down to earth and look after His flock, protecting them from evil."

Isaiah sees a vision of the Lord and the Temple shakes and fills with smoke

162

Hezekiah's Gold

*T*he kings of Israel had grown greedy and corrupt. They and their people had turned away from the Lord, worshipping false gods and idols again.

The Lord was not pleased. He warned them through his prophets, "Turn from your evil ways. Observe my commands and decrees, in accordance with the entire law that I commanded your fathers to obey and that I delivered to you through my servants, the prophets." But no one would listen.

The neighboring Assyrians, who had a powerful army, were a threat to Israel and Judah. Now they invaded Israel, pillaging and plundering. They laid siege to the capital, Samaria, and after three years, it fell to the enemy.

While Israel was occupied by the Assyrians, a king named Hezekiah came to the throne in Judah, to the south. He obeyed the Lord in everything he did. There had never been a king like him in Judah, and there never was again. He had also led his men to victory over the Philistines many times. But, when the Assyrians raced south and attacked the cities of Judah, Hezekiah had met his match. He sent a message to King Sennacherib of Assyria, saying, "Withdraw from Judah and I will pay whatever you ask."

> "God will defend you and save your city."

Sennacherib demanded three hundred talents of silver and thirty talents of gold. It was a huge amount. The only way that Hezekiah could pay was by stripping the gold from the doors of the Temple in Jerusalem. But Sennacherib did not keep his word. He took the treasure and ordered his troops to besiege Jerusalem. They stopped just outside Jerusalem, calling for the King. But Hezekiah sent his officials instead. At this, the commander of the Assyrian army addressed the people of Jerusalem. "Do not let Hezekiah deceive you. Do not believe that the Lord will protect you. Has the god of any nation ever delivered his land from the hand of the King of Assyria?"

The officials went back and told Hezekiah that the Lord's name had been taken in vain. Hezekiah put on sackcloth to show his humility. Before praying, he told his officials to ask the prophet Isaiah for help.

When the officials found Isaiah, he told them, "God will defend you and save your city."

That night, the angel of the Lord flew over the Assyrian camp. When King Sennacherib got up, thousands of his soldiers were dead. He looked in horror at the sea of bodies that surrounded him, and he fled, as fast as he could, away from Jerusalem. He did not stop until he got back to his home in Nineveh.

Hezekiah prays for help when his city is attacked by the Assyrians

163

Josiah and the Scroll of the Law

*J*osiah was only eight years old when he became the new ruler of Judah, after the assassination of his father, Amon. Unlike his father and his grandfather, King Manasseh, Josiah was obedient to the Lord.

During the previous decades, the splendid Temple that Solomon had built in Jerusalem had been neglected and had fallen into disrepair. In the eighteenth year of his reign, King Josiah decided that it was time for the Temple to be restored to its former glory. He asked the high priest, Hilkiah, to gather together the money that had been collected in the Temple over the years. It would be used to finance the repairs.

While Hilkiah was finding the money and having a good look around to see what needed to be done, he came across an old scroll hidden in a neglected corner of the Temple. It was festooned with cobwebs but, fortunately, the mice had not gotten their teeth into it. He dusted it off and was amazed to see that the yellowing parchment contained the Book of the Covenant. Hilkiah knew that there was only one

> "My people have forgotten God's Law!"

copy in the whole of Judah and Israel, and it had been missing for many, many years. This must be it. Gingerly, he picked it up and took it to his friend, Shaphan, who was the royal scribe. Shaphan's eyes opened wide when he saw the yellowing parchment scroll and, taking Hilkiah with him, he went straight to the palace with it. He bowed low before King Josiah and then unrolled the scroll very carefully. His voice trembled as he began to read the first few lines aloud.

Josiah listened intently and, as he heard the beautiful words bearing testimony to the Lord, he was filled with the deepest sorrow. He sprang up from his throne and began to tear at his clothes. "My people have forgotten God's Law!" he wept. "They are selfish and corrupt and God must be so angry with them! What will happen to them?" And he begged Shaphan and Hilkiah to find out what lay in store for the people of Judah.

"Great is the Lord's anger that burns against us because our fathers have not obeyed the words of this book," Josiah said. "They have not acted in accordance with all that is written there concerning us."

Shaphan and Hilkiah went to consult a prophetess named Huldah. She was married to the wardrobe keeper in the Temple and lived in a new part of Jerusalem. She told them that the Lord was going to bring disaster on the people of Judah because they had worshipped so many different gods. But King Josiah would be spared because he was a good man and had humbled himself in front of the Lord.

When King Josiah heard this, he called everyone together in the Temple— the elders and the priests, the prophets, and all the people of Jerusalem. He stood by the great pillar, solemnly unrolled the parchment scroll of the law, and read it to them, every word. And then, in the presence of the Lord, he renewed the covenant that had been made long ago by the people of Israel to follow the Lord and to keep His commands and decrees. The people listened in silence and gave their pledge.

After this, Josiah ordered a purge of the pagan gods and the priests who bowed down before them. All the trappings of worship were to go. The statues and altars were to be removed from the Temple and then destroyed and burned. Sacred stones and shrines to the false gods were to be smashed, ground up into fine powder, and scattered over the land. And the altar in the Valley of Ben Hinnom, where so many sons and daughters had been sacrificed in the flames by their parents, was to be reduced to dust. Then, when the whole of the country had been cleansed, Josiah commanded his people to celebrate the festival of Passover, which commemorated the Israelites' escape from Egypt.

Josiah reads from the scroll of the law

Jeremiah and the Potter's Wheel

The Lord told Jeremiah that He had chosen him to be a prophet. Jeremiah was astonished.

"Do not be afraid," answered the Lord. "I am with you." And He reached out His hand and touched Jeremiah gently on the lips with his fingers. "Now I have put words into your mouth," He said. "What do you see?"

"I see the branch of an almond tree in bloom," Jeremiah replied.

"That is right," said the Lord. "I am watching to see if my word is fulfilled. What else do you see?"

"I see a boiling pot, tilting away from the north," Jeremiah answered.

"It is from the north that I will bring disaster," said the Lord. "I am about to summon people to overrun Judah and punish the people for their wickedness in forsaking me and worshipping false gods. You must warn them. They will turn on you, but do not be frightened. I am with you."

The Lord sent Jeremiah to the house of a potter, who was busy in his workshop. The potter threw some clay on his wheel and shaped it with his hands. The lump of clay started to transform into a pot, but then it wobbled and collapsed in a heap. The potter scooped up the clay and started to make another pot. This time it was perfect.

> "Like the clay in the hand of the potter, so is the House of Israel in my hands!"

The Lord spoke to Jeremiah and said, "Like the clay in the hand of the potter, so is the House of Israel in my hands! If the people repent of their evil ways, I will make them good and strong. But, if they persist in worshipping false gods, they will be destroyed. Go and tell them this."

Some time later, Jeremiah bought a clay jar from the potter. Then he went to the Valley of Ben Hinnom and summoned everybody. He told them what the Lord had said. And, to illustrate his point, Jeremiah picked up the jar and threw it on the ground, destroying it. "This is what the Lord will do to you if you do not change your ways!" he warned.

As usual, no one listened, but soon enough, Jeremiah's prophecy came true. Under Nebuchadnezzar, the Babylonian army attacked Jerusalem. After months of suffering, the city was captured. King Jehoiachin and the people were exiled to Babylon. Nebuchadnezzar chose a new king, Zedekiah, to be king of Judah.

One day, the Lord showed Jeremiah two baskets of figs. One of them was full of perfect fruit. The other basket had only rotten figs. "What do you see, Jeremiah?"

"I see figs," he replied. "The good ones are very good, but the bad ones are rotten."

"Yes," said the Lord. "The people who have left Judah and gone to Babylon are like the ripe figs. They will repent and I will bring them out of captivity to be my people. But King Zedekiah and the people who remain in Jerusalem will not repent. They are rotten and I will destroy them!"

Jeremiah breaks the jar to show the people that
God will destroy them if they don't change

BABYLON

The city's gateway was built by Nebuchadnezzar in 575 BCE and was dedicated to the goddess Ishtar. Though little remains of Babylon, in 1899 archaeologists discovered some blue-glazed bricks from the gateway, decorated with dragons and young bulls. The gateway was reconstructed in Berlin, Germany.

*As the king was walking on
the roof of the royal palace of Babylon,
he said, "Is not this the great Babylon
I have built as the royal residence,
by my mighty power and for the
glory of my majesty?"*

Daniel 4:29–30

The Israelites in Captivity

*F*or years, the prophet Jeremiah had tried to warn the people that Jerusalem was in terrible danger. He knew that they could save themselves.

"The Lord has told me that, if you leave the city and go to Babylon, you will survive," he said to them. "But if you stay here in Jerusalem, you will be killed—either by the sword or by famine or plague. It is your choice!"

The people were infuriated by his constant warnings of doom and gloom and did not believe a word of them. Some army officers decided to take action. They went to King Zedekiah in the palace. "This man Jeremiah, who calls himself a prophet, has gone too far! He should be put to death!" they said. "He is demoralizing the troops—and everybody else who is left in Jerusalem. He pretends to be concerned with our well-being but, in fact, he is doing much more harm than good!"

"Do what you want with him," muttered the King. His thoughts were far away on more important business—he was plotting how to get his own back on the Babylonians, who made his life a misery.

> "All the most important people were deported from Jerusalem and sent into exile in Babylon."

So the officers seized Jeremiah and tied him up. They took him to their barracks where there was a courtyard with a large, empty water cistern. They lowered him over the side. Although there was no water, there was mud at the bottom, and Jeremiah sank into it up to his waist. He was left there, helpless, with no escape.

But when a palace official named Ebed-Melech heard what they had done to Jeremiah, he went to the king and protested. "My Lord," he said. "Those men are out of order! They have done a terrible thing to the prophet Jeremiah and thrown him into a huge cistern. He can't get out and he will surely starve to death!" The king agreed that Jeremiah must be rescued.

Ebed-Melech took some old rope and a bundle of old rags. Then, with thirty men, he went to the cistern. Ebed-Melech leaned over the side and peered down into the darkness. He could just see Jeremiah huddled at the bottom. "Put these rags under your arms to pad the ropes," he shouted, letting down the ropes and the rags. Jeremiah made a makeshift harness for himself and Ebed-Melech and his men slowly hauled him up to the surface.

After his lucky escape, Jeremiah renewed his efforts to warn the people of their fate, but still they would not listen. And soon, King Nebuchadnezzar of Babylon attacked the city again and laid siege to it. The people were starved into submission. After two long years, they finally opened the gates and let the invaders in.

When the Babylonian army entered the city, King Zedekiah fled as fast as he could. The Babylonians pursued him and caught up with him on the plains of Jericho. Zedekiah's two sons were put to death in front of his very eyes. Then they put out Zedekiah's eyes with burning stakes, and they took him to Babylon, blind and bound with shackles. All the most important people were deported from Jerusalem and sent into exile in Babylon. Only the very poor stayed in Judah, working in the vineyards and the fields.

The invaders swarmed into the holy Temple in the middle of the city, looting whatever they could get their hands on. They stole the precious gold treasures that had been there since the time of King Solomon. Then they set fire to the entire building, together with the royal palace and most of the houses. The whole city went up in flames, like a tinderbox, and was burned to the ground.

King Zedekiah is blinded and taken in chains to Babylon

The Golden Statue

Nebuchadnezzar had been king of Babylon for two years. He had conquered Jerusalem and brought back many of the people as slaves to his city.

One night, Nebuchadnezzar had a dream that disturbed him deeply. He summoned the wise men and asked for their help. "I have had a strange dream. I can't stop thinking about it," he told them. "Tell me what it means!"

"O King! Please live forever!" they flattered him. "Tell us your dream and we will interpret it for you."

"This is the deal," said the King. "If you cannot tell me my dream and what it means, I will have you cut into pieces and your houses reduced to piles of rubble. But, if you can interpret my dream, I will give you huge rewards and honors!"

There was a terrible silence. Not one of them had any idea what the dream was or what it meant. "O King! What you ask is impossible!" they cried. Nebuchadnezzar was furious and he immediately ordered the execution of every single wise man in Babylon.

One of them was a young man named Daniel who had been captured in Jerusalem.

> "If you cannot tell me my dream and what it means, I will have you cut into pieces."

He had been singled out, along with a few other captives from Judah, to be taught the language and history of Babylon. They were then taken into the King's service. Daniel soon became good friends with three of the other young men. They had been given new Babylonian names—Shadrach, Meshach, and Abednego. Daniel himself was now known as Belteshazzar. All four of them were clever, but Daniel had a special gift. He could interpret dreams.

So, when he heard about Nebuchadnezzar's terrible decree, Daniel went to the King and asked if he might be allowed to try to interpret the dream. The King agreed, but first Daniel went back to his house, where he and his three friends prayed for help from God. During that night, the mystery was revealed to him and, when he woke up in the morning, he knew what the dream meant. He gave thanks to the Lord. "Praise be to the name of God forever and ever. Wisdom and power are His."

He went to Nebuchadnezzar and said, "No wise man, enchanter, magician, or diviner can explain your dream, but God in heaven can reveal the mystery. He has shown me the meaning of your dream." Nebuchadnezzar told him to go on.

"You saw a gigantic statue in your dream. The head was made of pure gold, the chest and arms of silver, the belly and thighs of bronze. The legs were made of iron while the feet and toes were half iron and half baked clay." Nebuchadnezzar listened, open-mouthed, while Daniel continued.

"As you gazed at the statue, a rock suddenly came through the air from nowhere and hit the statue's feet, breaking them into tiny pieces. At once, all the other parts of the statue—the gold, silver, bronze, iron, and clay—were smashed to pieces, like chaff on the threshing-floor in summer. The wind swept them away without a trace. But the rock became a huge mountain and filled the whole earth." Daniel paused for breath while Nebuchadnezzar sat, transfixed, on his throne.

"Now I will tell you what it means," Daniel went on. "You, O King, are the king of kings. The God of heaven has given you dominion and power over your people, the beasts of the field, and the birds of the air. The statue's head of gold represents you. The silver represents another kingdom that will rise after you, but it will be inferior to yours. Next, there will be a third kingdom, one of bronze, which will rule over the whole earth. Finally, there will be a fourth kingdom, strong as iron. And, just as iron can break things, so this kingdom will crush and break all others. But, as you saw, the feet and toes of the statue were made of iron and baked clay, so this will be a divided kingdom.

The solid statue is smashed to pieces by a rock

"The rock that destroyed these kingdoms is the Kingdom of God. It is greater than any kingdom on earth and will never be destroyed."

King Nebuchadnezzar fell at Daniel's feet crying, "Surely your God is the God of gods and the Lord of kings. He is the revealer of mysteries!" The King heaped lavish gifts on Daniel and made him governor of Babylon. He also put him in charge of the wise men. And, at Daniel's request, he gave Shadrach, Meshach, and Abednego important positions, too.

Then, he ordered a statue to be made. It was gigantic and the whole thing was made of solid gold. Nebuchadnezzar summoned all the officials and told them to worship the statue. If they did not, they would be thrown into a blazing furnace.

But Shadrach, Meshach, and Abednego refused. "If we are thrown into the blazing furnace our God will save us. But even if He did not, we would never worship your golden statue," they said. Upon hearing this, the King told his men to stoke the furnace and make it seven times hotter than usual. Then he ordered his soldiers to take the three men, tie them up, and throw them into the flames. But as they did so, the flames licked out of the furnace and devoured the soldiers themselves.

The King looked into the fire. "Look!" he shouted. "I can see four men wandering around in there. They aren't tied up and they seem completely unharmed. The fourth one looks like a son of the gods!" Cautiously, he crept nearer. "Shadrach, Meshach, and Abednego," he shouted. "Come out at once!"

They obeyed and walked calmly out of the furnace, not a hair singed. Everyone crowded around them in amazement. Then Nebuchadnezzar proclaimed, "Praise be to the God of Shadrach, Meshach, and Abednego, who has sent His angel and rescued His servants! They trusted in Him and defied my command. They were willing to give up their lives rather than worship any god except their own. I decree that my people shall worship their God alone!"

*A fourth man appears
in the furnace*

Belshazzar's Feast

King Belshazzar gave a great banquet for a thousand of his nobles. He ordered his servants to bring in the gold and silver cups that his father, Nebuchadnezzar, had plundered from the Lord's Temple in Jerusalem.

מנא מנא
תקל ופרסין

The precious cups were filled to the brim. Belshazzar and his guests raised them high in the air. And then they drank from them, toasting their gods. But, suddenly, the King turned pale. He stared at the wall across from him. A ghostly hand had appeared from nowhere and was floating there, all on its own. Slowly its finger wrote some words on the wall. It looked like a secret code: MENE, MENE, TEKEL, PARSIN. Then the hand melted away, leaving its message behind. Belshazzar asked his wise men what the words meant, but they were baffled.

The Queen, however, knew what to do. "There is a man in your kingdom named Daniel—or Belteshazzar to his Babylonian friends. He will tell you what the writing means."

Daniel was found and brought to the palace. Belshazzar showed him the writing and said, "If you can tell me what it means, you will be clothed in purple with a gold chain around your neck, and you will be made the third highest ruler in the kingdom."

"You may keep your gifts and rewards," replied Daniel. "But I will read the writing and tell you what it means." And he examined the wall carefully. Then he said, "God sent the hand you saw that wrote on the wall. MENE, MENE, TEKEL, PARSIN means three things. First, God has numbered the days of your reign.

> "God sent the hand you saw that wrote on the wall."

Secondly, you have been weighed on the scales and been found wanting. And thirdly, your kingdom will be divided and given to the Medes and the Persians." Belshazzar listened in horror to Daniel's words.

That very night, the Persian army launched a surprise attack on Babylon under King Darius the Mede. And, just as the cryptic words predicted, the city fell and was taken by the Medes and the Persians, and Belshazzar was killed.

175

Daniel and the Lions

*A*fter Babylon was conquered, it became one of the great Persian Empire's royal cities. King Darius made Daniel one of his chief administrators and planned to put him in charge of the entire kingdom.

This made the other officials at court very jealous. They tried to undermine Daniel and put him down whenever they could, but there was simply no way of getting at him. "We will never be able to pin anything on him," they said. "The only way is to make him disobey his God." And together they hatched a plan.

They went to the Darius and said, "O King Darius! Live forever! We ask you to issue a decree that, for the next thirty days, the worship of any god, other than you, the king, is forbidden. Anyone caught worshipping another god will be thrown into the lions' den. Please make sure that it is written down so it cannot be changed." Darius agreed and called for the royal scribe.

Daniel heard about the decree, but went on praying to the Lord three times a day, as usual, at home in his room upstairs. The big windows opened toward Jerusalem and everyone could see him clearly, kneeling down to worship his God. His enemies gathered in the street below and watched him.

> "May your God, whom you serve so well, rescue you."

Then they went straight to the palace to denounce him. "Daniel pays no attention to you, O King. Or to the decree you put in writing," they told him gleefully. "He still prays to his God three times a day."

Darius was distressed when he heard this. Daniel was one of his most trusted men. He spent the rest of the day trying to think how he could save him. But the conspirators were not going to give up. "Remember, O King, that, according to the law of the Medes and the Persians, no decree that the King issues can be changed."

With a heavy heart, Darius gave the order to arrest Daniel, who was seized as he kneeled at his window to pray. He was taken to the lions' den, and the King accompanied him. As they approached the enclosure, they could hear blood-curdling roars from inside. "May your God, whom you serve so well, rescue you," Darius said, sadly, as Daniel was thrown inside and left to his fate.

A huge stone was rolled across the mouth of the den. Darius sealed it with his signet ring. He returned to the palace, but he could not sleep.

At dawn, he hurried to the lions' den, dreading what he would find. All was quiet. He called out, his voice trembling with fear. To his amazement, he heard Daniel saying, "O King! Live forever! My God sent His angel and he shut the mouths of the lions. They have not hurt me because I am innocent in His sight. Nor have I ever done wrong to you, O King."

Darius was overjoyed and ordered Daniel's release. The stone was duly rolled away and he walked out calmly, without even the tiniest scratch. Behind him, the lions opened their great jaws and yawned, watching him go. Darius ordered his men to arrest the conspirators. They were thrown into the lions' den, and this time, it was a very different story. Before their bodies reached the ground, the lions pounced, tearing them limb from limb. The lions devoured their flesh and lay there happily, gnawing on the bones.

Esther Becomes Queen

King Xerxes ruled over all the different provinces of the Persian Empire, from India to the Nile.

In the third year of his reign, he gave a lavish banquet for his nobles and military leaders at his palace in Susa. It lasted a week and was a glittering occasion. On the seventh day, when King Xerxes was in particularly high spirits, he sent for Queen Vashti. She had been entertaining her women friends in another part of the royal palace. And now, Xerxes wanted to show off his beautiful wife in front of everybody. But the Queen refused to come.

King Xerxes exploded with fury. He had been snubbed in front of all the important dignitaries. Immediately, he called for his wise men. "According to the law, what must be done to Queen Vashti?" he asked them, still seething with rage. "She has not obeyed my command!" They told him to find a new wife who was more suitable.

Xerxes followed their advice, and emissaries were sent far and wide to find a new queen. Hundreds of suitable candidates were brought back—all beautiful and young. They were looked after well and were taught how to make themselves look even more beautiful. But it was a whole year before Xerxes was allowed to see them and choose his queen.

One of the girls was named Hadassah—or Esther. She had been brought up by her cousin, Mordecai, after her parents died. Mordecai was a Jew who belonged to the tribe of Benjamin and he had been captured in Jerusalem by King Nebuchadnezzar. When she joined the other girls at the royal palace, Esther was warned by Mordecai not to tell anyone about her family background. He thought that Xerxes would not look kindly on a Jewish girl.

> "There is a certain people whose customs are different from those of other people in your kingdom."

At last, after a year of preening and polishing, the girls were presented to the King. They shone like jewels as they appeared before him. It was an impossible choice. But when Xerxes saw Esther, he fell helplessly in love. He knew that she was the one. He beckoned her to him immediately and sent the other girls back to their quarters. He made Esther his wife soon after, and gave a great banquet, proclaiming a special holiday.

One day, during the course of his duties at court, Mordecai overheard two of the officers, on guard at the gate, discussing a plan to assassinate Xerxes. He went straight to his cousin, Esther, and told her about the plot. She immediately informed the King, and the two conspirators were arrested. King Xerxes's life had been saved. The chief scribe carefully noted this down, along with the rest of the day's events, in the Book of Chronicles.

But Mordecai was not happy when Xerxes appointed Haman, who was an Amalekite, as chief minister. The Israelites and the Amalekites had been fierce enemies since the time when the Israelites left Egypt. All the royal officials were commanded to bow down before Haman and honor him, but Mordecai refused

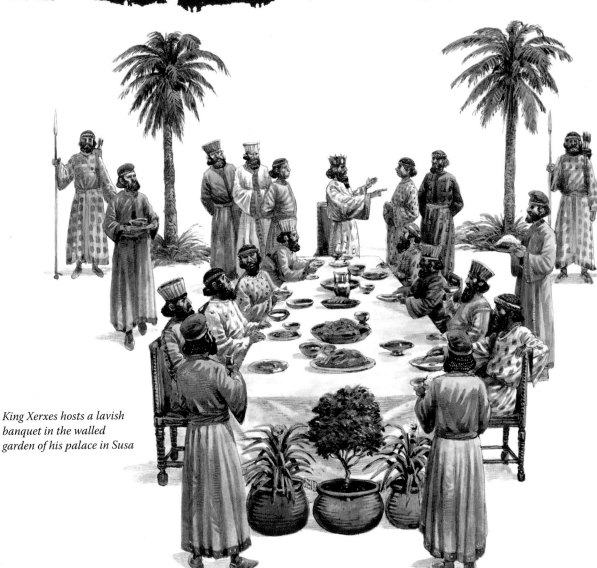

King Xerxes hosts a lavish banquet in the walled garden of his palace in Susa

point-blank. Haman was infuriated by Mordecai's lack of respect. When he discovered that Mordecai was a Jew, he decided that he would have him killed. And not only Mordecai—all his people, too.

Haman and his men cast the little stones known as the pur—or the lot—to choose a time for the massacre of the Jews. The lot fell on the thirteenth day of the twelfth month. Haman went straight to Xerxes. "There is a certain people whose customs are different from those of other people in your kingdom," he said. "They do not obey your laws. If it pleases the King, let a decree be issued to destroy them."

The King agreed and gave him his signet ring. "Do as you please with these people," he said. So the royal scribes were summoned and they wrote out the decrees in all the many different languages of the empire, telling the governors to kill all the Jews on the thirteenth day of the twelfth month.

When Mordecai heard the terrible news, he told Esther of Haman's plans to get rid of the Jewish people. She replied, "Go, gather together all the Jews who are in Susa and fast for me. Do not eat or drink for three days, night or day. I and my maids will fast as you do. When this is done, I will go to the King, even though it is against the law. And if I perish, I perish."

Esther Saves Her People

After Esther had fasted for three days, she put on her ceremonial robes and went to the inner court of the palace, in front of the King's great hall.

Xerxes was sitting on his magnificent throne opposite the door, deep in thought. When he saw her, his face lit up and he held out the golden scepter in his hand toward her. This was the sign that she was allowed to approach him. She smiled and went straight to him, touching the tip of the scepter.

"What is it, my dearest?" he asked fondly. "What is your request? You know I would give you half my kingdom!"

"If it pleases, my Lord, I would like to prepare a banquet for you tomorrow evening. Please come—and bring the chief minister, Haman, with you. Then I will answer your question." Xerxes agreed, gladly, knowing that his wife would make sure that he was offered all his favorite dishes.

Haman was delighted when he got the invitation and boasted about it to his wife and friends. "I am the only person that Queen Esther has invited to accompany the king to her banquet!" he gloated, pink with pleasure. Then his face darkened. "But all this gives me no satisfaction as long as I see that Jew Mordecai sitting at the King's gate!"

> "My people and I are about to be put to death like animals. We are going to be exterminated."

His wife, Zeresh, and his friends said, "Have a gallows built and tomorrow morning ask the king to have Mordecai hanged on it. Then go to the banquet and be happy!" The suggestion delighted Haman and he immediately ordered the huge gallows to be built just outside his house.

That night, Xerxes could not sleep, so he asked for the Book of Chronicles to be brought to him. He opened the book and started to skim through it. When he came to the part that described how Mordecai had saved his life by uncovering a plot against him, he sat bolt upright. "What honor and recognition did this man, Mordecai, receive?" he asked his attendant in the bedchamber.

"Nothing, my Lord," the attendant replied.

Early next morning, when Haman requested an audience with the king to discuss hanging Mordecai, Xerxes asked him, "There is someone I want to honor for a great service that they did for me. How can I reward him?"

Naturally, Haman thought that the king was talking about him, and that he was about to be heaped with yet more favors. "He should be proclaimed a hero! He should be dressed in a magnificent royal robe and put on the king's horse," he replied. "Then he should be led through the streets of the city in triumph!"

"Excellent!" said Xerxes. "What a good idea! Go and get my finest robe for my servant Mordecai, put him on my very best horse, and parade him through the streets! You can walk by his side!" Haman went very pale!

That evening, Xerxes and Haman went together to Esther's banquet. The three of them sat down to eat and Xerxes repeated his question. "What is it, Queen Esther? What is your request? You know I will give you half my kingdom!"

"If I have found favor with you, O King, and if it pleases your majesty, grant me my life—that is my request," she replied. "For my people and I are about to be put to death like animals. We are going to be exterminated."

The king leaped up from the table. "What? Who is he? Where is the man who would dare do such a thing?" he thundered.

Esther stared at Haman. "That is your man. He is sitting there right in front of you! It is the unspeakable Haman," she said.

Xerxes gasped in disbelief. Then he turned and left the room, without saying anything. He paced up and down in the palace garden as the full horror sank in. While he was gone, Haman threw himself on Esther, begging for his life. He was hysterical and, just as the king returned, he was clutching at the queen like a madman. Xerxes thought he was harming her, so he gave the order for Haman to be taken away immediately.

"There is a huge gallows just by his house," said one of the attendants, helpfully. "He had it made for Mordecai, the loyal servant who saved your life!" So they hanged Haman on the gallows he had prepared for Mordecai.

Esther acuses Haman of plotting against the Jews

Exile and Return

In 597 BCE, King Nebuchadnezzar II of Babylon captured Jerusalem, taking away many of the people into captivity. He returned in 586 BCE, when he destroyed the city and its Temple, taking even more Jews into exile. The loss of Solomon's Temple was a disaster for the Jews. Even so, throughout the long years of exile, they held on to their religion and their national identity.

Cyrus

In 539 BCE, the Babylonians themselves were overthrown by King Cyrus the Great of Persia. This clay cylinder is inscribed with Cyrus's account of his conquest of Babylon. He also records his decision to allow exiled peoples to return home.

Babylon

These are the ruins of Babylon, where the Jews were exiled for more than 50 years. During this period, they stopped speaking Hebrew as an everyday language and started speaking Aramaic, the Babylonian language. They continued to write in Hebrew.

Ishtar Gate

Babylon's grand Ishtar Gate was built by Nebuchadnezzar during the time of the Jewish exile. Babylon was a wealthy city, much larger and more impressive than Jerusalem. For the Jews, it came to stand for all wicked states opposed to God.

Subjects of Persia

The Persians respected the customs of the peoples they ruled. Reliefs from their palace at Persepolis show subject peoples bringing tribute. Here you can see a Lydian, from western Turkey, three Medes, from northwest Iran, and a Nubian, from Africa.

Persian Province

Under Persian rule, many Jews returned home where, in 515 BCE, they completed rebuilding their Temple on a smaller scale. Judah was now a minor Persian province named "Yehud." This is a coin of Yehud issued in the 4th century BCE.

This map shows the Persian Empire at its height, under King Darius I, who ruled from 522–485 BCE.

TIMELINE

597 BCE
King Nebuchadnezzar II of Babylon captures Jerusalem, taking 10,000 Jews into captivity. He places Zedekiah on the throne of Judah.

c. 590 BCE
The prophets Ezekiel, in exile, and Jeremiah, in Judah, warn that Jerusalem is faced with destruction.

587 BCE
Zedekiah rebels against Nebuchadnezzar.

586 BCE
Nebuchadnezzar captures Jerusalem and destroys the Temple, taking more Jews into captivity.

586–571 BCE
Ezekiel offers hope to the exiled Jews, promising that Jerusalem will be restored.

586–539 BCE
Exile poems grieving over the destruction of Jerusalem are collected to form the Book of Lamentations.

539 BCE
King Cyrus the Great of Persia overthrows Nabonidus, the last king of Babylon. Cyrus allows the Jews to go home to Judah.

520–515 BCE
The Jews rebuild their Temple in Jerusalem. The prophets Haggai and Zechariah provide leadership.

The Rebuilding of Jerusalem

Over the years, some of the people who had been exiled from Judah and taken to Babylon were given their freedom by King Artaxerxes and allowed to return home.

A few came back to court again with sad tales of the city of Jerusalem. Nehemiah, who was the cupbearer to King Artaxerxes, heard the stories and was deeply affected. He mourned and he fasted and prayed to God, asking for mercy. "I confess the sins we Israelites have committed against you. We have not obeyed the commands, decrees, and laws you gave your servant Moses. You said that if we were unfaithful, we would be scattered among the nations. But if we came back to you and obeyed your commands, we would be together again and returned to your dwelling place."

That day, when he took a goblet of wine to Artaxerxes, the King looked at him and asked, "Why do you look so sad? What grieves you so deep in your heart?"

"May the King live forever!" said Nehemiah. "But why should I not look sad when the city where my fathers are buried lies in ruins and has been destroyed by fire?" And he asked the King if he could go to Jerusalem to help rebuild it. Artaxerxes agreed and helped him on his way with letters of safe passage and an armed escort. It was a journey of four months from the royal palace in Susa to Judah.

> "Our great city lies in ruins. It is a disgrace. Let us pray to the Lord our God to help us!"

As Nehemiah reached Jerusalem, he saw that the city was in ruins. The walls were rubble, and the holy Temple and royal palace were charred. One night, he set out to inspect the city on his donkey, then summoned the people. "Let us rebuild the walls of Jerusalem!" he said. "Our great city lies in ruins. It is a disgrace. Let us pray to the Lord our God to help us!"

Some people mocked him. "You don't have a chance," they jeered.

"The God of heaven will give us success," said Nehemiah quietly. "We will start rebuilding the city."

Sanballat, the governor of Samaria to the north, was incensed when he heard that Nehemiah was organizing the rebuilding work. "What are those feeble Jews doing?" he asked. "Do they think that they can build those great walls again? Can they bring back to life the stones that have been reduced to piles of rubble?"

But, despite the resentment and threats from the neighboring countries, Nehemiah and his people started rebuilding the great wall of Jerusalem. Nehemiah put some men in front of the weakest places, armed with swords, spears, and bows, to prevent attack. "Do not be afraid," he said to them. "Remember the Lord, and fight for your brothers, your sons, your daughters, your wives, and your homes."

*When night falls, Nehemiah
inspects the ruins of Jerusalem*

From then on, half of the workforce continued building while the other half stood guard. After only fifty-two days, the walls were finished and Jerusalem stood, safe and secure, once more. The neighboring nations could not believe their eyes and they were filled with fear. They realized that the work had been done with the help of God. And the people of Judah flooded back from exile to the land of their fathers. There were more than forty-two thousand of them.

The people assembled in the square in front of the Water Gate, and Ezra brought out the Book of the Law of Moses and read it aloud. He praised the Lord and the people cried "Amen! Amen!" Together, they bowed down and worshipped God. And the Levites came to dedicate the great new walls to the Lord, and to celebrate with songs of thanksgiving and with the music of cymbals, harps, and lyres.

Jonah 1–4

Jonah and the Big Fish

A nd God told his prophet Jonah that he must go to Nineveh, the capital of Assyria, to warn the people that their great walled city would be destroyed if they did not give up their wicked ways.

But Jonah did not like the people of Nineveh and did not want to see them saved, so he disobeyed the Lord. He fled to Joppa, a harbor in Israel, and boarded a ship to Tarshish, on the eastern shores of the Mediterranean.

The sea was calm and the skies were clear but, as soon as the ship set sail, dark clouds gathered and a violent storm howled across the water, whipping it into towering waves that crashed wildly onto the little ship. Terrified, the sailors prayed to their different gods and threw the cargo overboard to lighten the ship's heavy load.

Jonah, meanwhile, had fallen fast asleep below deck and was dead to the world. The captain raced down and shook him furiously. "Wake up! How can you sleep at a time like this? Pray to your God that we are saved." Up on deck the rest of the crew were busy drawing straws to find out who was responsible for their terrible predicament. It was Jonah.

The crew challenged Jonah and he admitted that the storm was his fault because he had disobeyed his God. "Pick me up and throw me into the sea, and it will become calm," he said. The sailors were doubtful about this and tried to row for shore, but the waves became wilder. Reluctantly, they threw Jonah over the side and into the sea. As if by magic, the raging waters grew calm and they were saved. The sailors, amazed and a little afraid at the power of Jonah's God, offered up prayers and gave thanks.

Jonah sank to the bottom of the sea, long streamers of seaweed trailing behind him. Suddenly, a huge fish appeared out of the gloom, opened its jaws, and swallowed Jonah whole. He slid headfirst into the creature's great empty belly and stayed there, praying to God, for three days and nights in the dark.

"But Jonah was angry with God for sparing Nineveh."

Finally, he proclaimed, "Salvation belongs to the Lord!" The fish opened its mouth and dropped Jonah onto dry land, safe and sound.

Again, the Lord told Jonah to go to Nineveh. This time he obeyed and set off on the long journey. The King welcomed him and heeded his warning. He promised that his people would turn to God. They started to fast and wear clothes of sackcloth to show how sorry they were for their bad behavior. Even the King took off his royal robes and covered himself with sackcloth. The city was saved.

But Jonah was angry with God for sparing Nineveh. He built a shelter outside the city walls and waited there, hoping that the city would fall after all. God watched over him and planted a tall shrub to shade him from the sun. Jonah was thankful for the cool leaves. But the next day, God sent a worm that ate the roots of the plant and killed it. Despite the hot sun and strong wind, Jonah kept watch, weak and angry that the plant had died. "It would be better for me to die," he moaned.

"Jonah, why are you so angry about a plant that you did not grow or tend?" God asked. "Yet you resent my concern for the great city of Nineveh and the thousands of people who live there?"

The Book of Psalms

The Book of Psalms is also known as the Psalter.
In Hebrew, it is called the Book of Praises.

It contains one hundred and fifty different prayers addressed to God, including laments, praises, and thanksgivings. Many of them are thought to have been written by King David, who was a poet as well as a singer and musician.

The very first psalm, whose author is not known, introduces the themes that recur throughout the whole book—devotion, thanksgiving, and unwavering faith in God. It says that only those who follow the path of righteousness will ultimately be blessed by God.

"Blessed is the man who does not walk in the counsel of the wicked
or stand in the way of sinners or sit in the seat of mockers.
But his delight is in the law of the Lord, and on His law he meditates
day and night."

In ancient Israel, the law was studied every day. A deep knowledge of the law was a way of getting closer to God.

Psalm 8, attributed to King David, celebrates man's dominion over the earth. It is a reflection of God's greatness and recognizes man's insignificance in comparison to the glory of God's creation.

"O Lord, our Lord, how majestic is your name in all the earth!
You have set your glory above the heavens.
From the lips of children and infants you have ordained praise.
because of your enemies, to silence the foe and the avenger.
When I consider your heavens, the work of your fingers,
the moon and the stars, which you have set in place,
what is man that you are mindful of him,
the son of man that you care for him?
You made him a little lower than the heavenly beings
and crowned him with glory and honor.
You made him ruler over the works of your hands;
you put everything under his feet:
all flocks and herds, and the beasts of the field,
the birds of the air, and the fish of the sea,
all that swim the paths of the seas."

God gives humankind dominion over His creation

Like a good shepherd, God will protect His flock

People can live free from evil because God watches over them

Psalm 23, one of the most famous psalms, is also attributed to David. It describes God as a good shepherd, looking after His sheep. Man can live free from fear because He is always there to protect and guide His flock.

"The Lord is my shepherd, I shall not be in want.
He makes me lie down in green pastures,
He leads me beside quiet waters, He restores my soul.
He guides me in the paths of righteousness for His name's sake.
Even though I walk through the valley of the shadow of death,
I will fear no evil, for you are with me;
your rod and your staff, they comfort me.
You prepare a table before me in the presence of my enemies.
You anoint my head with oil; my cup overflows.
Surely goodness and love will follow me all the days of my life,
and I will dwell in the house of the Lord forever."

Psalm 121 is the second in a collection of fifteen psalms called "Songs of Ascents." These psalms were sung during the annual religious pilgrimages to Jerusalem.

"I will lift up my eyes to the hills—where does my help come from?
My help comes from the Lord, the Maker of heaven and earth.
He will not let your foot slip—He who watches over you will not slumber;
indeed, He who watches over Israel will neither slumber nor sleep.
The Lord watches over you—the Lord is your shade at your right hand;
the sun will not harm you by day, nor the moon by night.
The Lord will keep you from all harm—He will watch over your life;
the Lord will watch over your coming and going both now
and for evermore.

Hellenism

In 332–323 BCE, King Alexander the Great of Macedonia, to the north of Greece, conquered the Persian Empire. Alexander and the kings who followed him spread their Hellenistic, or Greek, way of life across the lands they ruled. Greek became an international language, used by educated people from Egypt to Afghanistan.

Alexander's empire covered some two million square miles (five million square kilometers), stretching across three continents. After his death, it broke up into rival Hellenistic kingdoms.

Alexander

This Roman mosaic shows the young Alexander charging into battle riding his favorite horse Bucephalus, against King Darius of Persia. A brilliant general, Alexander won an unbroken series of victories over his enemies before dying in Babylon, aged just 33.

TIMELINE

333–323 BCE
Alexander the Great conquers his empire, which stretches from Egypt to the borders of India.

323–301 BCE
After Alexander's death, his generals fight a series of wars for control of his empire.

305 BCE
Ptolemy, one of Alexander's generals, is proclaimed king of Egypt. Another general, Seleucus, makes himself king of the eastern part of the empire.

300–200 BCE
The Jewish homeland, now called Judea, is ruled by the Ptolemies of Egypt.

281–246 BCE
Rule of Ptolemy II, who has the Hebrew Bible translated into Greek by Jewish scholars in Alexandria, Egypt.

200 BCE
Antiochus III, the sixth Seleucid king, wins control of Judea from Ptolemy V.

168 BCE
Antiochus IV rededicates the Jewish Temple in Jerusalem to the Greek god Zeus.

168–160 BCE
The Jews, led by Judas Maccabeus, rebel against Antiochus IV and drive him out.

160–37 BCE
Judea is ruled by the Jewish Hasmonean dynasty, founded by Judas Maccabeus.

Architecture

One effect of Hellenism was to spread Greek styles of architecture across the Middle East. This monument, from Petra in what is now Jordan, has distinctive columns based on those of Greek temples. It was carved out of the cliff face.

Judaism banned
In 168 BCE, the eastern ruler Antiochus IV tried to stamp out the Jewish religion. He set up an altar to the Greek god Zeus in the Temple of Jerusalem, where he sacrificed pigs. The Jews rebelled and drove him out.

Naked exercise
The Jewish high priest Jason, who served from 175–172 BCE, admired Greek culture. In Jerusalem he built a gymnasium, a place where Greek men gathered to exercise naked. Many Jews were shocked by public nudity in their holy city.

Greek Bible
In about 250 BCE, the Hebrew scriptures were translated into Greek by 72 Jewish scholars in Alexandria, Egypt. Their translation (right) was called the Septuagint (from "seventy" in Greek). Later, the New Testament would be written in Greek.

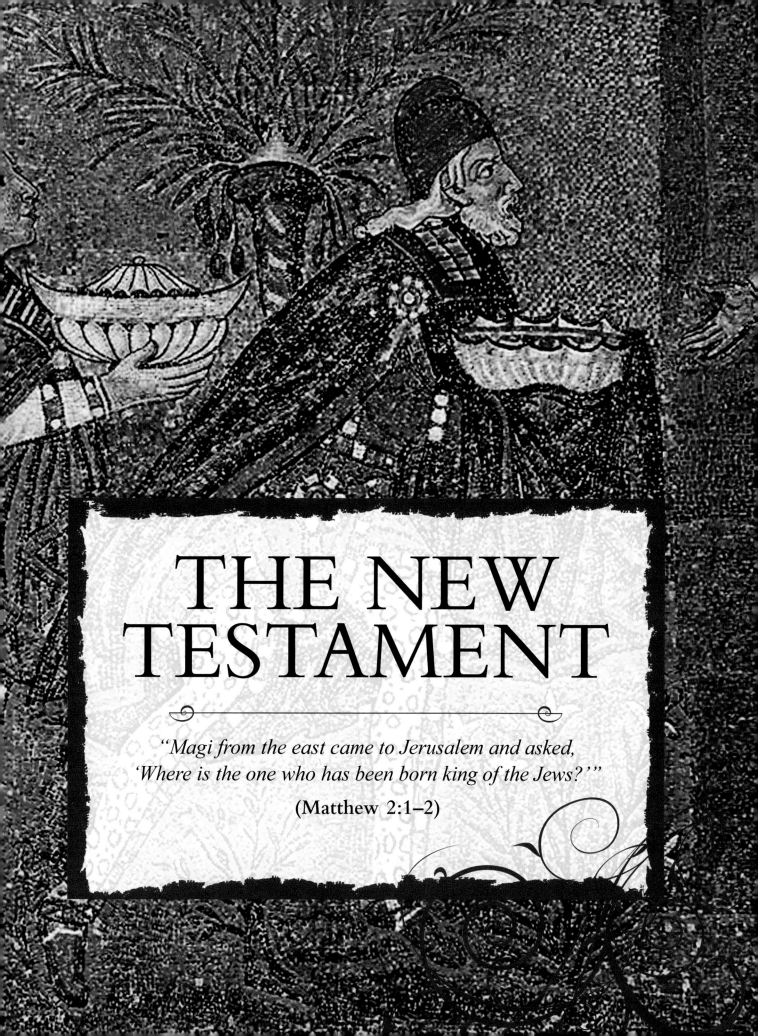

THE NEW TESTAMENT

"Magi from the east came to Jerusalem and asked, 'Where is the one who has been born king of the Jews?'"

(Matthew 2:1–2)

New Testament

The New Testament is a collection of Christian writings, composed in Greek in the second half of the 1st century CE. It includes four versions of Jesus's life story called Gospels, the Acts of the Apostles—the story of the early Church, and a collection of 22 epistles, or letters, written by early Christian leaders.

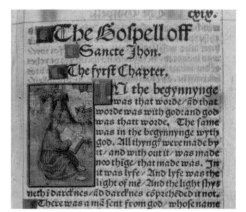

Gospel authors
The Gospels (meaning "good news") were not written as biographies but to present teachings about Christ. Each presents Christ from a different viewpoint. Later, Church tradition assigned them to four authors—Matthew, Mark, Luke, and John.

Paul's epistles
The earliest books of the New Testament are Paul's letters to the churches he founded. There are at least eight genuine letters, while the remaining six are thought to have been written by Paul's followers. These letters focus more on the message that Jesus had risen from the dead than on Jesus's life and teachings.

Parables
The first three Gospels preserve many teachings of Christ in the form of parables—short, colorful stories, drawn from everyday life. A typical parable (Mark 40:32) compares the "Kingdom of God" to a tiny mustard seed, the smallest of all seeds, which grows into the biggest garden plant.

Miracles
All the Gospel authors believed that Christ was able to perform miracles—supernatural acts in which the ordinary laws of nature were set aside. He could raise the dead, walk on water, turn water into wine, and calm storms.

Mark

The earliest and shortest Gospel focuses on Christ's urgent message that the "Kingdom of God" was at hand: humanity was being given a new start, but time was short. Mark's Jesus is emotional, angry, and impatient with his disciples, who often misunderstand him.

Matthew

Matthew's Gospel was written to demonstrate that Christ was the Messiah. The proof lies in Jesus's miracles and his fulfilment of Jewish prophecies. Matthew took much of his material from Mark, but changed it to fulfil prophecies, and he added more miracles.

Luke

Luke was probably the only non-Jew to write a book in the Bible. His work was aimed at his fellow gentiles to show that Jesus came to offer salvation to "all the nations" (Luke 24:47). Like Matthew, Luke took material from Mark. Women, such as Mary Magdalene (right), play an important role.

John

The last Gospel is very different from the other three. It follows a different chronology (three years instead of one), and there are no parables and no casting out of devils. John's Jesus is fully divine, a visitor from heaven, who says, "I have come down from heaven not to do my will but to do the will of Him who sent me" (John 6:38). Here Christ is shown after his return to heaven, where he sits on a throne, surrounded by saints.

Revelation

The Book of Revelation, the last book in the New Testament, was written by John—a Jewish Christian visionary on the island of Patmos. It takes the form of a letter to the seven churches of Asia and describes a series of dreamlike visions of Christ's return in glory.

A Son for Zechariah

In the time of King Herod of Judea, there was a priest named Zechariah, who served in the splendid Temple at Jerusalem. He was a descendant of Aaron, the brother of Moses, and so was his wife Elizabeth.

They were good people who lived righteous lives and obeyed all the Lord's commandments. But they were both growing old and, to their great sadness, they had no children. This was considered something of a disgrace, and their neighbors pitied them.

One day, when he was on duty, Zechariah was chosen by the casting of lots—as was the custom—to go into the inner sanctuary of the Temple to burn the incense before the morning sacrifice. It was a huge honor and privilege. He walked through the doors adorned with embroidered curtains, which hid the inner and most sacred part of the Temple. Only the priest on duty was allowed to go there. Outside, in the main part of the building, the people had gathered to pray. Zechariah approached the magnificent golden altar in front of the Holy of Holies, where the Ark of the Covenant had once stood.

Slowly, he lit the incense and little clouds of smoke danced through the air, filling the sanctuary with a sweet and heady scent. And, when Zechariah looked up, he saw an angel standing there just to the right of the altar. He nearly jumped out of his skin.

> "God has sent me to tell you the good news. But, because you did not believe me, you have been struck dumb."

But the angel held out his hands and said to him, kindly, "Do not be afraid, Zechariah. Your prayer has been heard. Your wife, Elizabeth, will bear you a son and you are to give him the name John. He will be a joy and delight to you, and many will rejoice because of his birth, for he will be great in the sight of the Lord. He is never to take wine or other fermented drink, and he will be filled with the Holy Spirit even from birth. Many are the people of Israel that he will bring back to the Lord their God."

Zechariah listened in amazement to the angel's words. "How can this be possible?" he asked. "I am an old man already—and my wife, Elizabeth, is well advanced in years, too."

"I am Gabriel," the angel replied. "God has sent me to tell you the good news. But, because you did not believe me, you have been struck dumb. You will not be able to speak a single word until what I have just told you comes true."

Meanwhile, the worshipers, waiting outside the sanctuary, were beginning to wonder why Zechariah was taking so long. He should have come out by now.

Finally, he appeared from behind the doors and stood before them, unable to say a word. He made signs with his hands, pointing to the sanctuary and to his eyes and to the air, and they realized that he had seen a vision.

When Zechariah had finished his duties in the Temple, going silently about his business, he went home to his wife, Elizabeth. He was, of course, not able to tell her what he had seen and what he had been told. But, before very long, she discovered, to her great delight, that she was pregnant. She was overjoyed. For the next few months, she stayed at home, counting her blessings. "The Lord has done this for me," she said, gratefully. "He has shown me great mercy and taken away my disgrace."

The angel Gabriel appears before Zechariah with the news that his wife shall have a son

An Angel Appears to Mary

G od sent His messenger, the archangel Gabriel, to find a young woman named Mary, who lived in the small town of Nazareth in southern Galilee.

Mary, like her cousin Elizabeth, was descended from Aaron, the first high priest of Israel. She was betrothed to Joseph, a carpenter who lived and worked in Nazareth, and they would be married soon. Joseph's family tree went back through the generations to David, the first king of Israel.

The angel Gabriel appeared as Mary was sitting alone in her small garden. There was no one else around. She looked at him, astonished, as he stood there in front of her. "Greetings, you are highly favored," he said. "The Lord is with you!"

> "You will be with child and give birth to a son, and you are to give him the name Jesus."

Mary was deeply troubled by the apparition, which had arrived so suddenly, from nowhere. She did not understand why he had come to find her or what he was talking about. Then, as if he could read her mind, the angel went on, "Do not be afraid, Mary, you have found favor with God. You will be with child and give birth to a son, and you are to give him the name Jesus. He will be great and will be called the Son of the Most High. The Lord God will give him the throne of his father David, and he will reign over the house of Jacob forever. His kingdom will never end."

"How can this be?" asked Mary. "I am not married."

"The Holy Spirit will come upon you and the power of the Most High will overshadow you," the angel replied. "So the holy one to be born will be called the Son of God."

Mary said to the angel, "I'm ready for whatever God wants from me! If that's His will, then let it be."

*The angel Gabriel appears before Mary
and tells her that she will give birth to
a child who will be named Jesus*

And the angel went on to tell Mary that her elderly cousin Elizabeth,
who was thought to be barren, was now in her sixth month of pregnancy.
"For nothing is impossible with God," he said. Then he left her standing
in the garden, her thoughts full of excitement and trust.

The Birth of John

Mary went straight to the town in the hills near Jerusalem, where her cousin Elizabeth lived with her husband Zechariah. She wanted to tell them the good news.

Mary went into the little house and greeted her cousin warmly. When Elizabeth heard her voice, she could feel the baby in her womb leap for joy and she was filled with the Holy Spirit. "Blessed are you among women and blessed is the child you will bear!" Elizabeth cried. "But why am I so favored that the mother of my Lord should come to me? Blessed is she who has believed that what the Lord has said to her will be accomplished!"

Mary replied with a beautiful song of praise. Her sweet voice filled the air:
"My soul glorifies the Lord and my spirit rejoices in God my Savior,
for He has been mindful of the humble state of His servant.
From now on all generations will call me blessed,
for the Mighty One has done great things for me—holy is His name.
His mercy extends to those who fear Him, from generation to generation."

Mary stayed for about three months and then went home to Nazareth. Soon after, Elizabeth gave birth to her son, and her relatives and friends and neighbors rejoiced. He was a precious gift to his parents, late in life. Eight days after he was born he was circumcised, as was the custom, and was about to be named Zechariah, after his father. But Elizabeth protested. "No! He is to be named John!" she insisted, much to everyone's surprise.

> "Blessed is she who has believed that what the Lord has said to her will be accomplished!"

"But no one in your family has ever been named John," they replied, mystified by her sudden outburst. They turned to Zechariah and asked his opinion, using sign language because he had been struck deaf and dumb after he doubted the angel's message in the Temple. He pointed for his wooden writing tablet. Then, in big, clear letters he wrote, "His name is John." There was nothing more to be said. And, immediately, his tongue woke up from its long sleep. He started to speak and was filled with the Holy Spirit, prophesying and proclaiming God's word:

Family and friends make signs to Zechariah, asking him about the baby's name

"Praise be to the Lord, the God of Israel,
because He has come and has redeemed His people.
He has raised up a horn of salvation for us
in the house of His servant David
(as He said through His holy prophets of long ago),
salvation from our enemies
and from the hand of all who hate us—
to show mercy to our fathers and to remember His holy covenant,
the oath He swore to our father Abraham. . .
And you, my child, will be called a prophet of the Most High;
for you will go on before the Lord to prepare the way for Him,
to give His people the knowledge of salvation
through the forgiveness of their sins,
because of the tender mercy of our God,
by which the rising sun will come to us from heaven
to shine on those living in darkness
and in the shadow of death,
to guide our feet into the path of peace."

Everyone looked at each other, wide-eyed. And word soon spread that the Lord was with the baby who had been born to Elizabeth and named that day.

Zechariah asks for his wooden tablet so that he can write his son's name

Elizabeth says that her baby will be named John

The Birth of Jesus

Joseph was an honorable man. He was pledged to Mary in marriage and, when he learned that she was expecting a child that was not his, he wanted to protect her from disgrace.

But, while he was considering what to do, an angel appeared to him in a dream. "Joseph, son of David, do not be afraid to take Mary home as your wife, because what is conceived in her is from the Holy Spirit. She will give birth to a son, and you are to give him the name Jesus, because he will save his people from their sins."

The Lord's words, which had been spoken by the great prophet Isaiah many years before, would now come true. And, as promised, the baby would be the son of David because Joseph, who would become his father, was a descendant of King David. And so, Joseph and Mary kept their pledge and soon they were married.

Meanwhile, the emperor, Caesar Augustus, ordered that a census should be taken of all the people in the Roman Empire. This happened every fourteen years. It meant that everybody had to go back to their home town to register and to be counted. So Joseph and Mary set off from Nazareth in Galilee and made the long journey south to Bethlehem in Judea, where Joseph was born. They were cold and tired by the time they eventually arrived in Bethlehem, the City of David.

> "That night, Mary gave birth to her firstborn. It was a boy, perfect and new."

Bethlehem was bursting at the seams—the streets crowded, and every inn full. Mary knew that soon it would be time to give birth to her baby and she must find somewhere safe and warm. Eventually, they found some shelter. There was straw on the ground, and it was dry and protected from the cold.

That night, Mary gave birth to her firstborn. It was a boy, perfect and new. Tenderly, she nursed him and wrapped him in strips of linen, as was the custom. She laid him in the stone manger, where the animals fed. It was lined with straw and would make a comfortable little bed for her newborn son. There was nowhere else for him to sleep.

The Shepherds' Visit

Some humble shepherds were looking after their flocks in the fields near Bethlehem that night. It was dark and clear, with a thousand stars shining.

The men tucked their thick, fleecy cloaks around their legs to keep out the biting cold. Eagle-eyed, they watched their sheep, on the lookout for any hint of danger from thieves or wild animals.

Suddenly, the peace was shattered and an angel appeared in the sky, surrounded by a brilliant white light. The stars disappeared, outdazzled. It was the Glory of God shining in the darkness. The shepherds dropped their crooks, shielding their eyes from the blinding light.

"Do not be afraid!" the angel said, looking down at them. "I bring you good news of great joy for everyone. Today, in the town of David, a Savior has been born to you. He is Christ the Lord. This will be a sign to you. You will find a baby wrapped in cloths and lying in a manger." And then, he was joined by a whole army of angels and archangels, stretching across the sky. Their voices rang out, a heavenly choir, praising the Lord: "Glory to God in the highest and on Earth, peace to men on whom his favor rests!"

> "Glory to God in the highest and on Earth, peace to men on whom his favor rests!"

As the last note lingered and died away, the angels vanished into thin air and the shepherds looked at each other in wonder. "Let's go to Bethlehem and see this thing that has happened, which the Lord has told us about," they said. They hurried off, leaving their flocks behind.

When they got to Bethlehem, they found their way to the stable where Joseph and Mary had taken shelter. They crept in quietly, past the ox, the ass, and the sheep asleep on the ground. Through the gloom, they could just make out the figure of a tiny baby lying fast asleep in the manger, with Mary and Joseph by his side. They went over and knelt down before him. They gazed at him in awe, the angel's words ringing in their ears. Then they told Joseph and Mary about the heavenly visitation earlier that night, and the astonishing things they had been told.

After a while, they left the little family in the stable. They could not believe that they had been the first to see the newborn Savior.

Dawn was just breaking and they went straight into town. Full of joy, they told everyone the amazing news that Christ the Lord had been born that very night in Bethlehem. Word traveled fast and soon the whole town knew. In the stable, Mary sat quietly, holding her baby in her arms, thinking on what the shepherds had told her. She turned their words over in her mind and treasured them.

The shepherds themselves returned to their flocks in the fields and found them safe and sound. They rejoiced and praised God for all the wonderful things they had heard and seen that night.

The shepherds visit the Savior in the stable

The Presentation in the Temple

*W*hen Mary's baby was eight days old, he was circumcized, as was the custom. And he was named Jesus, just as the angel had said.

Under the Law of Moses, every firstborn son had to be consecrated to the Lord, but Mary had to wait forty days—the time of purification—before she was allowed to enter the Temple in Jerusalem. So, it was more than a month before Mary and Joseph set off from Bethlehem with the baby Jesus, to present him to the Lord in the Temple and to dedicate him to God's service. They would make an offering of two turtle doves, since they did not have enough money to buy a lamb.

When they arrived in Jerusalem, Mary and Joseph joined the stream of pilgrims flooding into the Temple. They walked up the great steps into the outer courtyard where the money changers were doing a roaring trade. No one took any notice of the young couple with the baby, as they wove their way through the crowds. Mary and Joseph paid their tax, as everyone had to before they went into worship, sliding their money into the narrow mouth of one of the treasure chests.

An old man named Simeon had come to the Temple that day, filled with the Holy Spirit. He was a good man, virtuous and devout, and he had been told by God that he would not die before he had seen the Messiah.

Simeon gives thanks to the Lord and blesses the infant Messiah

He went right up to Mary and Joseph, and he knew, at once, that the baby he was looking at was the Savior he had been waiting for. Gently, he took Jesus in his arms and praised God, saying, "Sovereign Lord, as you have promised, I may now die in peace. With my own eyes I have seen the son you have sent to bring salvation to all people—a light for revelation to the gentiles and for glory to your people Israel."

> "With my own eyes I have seen the son you have sent to bring salvation to all people"

Mary listened, marveling at his words. Simeon blessed them and said, "This child will be a turning point in the life of Israel and will cause the falling and rising of many. But he will make powerful enemies who will do their utmost to cause his downfall." As he passed Jesus carefully back to Mary, he added, "And a sword will pierce your own soul, too."

Then an old woman shuffled up to them out of the gloom. She was a prophetess named Anna, who belonged to the tribe of Asher. She was eighty-four years old and had been a widow for many years. The Temple was her home now and she worshiped day and night, fasting and praying. She gazed at the baby in Mary's arms, but did not touch him. Then she gave thanks to the Lord that she had been allowed to see him and shuffled off again. She told everyone that the baby she had just seen would be the Savior of Jerusalem.

When they had finished at the Temple, Mary and Joseph left Jerusalem and went home with Jesus. He grew healthy and strong, and was filled with wisdom and the grace of God.

The Wise Men

*A*fter Jesus had been presented in the Temple, the news *of his birth spread far and wide. A group of highly respected wise men traveled from the east to Jerusalem.*

Although they were not Jewish themselves they had heard about the new infant king and they wanted to pay their respects. "Where is the one who has been born king of the Jews?" they asked. "We saw his star in the east and have come to worship him."

When King Herod heard about the newborn child who was to lead the Jews, he was deeply disturbed. He thought a new king was a terrible threat to his power. He called together all his chief priests and teachers of the law and asked them where the child might have been born. "In Bethlehem in Judea," they replied. His worst fears were confirmed. Bethlehem was not very far from Jerusalem.

Secretly, King Herod summoned the wise men to the palace. First, he found out the exact time the star had appeared in the sky and then he asked them if they would go to Bethlehem on his behalf. "As soon as you find him, report to me so that I may go and worship him." He had no intention of doing this, of course, and was hatching a very different plan.

The wise men agreed and left for Bethlehem on their camels. The star still guided them on their way, shining brightly ahead in the night sky. It stopped over a little stone stable on the outskirts of town and they knew that this must be the place that they had traveled so far to find. They saw the child with his mother Mary, and they bowed down and worshiped him.

"We saw his star in the east and have come to worship him."

Then they opened the heavy caskets that they had brought with them from the east and laid their magnificent gifts before him. There was gold to pay tribute to him as a king, frankincense to honor him as God, and myrrh as a sign that he, too, would die. Later, when it was time to go, the wise men got back on their camels and set off on the journey home. This time they took a different route, avoiding Jerusalem completely. They had been warned in a dream that they must not go back to see Herod again, whatever happened.

King Herod

In the 1st century BCE, the Hellenistic kingdoms of the East were conquered by the Romans. One Roman custom was to rule through local "client kings," loyal to Rome. From 37–4 BCE, the client king of Judea was Herod the Great. Jesus Christ was born at the end of his reign.

Herod's coin
Herod came from Idumea, south of Judea, whose people had recently converted to Judaism. He showed respect for Jewish law by issuing coins decorated with a helmet rather than his portrait.

Herodium
Between 24 and 15 BCE, Herod built this fortified summer palace, called Herodium, 7 miles (12 km) south of Jerusalem. Herod reshaped this hill, cutting off its top and hollowing it out, using the ground to build up steep sides.

Herod's Palace

This cutaway model shows Herodium in Herod's lifetime. Its circular towers provided wonderful views across Judea. Inside, there were luxurious apartments, baths, and a garden surrounded by columns. Herod was buried here after his death in 4 BCE.

Caesarea

Between 22–10 BCE, Herod built a new port city, which he named Caesarea in honor of Emperor Augustus Caesar. This aerial view shows Herod's theater (top), which could hold an audience of 3,500 people.

The Temple

This model shows Herod's greatest achievement, the new Jerusalem Temple Mount complex, which he began to rebuild around 19 BCE. The Temple building, at the center, was so sacred that it had to be built by priests, who were retrained as masons.

TIMELINE

73 BCE
Herod is born in Idumea, the southernmost part of the Jewish kingdom, ruled by the Hasmonean dynasty.

67 BCE
The Hasmonean Hyrcanus II becomes king.

63 BCE
Judea is brought under Roman control. The Romans allow Hyrcanus to remain as high priest. Real power is held by Herod's father, Antipater, a general loyal to Rome.

47 BCE
Herod, aged 25, is made governor of Galilee by Antipater.

43 BCE
Antipater is poisoned by Malichus, a follower of Hyrcanus. Herod kills Malichus, avenging his father's death.

40 BCE
The Parthians invade Judea and place Antigonus, another Hasmonean, on the throne. Herod flees to Rome, where he is declared king of the Jews.

37 BCE
Backed by a Roman army, Herod defeats Antigonus, who is beheaded by the Romans.

29 BCE
Herod executes Mariamne, the second of his ten wives, for plotting against him.

19 BCE
Herod begins to rebuild the Jerusalem Temple on a grand scale.

7 BCE
Herod executes his two sons by Mariamne.

4 BCE
Herod executes his eldest son and heir a few days before dying himself.

The Flight into Egypt

A fter the wise men had left Bethlehem, an angel of the Lord appeared to Joseph in a dream.

"Take the child and his mother and escape to Egypt. Stay there until I tell you, for Herod is going to search for the child to kill him."

Joseph woke immediately and jumped up. He stood there for a moment as the full meaning of the angel's words sank in. He looked down in wonder at the baby Jesus, sleeping so quietly in the little manger. Then, he went over to Mary and shook her gently. He told her about his dream and what they must do. She rubbed her eyes sleepily and listened. She gathered her things together and tenderly picked up the sleeping Jesus, as Joseph prepared the donkeys for the long journey ahead.

They left as soon as they could, creeping quietly out of the little stable into the night. Like shadows they flitted past the darkened houses, through the empty streets, and out of the peaceful, sleeping town. By the time dawn broke, they had left Bethlehem far behind and were heading into the wilderness, far from human habitation.

The family leave Bethlehem at night and make their way to Egypt

Meanwhile, Herod had waited and waited for the wise men to return to the royal palace in Jerusalem with news of the baby Jesus. He paced impatiently up and down his throne room. When he finally realized that he had been outwitted by the wise men from the east and that they were not coming back, he was furious. How would he find the newborn king that was such a threat to his throne now? How would he get rid of him? Insane with rage, he issued a decree that all boys under the age of two in the Bethlehem area should be killed immediately.

> "Take the child and his mother and go back to Israel, for those who were trying to take the child's life are dead."

Herod's most trusted soldiers were dispatched at dawn to carry out his terrible order. And that very day, as Mary and Joseph hurried on their way with the infant king, every little boy in Bethlehem was butchered. Their mothers pleaded and wept for their children's lives as the soldiers obeyed the king's command. It was the massacre of the innocents that the prophet Jeremiah had predicted many years before: "A voice is heard in Ramah, weeping and great mourning, Rachel weeping for her children and refusing to be comforted, because they are no more."

Unaware of the slaughter in Bethlehem, Mary and Joseph traveled south, looking out for any sign of Herod's men. They avoided the main routes as much as they could, keeping to the ancient animal tracks that wound through the landscape. Mary held her baby tightly to her, hidden safely under her thick cloak. On and on they went, through the wild countryside, stopping only to rest at night. It was a long and difficult journey. When they reached the bleak and rocky desert, the Sun beat down relentlessly on the little family.

Eventually, they arrived in Egypt—a strange and exotic land from which their ancestors had escaped so long ago. They found sanctuary there, as the angel had told Joseph, far from King Herod and his henchmen in Jerusalem.

Some time later, an angel appeared to Joseph again in a dream. "Get up," he said. "Take the child and his mother and go back to Israel, for those who were trying to take the child's life are dead." And so, the Lord's words spoken through the prophet Hosea were fulfilled: "Out of Egypt, I called my son."

On hearing this message, Joseph and Mary set off with Jesus to make the long journey home. But, when they arrived in Israel, they discovered that Herod's kingdom had been divided into three parts following his death. His cruel son, Archelaus, was now reigning over Judea. Fearful at the news, they decided to travel farther north and to settle in Nazareth in Galilee, where they had lived before.

Jesus is Found in the Temple

Mary and Joseph set off with their friends and relatives during Nisan, the first month of the year, to go to Jerusalem for the Feast of Passover.

It was held in the evening of the fourteenth day of the month, and it was important to arrive on time. Passover celebrated the deliverance of the Israelites from Egypt and was one of the greatest feast days of the year. The roads were always crowded with pilgrims coming from all over the country.

Jesus was twelve years old now, and he was allowed to go with Mary and Joseph for the first time. He was excited at the thought of going into the Temple with them and taking part in the celebrations. It would be an important moment in his life, preparing him for the next year, when, at the age of thirteen, he would be considered a man.

After the Feast, Mary and Joseph left Jerusalem and started the journey back to their home in Nazareth with everyone else. Tired after the festivities, they traveled slowly along the road toward Galilee. It was not until the evening, when they stopped for the night, that Mary and Joseph noticed that Jesus was not with them. They looked at each other, puzzled. Then they looked around, but there was no sign of him. They were both filled with a terrible, sinking feeling. Desperately, they asked people if they had seen him, but no one could help. Jesus seemed to have vanished into thin air. As night fell, Mary and Joseph turned around and headed back to Jerusalem, scouring the road as they went.

Joseph, Jesus, and Mary travel to Jerusalem for Passover

For three days they searched the city high and low, consumed with fear and hoping against hope that they would find him safe and sound. Finally, in desperation, they went back to the Temple and walked up the great steps.

Suddenly, in the inner courtyard, they saw Jesus. He was sitting on the ground, deep in conversation with some of the religious teachers. Wise beyond his years, he was asking them question after question and listening intently to their answers. The teachers were clearly amazed by his intelligence and understanding. They talked to him as if he were an adult and chose their words carefully.

"Didn't you know that I had to be in my Father's house?"

Mary and Joseph stood and watched, fascinated by the scene. Then they rushed forward and threw their arms around Jesus. "My son, why did you do this to us?" asked Mary, holding back the tears. "Your father and I have been so worried. We have been looking everywhere for you."

Jesus looked at them, wide-eyed. "Why were you searching for me?" he asked innocently. "Didn't you know that I had to be in my Father's house?" But neither Mary nor Joseph understood what he meant. He got up and said goodbye to the teachers, then left the Temple with his parents.

Together, they set off from Jerusalem and started their journey home to Nazareth. But Mary could not stop thinking about her son, sitting there in the Temple and talking so seriously with the teachers. She turned the image over in her mind and smiled to herself.

Joseph and Mary find Jesus talking to religious teachers in the Temple

THE JORDAN RIVER
On the banks of the Jordan River, the preacher John the Baptist launched a religious revival. Crowds came to be plunged in the water. Their baptism showed that they had been spiritually reborn and would live a new, holy life.

Then Jesus came from Galilee to the Jordan to be baptized by John. But John tried to deter him, saying, "I need to be baptized by you, and do you come to me?" Jesus replied, "Let it be so now; it is proper for us to do this to fulfil all righteousness." Then John consented. As soon as Jesus was baptized, he went up out of the water. At that moment heaven was opened, and he saw the Spirit of God descending like a dove and lighting on him. And a voice from heaven said, "This is my Son, whom I love; with him I am well pleased."

Matthew 3:13–17

John Baptizes Jesus

It was the fifteenth year of Tiberius Caesar's reign as Roman Emperor. Judea, in the south, was ruled by his governor, Pontius Pilate. Galilee, in the north, was governed by Herod Antipas, son of Herod the Great.

Nearly four centuries had passed since the last of the prophets had spoken to the Jewish people. They remembered the promise that a new Messiah was coming—and a new prophet who would prepare the way for him. But they had waited a long time.

John, the son who had been miraculously born to Elizabeth and Zechariah late in life, lived a solitary life in the desert far from the Roman garrisons and Herod's splendid Temple in Jerusalem. He wandered alone through the remote countryside, preaching and baptizing the people. He had a special gift for speaking, and the words from his tongue were eloquent and pure. His clothes were made of the roughest camels' hair, held in place by a leather belt around his waist, and he lived on wild food, like locusts and honey from the desert bees. When he stopped to preach, he urged the people to turn away from evil. He told them to return to God because Judgment Day was near. And then, when they had repented of their sins, he baptized them in the cool waters of the River Jordan.

Word spread, and soon people from all over Galilee and beyond were talking about the prophet in the wilderness who could wash away their sins. They called him John the Baptist. People wanted to see for themselves and soon they started to flock to the desert to find him.

> "I baptize you with water. But one more powerful than I will come"

When he saw the wealthy and powerful Sadducees and the Pharisees who had come all the way from the Temple in Jerusalem, John berated them. "You brood of vipers! Repent your sins!" he said. "Do not think that you are safe just because you are the children of Abraham. Trees that produce rotten fruit will be cut down and thrown on the fire."

"What should we do?" the people asked.

"The man with two tunics should share with him who has none. And the man who has food should do the same," John replied.

"And what about us?" asked the tax collectors. "What should we do?"

"Do not collect any more than you are required to," John told them.

Then some soldiers stepped forward. "What should we do, Teacher?"

"Do not extort money and do not accuse people falsely. Be content with your pay."

The people listened and wondered whether John the Baptist might be the Messiah himself. As if he could read their minds, John said, "I baptize you with water. But one more powerful than I will come; the thongs of his sandals I am not worthy to untie. He will baptize you with the Holy Spirit and with fire. His winnowing fork is in his hand to clear his threshing-floor and to gather the wheat into his barn, but he will burn up the chaff with unquenchable fire."

Jesus came from Galilee to be baptized by John in the river. John bowed down. He knew that Jesus had never sinned and had nothing to repent. "I am the one who should be baptized by you," he said.

"No, you must baptize me," answered Jesus. "It is God's will. We must obey Him." Jesus did not want to separate himself from the sins of his people, and his baptism would be an example to his followers.

Together, they waded into the river as the crowd watched. John cradled Jesus in his arms and lowered him into the water, submerging him for a few moments. As he lifted him back out of the water, the clouds parted and a white dove flew down from heaven, bathed in light. It was the Spirit of God and it hovered over Jesus. At the same time, a voice from above said, "This is my Son, whom I love; with him I am well pleased."

John baptizes Jesus in the River Jordan

The Temptations in the Wilderness

After Jesus was baptized he came back from the Jordan and went into the wilderness to be alone—away from the distractions of daily life.

It was a bleak and barren landscape, unbearably hot by day and bone-numbingly cold at night. His only companions were the great eagles and vultures that flew high above and the desert snakes that slithered into the shade under the hot rocks.

For forty long days and nights, Jesus fasted and prayed in complete solitude. At the end of this time, he was exhausted and weak with hunger, and the Devil came to tempt him and test his faith. "If you really are the Son of God, as you say, prove it. Turn these burning desert stones into bread."

Jesus, obedient to the will of God, refused to break his fast. He replied, "It is written that man cannot live by bread alone, but must find strength in God's words."

But the Devil refused to give up. He took Jesus to the very top of Herod's magnificent marble Temple in the heart of Jerusalem.

For forty days, Jesus prays alone in the wilderness

The Devil takes Jesus to the top of Herod's Temple

From the top of a mountain,
the Devil tempts Jesus with
all the kingdoms of the world

"It is written that God alone is Lord of all"

The Devil turned to Jesus and said, "You say you are the Son of God. Jump off the Temple! The angels will catch you."

Jesus, steadfast in his obedience to God, replied calmly, "It is written that God must never be put to the test."

The Devil remained undeterred. He took Jesus to the highest mountain peak and showed him all the kingdoms of the world spread out like a patchwork quilt beneath them. "I will make you lord and ruler of all these lands if you will just kneel down and worship me."

And, once again, unwavering in his devotion to God, Jesus replied, "Get behind me, Satan. It is written that God alone is Lord of all, and it is God alone whom you should worship."

With that, the Devil vanished and a host of angels appeared from nowhere and flew down to strengthen Jesus after his struggle.

Jesus Calls his Disciples

Jesus returned to Galilee and went to live in Capernaum, a little town on the shore of the big freshwater lake known as the Sea of Galilee.

One morning, Jesus was preaching at the edge of the water and, as usual, a crowd had gathered to listen. As he spoke, he noticed two little fishing boats moored nearby. Peter and his brother, Andrew, were scrubbing their nets in the water. Jesus stepped onto the boat belonging to Peter, and asked him to cast off from the shore. The little vessel plowed slowly out to sea, while Jesus sat down and continued to preach from it. When he had finished, he said to Peter, "Put out into deep water and let down the nets for a catch."

The fisherman looked at him doubtfully. "Master," he replied. "We worked hard all night and haven't caught anything. But, because you say so, I will let down the net."

They headed toward the middle of the sea, and Peter threw the big cast net over the side. Suddenly, there was a great surge and the net ballooned with fish. Peter watched in amazement. He had never before seen such a catch.

Jesus chooses his twelve disciples

He signaled to his brother Andrew, far away on the shore, to join them with the other boat. Together, the brothers heaved in the haul of fresh fish. And then the two little boats turned, both piled high and perilously low in the water. They just made it back to dry land before they sank.

Two other fishermen, James and John, the sons of Zebedee, came over, astonished at the miraculous catch and, along with Peter and Andrew, they fell down to the ground, consumed with fear. "Do not be afraid," said Jesus. "Follow me and I will make you fishers of men."

So the four men left their boats and said goodbye to their families. They set off with Jesus and went with him all over Galilee as he taught in synagogues and preached by the wayside, spreading the word of God. He spoke with such authority that people were amazed and flocked to hear him. And he healed the sick and the diseased. News spread far and wide, and soon people came not only from Galilee but from Jerusalem, Judea, and far beyond the River Jordan.

> "Follow me and I will make you fishers of men."

One day, Jesus saw a tax collector named Matthew, counting out the money he had taken that day. He was disliked by the Jewish people because he worked for the Romans. Jesus went up to him, saying, "Follow me!" Matthew got up immediately and went with him. That evening, Jesus and his followers went to Matthew's house and sat down to eat with him. A few other tax collectors and some undesirable people joined them.

When the Pharisees saw this they were shocked. "Why does your teacher break bread with such characters?" they asked.

Jesus heard their pious words and replied, "It is not the healthy who need a doctor, but the sick. I am not looking for the righteous. I have come to find sinners. It is they who need me."

Later, Jesus went to the top of a high mountain to be on his own. He stayed there all night, deep in prayer. The next day, he came down and called all of his followers together and chose twelve disciples to his side. They were Peter and his brother Andrew, James and his brother John, Philip, Bartholomew, Matthew, Thomas, James son of Alphaeus, Simon the Zealot, Thaddeus, and Judas Iscariot.

Galilee

Jesus spent most of his life in Galilee, the fertile northern region of Palestine. Most Galileans lived in villages, farming or fishing on the Sea of Galilee. Jesus's teaching is full of details of country life, including the care of fig trees (Luke 13:6–9) and how to predict fine weather by a red sky at night (Matthew 16:1–3).

After Herod the Great's death, his kingdom was divided among his three sons. From 4 BCE to 39 CE, Herod Antipas governed Galilee and Perea.

Herod Antipas

Galilee was governed by Herod Antipas, son of Herod the Great. Antipas, who Jesus called "that fox" (Luke 13:32), is best known for executing John the Baptist. The letters "TIB" on his coin stand for his capital city, Tiberias.

Tiberias

Antipas named his capital, which he built beside the Sea of Galilee, in honor of Emperor Tiberius. Unfortunately, he built it on top of a Jewish cemetery and no pious Jews would live there. This is the city's bath house.

GOSPEL LOCATIONS IN GALILEE

Bethsaida
Town by the Sea of Galilee, home to the disciples Peter, Andrew, and Philip (John 1:44).

Cana
Village northeast of Nazareth where Jesus was said to have performed his first miracle (John 2:11).

Capernaum
Town on the northwestern shore of the Sea of Galilee where Jesus lived and taught after leaving Nazareth (Matthew 4:13).

Nazareth
Hill town, between the Sea of Galilee and the Mediterranean, where Jesus grew up (Luke 4:16).

Nain
Village southeast of Nazareth where Jesus was said to have raised a man from the dead (Luke 7:12).

Tiberias
Herod Antipas's capital in Galilee. Jesus avoided Tiberias, and it is only mentioned in passing in the Gospels, such as when the Sea of Galilee is called the Sea of Tiberias (John 6:1).

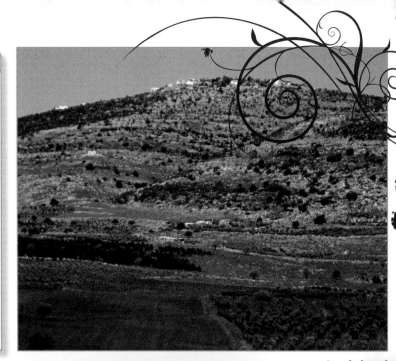

Lush land
With good rainfall, Galilee was far more fertile than Judea—the dryer southern region. Galilean farmers grew wheat, vines, olives, dates, and flax for linen. Judeans looked down on Galileans as ignorant country folk, and made fun of their thick accent.

Jesus taught here
This is the synagogue of Capernaum, where local Jews met to study, pray, and read the scriptures. Although these ruins belong to a synagogue built after Jesus's lifetime, they stand on the very site where he often taught.

227

The Marriage Feast of Cana

*J*esus, *his mother Mary, and the twelve disciples were all invited to a wedding feast at Cana, just north of Nazareth in Galilee.*

Everybody was sitting in the sun as the musicians played on their harps and pipes and tambourines. The women were dancing and singing to the music. The celebrations had been going on for some days now, as was the custom, and everybody was enjoying the fine food at the banquet.

Mary, who was sitting next to Jesus, suddenly noticed that the wine had completely run out. There was not a single drop left although the banquet was still in full swing. She turned to Jesus and told him, whispering quietly so that no one else would hear. He turned to her and said, "Dear mother, why do you involve me? My time has not yet come."

Then Mary called one of the servants over and said, "Do whatever he tells you." There were six huge stone water jars standing nearby, the kind that were used to store the water for washing before a meal or for a religious ceremony.

Jesus pointed to the jars and said to the servants, "Fill them with water, please!" The servants did as he said, slowly filling the great jars with their water carriers. It took some time. Then Jesus said to one of them, "Now pour some out and take it to the guest of honor who is sitting over there."

A servant fills the water jar just as Jesus commanded

The servant looked at him, surprised, as this water would never normally be used for drinking. But he went to fetch a clean goblet and filled it carefully from the jar. He took it to the guest of honor who thanked him and raised it to his lips. The guest of honor had no idea that it had just been poured from the water jar. The servant watched curiously as he tasted the first few drops, and then drained the goblet.

> "And so, Jesus turned the water into wine at the wedding feast in Cana."

The guest of honor called the bridegroom over and said, "Delicious! Thank you so much! Most people give their guests the finest wine first and then bring out the cheaper wine later, when the guests have had too much to drink. But you have saved the best till now!" The bridegroom glowed with pleasure. The servant was still standing there. He opened his mouth in amazement, but said nothing.

And so, Jesus turned the water into wine at the wedding feast in Cana. It was the first miracle that he performed.

The guest of honor thanks the bridegroom for the delicious wine, not knowing that Jesus had performed a miracle

Jesus speaks to the crowd from the mountain

The Sermon on the Mount

So many people had come to listen to Jesus that he went up the mountain to speak to the crowd from there. The words he spoke are known as the Beatitudes, from the Latin for "blessed."

"Blessed are the poor in spirit, for theirs is the kingdom of heaven.
Blessed are those who mourn, for they will be comforted.
Blessed are the meek, for they will inherit the Earth.
Blessed are those who hunger and thirst for righteousness,
for they will be filled.
Blessed are the merciful, for they will be shown mercy.
Blessed are the pure in heart, for they will see God.
Blessed are the peacemakers, for they will be called sons of God.
Blessed are those who are persecuted because of righteousness,
for theirs is the kingdom of heaven."

The great crowd listened from a distance, drinking in his words. Jesus continued, "Do not think that I have come to destroy the law or the words of the prophets. I have come to uphold them. The law must be obeyed. You are the light of the world, do not hide it. Let your light shine brightly before men so that they may see your good deeds and praise your Father in heaven.

"You have heard it said that you must not kill. But do not be angry with your brother, either. If you have quarreled with him, be reconciled. Forgive anyone who has made you angry. You have heard it said, 'An eye for an eye, a tooth for a tooth.' But I tell you, do not resist an evil person. If someone strikes you on the right cheek, turn the other cheek to him, also. Some people say that you must love your neighbor and hate your enemy. But I tell you to love your enemies and pray for those who persecute you.

"You are the light of the world, do not hide it."

"Do not boast about your good deeds. When you give to the needy, do not announce it with trumpets as the hypocrites do in the synagogues and on the streets. When you pray to the Lord, do it quietly, without being seen. Go into your room, close the door, and pray to your Father, who is unseen. You do not need to babble like the pagans, who think the more words they use the more they will be heard.

"Pray simply to God, using words like these: Our Father, who is in heaven, hallowed be your name. Your kingdom come, your will be done on Earth as it is in heaven. Give us this day our daily bread and forgive us our sins, as we forgive those who sin against us. Do not lead us into temptation, but deliver us from evil.

"I tell you not to worry about what you will eat or wear. Life is more than food and the body is more than clothes. Consider the ravens. They do not sow or reap, they have no storeroom or barn. Yet God feeds them. The lilies of the field do not labor or spin, but God clothes them in splendor.

"Do not store up treasures for yourself on Earth, where moth and rust destroy. Store up treasures in heaven, where thieves do not break in and steal. No one can serve two masters. You cannot serve both God and money.

"Do not judge, or you, too, will be judged. Why do you criticize the speck of sawdust in your brother's eye when you have a plank in your own eye? First, take this out, then you will see clearly to remove the speck from your brother's eye.

"Ask and it will be given to you, seek and you will find. Watch out for false prophets because they come to you in sheep's clothing, but inwardly they are ferocious wolves.

"You have heard my words. If you put them into practice, your house will be safe. The rain will come and the wind will blow and the floodwaters will rise, but it will not fall down because the foundations are built on rock."

Healing the Sick

*P*eople came from all over Galilee to hear Jesus teach
and huge crowds followed him wherever he went.

One day, in Capernaum, a leper approached Jesus, ringing
a little bell and shouting, "Unclean! Unclean!" People fled
from him. The poor man's skin was white and scaly and his
clothes were tattered and torn. He went up to Jesus and
knelt down on the ground before him. "Lord, if you are
willing, please cure me!" he begged. Jesus looked at
him and, filled with compassion, he reached out and
touched him on the hand. "Of course, I am willing,"
he said. "Be clean!"

*The leper is
healed by Jesus*

Immediately, the leprosy vanished and the man's skin
became soft and smooth. He was completely cured, and
he bowed down low on the ground in thanks. Jesus said
to him, "See that you don't tell anyone. Just go and show
yourself to the priest, who will confirm that you are healed.
And make sacrifices, as Moses commanded." But the man was
so overwhelmed by the miracle that he rushed around telling everybody.
And, as a result, even more people came to Jesus to be healed. He was
mobbed wherever he went.

A few days later, Jesus was preaching in a house, full of people. Some people
could not even get into the little house but stood outside, trying to hear a word
or two. As the day wore on, more and more
people arrived, including a man who was
completely paralyzed. He was carried by his
friends, but their hearts sank when they saw
the huge crowd of people. They had come
from far away and they were determined to get to Jesus. Carefully, they carried
their friend up the outside steps and onto the little flat roof. Then they cut a big
hole in the roof, and gently lowered him down into the house on his mat. He
landed just in front of Jesus.

"We have seen remarkable
things today!"

Jesus saw the faith they had and he said to the paralyzed man, "My son, your
sins are forgiven." The Pharisees and the teachers of the law, who had been there
since the crack of dawn, looked shocked and raised their eyebrows. "Who is this
fellow who speaks such blasphemy?" they said to each other. "Who can forgive
sins but God alone?"

Jesus, who could read their minds, said, "Why are you thinking these things in your hearts? Tell me, which is easier? To say 'Your sins are forgiven' or to say 'Get up and walk?'" And he turned to the paralyzed man and said, "Get up, take your mat, and go home."

Immediately, the man sprang to his feet in front of everyone, praising God. He bent down and picked up the mat he had been lying on and went home. Everybody watched him in amazement and gave thanks to God. "We have seen remarkable things today!" they said to each other.

The paralyzed man picks up his mat and walks

The Centurion's Servant

*J*esus preached all over the country, drawing bigger and bigger crowds. But he always went back to Capernaum on the northern shore of the Sea of Galilee.

Capernaum was a busy fishing town and Jesus used it as his base during his ministry. He performed many miracles there. Like so many others, a Roman centurion had heard the stories about a teacher named Jesus, who preached the word of the Lord and had astonishing powers. The centurion had a much-loved and most loyal servant, who had been with him for many years. The servant had fallen dangerously sick and was now on the brink of death.

The Roman centurion meets Jesus

The centurion did not know what to do. He wondered whether he might ask for Jesus's help. He thought about it for some time and, finally, enlisted the help of some elders from the synagogue in Capernaum. He asked them if they would go to Jesus on his behalf. They agreed, gladly, as they liked the Roman centurion and were fond of his old servant.

The elders approached Jesus and begged him to come to the centurion's house to save the life of the servant. "Our friend, the Roman centurion, is well-deserving of this," they said to Jesus. "He loves our nation and has built a synagogue." Jesus listened with interest and agreed to go with them.

> "I have not found anyone in the whole of Israel with such great faith."

He was not far from the house, where the servant lay so dangerously ill, when the centurion himself came out to meet Jesus. He was a fine figure of a man, resplendent in his shining chain mail, but he greeted Jesus respectfully. "Lord, do not trouble yourself for I do not deserve to have you come under my roof," he said, bowing low. "That is why I did not even consider myself worthy to come to you. But I know that, if you just say the word, my servant will be healed. For I myself am a man well acquainted with authority. I am used to giving orders to soldiers and having them obeyed."

When Jesus heard this he was astonished and said to his followers, "I tell you the truth, I have not found anyone in the whole of Israel with such great faith." And, without further ado, the centurion turned around and went home to find that his servant, who had been at death's door, was completely recovered.

Jesus Calms the Storm

One evening, Jesus and his disciples were walking by the Sea of Galilee. It had been a beautiful day and the orange ball of the Sun was sinking low in the sky.

The waters were calm and tranquil, and the fishermen were preparing for the night ahead. "Come, let us go to the other side," said Jesus. They climbed into their little fishing boat, the disciples took the oars, and they sailed out to sea.

A gentle breeze tickled the water and soon Jesus had fallen asleep, lulled by the rocking motion of the boat. The disciples looked at him and smiled at each other. On and on they rowed and they were far out at sea when, without warning, the sky darkened. A sudden violent wind appeared from nowhere, whipping the waters into gigantic waves. Water crashed down onto the little boat, threatening to swamp it. Jesus was still fast asleep in the stern of the boat.

> "Master! Master! Wake up! Save us!"

"Master! Master! Wake up! Save us! We are going to drown!" the disciples shouted, shaking him. Jesus opened his eyes and got to his feet, holding the side of the boat. He lifted his arm above the sea, which raged below, and said to the waves, "Quiet! Be still!"

Immediately, the waters calmed and the wind dropped. The Sea of Galilee lay flat once more. The disciples looked at each other, pale with fear and amazement. "How great is he? Even the winds and the water obey him!"

The disciples watch in amazement as Jesus calms the storm

234

The Gadarene Swine

Jesus and the disciples crossed the sea and landed in the country of the Gadarenes. As they stepped out of the boat, a man rushed up to Jesus, screaming and gibbering.

The man was bleeding, with cuts on his arms and legs. His wrists and ankles were bound in chains and his torn clothes were filthy. He was possessed with demons and had lived among the tombs of the dead for years, terrifying anyone who came near.

He fell at Jesus's feet, clutching at his robes with blackened hands. "What do you want with me, Jesus, Son of the Most High God? I beg you, do not torture me!"

"What is your name?" asked Jesus politely.

"My name is Legion," he replied. "Because I have so many demons inside me."

Jesus listened and looked at the huge herd of pigs, rooting around on the hillside that led down to the sea. "Be off!" he said to the demons possessing the wild man. "Go and find a new home. Go to the pigs. There are plenty of them, at least two thousand. Leave this man in peace."

> "Go home and tell everyone what God has done for you."

Obediently, the evil spirits swarmed out of the man toward the herd. They possessed the pigs like a terrible virus. The creatures squealed and shivered. Then, they charged down the hill. They ran to the edge of the cliff and straight over it and into the sea below. They plunged under the water and drowned.

The astonished herdsmen who had been looking after the pigs rushed off to tell everyone. Naturally, people came to have a look. But when they arrived, all they saw was a normal man, sitting at Jesus's feet, talking quietly. And not a pig in sight.

People were confused by what they saw. They asked Jesus and his disciples to leave. As they left, the man who had been cleansed of his demons, begged to go with them. But Jesus turned to him and said, "Go home and tell everyone what God has done for you."

Jesus tells the demons to leave the man and enter a herd of pigs

Jairus's Daughter

*J**esus got back to the other side of the Sea of Galilee and a crowd was waiting for him on the shore.***

One of the leaders of the synagogue, a very important man named Jairus, came up to him in a terrible state. He fell at Jesus's feet, pleading with him to come to his house. His only daughter, a little girl of twelve years old, lay there dying.

> "Just believe and she will be healed."

As Jesus went with Jairus through the crowd, he was jostled and squashed by people trying to get near him. Among them was a woman who had been sick for many years, suffering from bleeding. She had tried everything, but nothing stemmed the flow. "If only I can touch his cloak, I will be healed," she said to herself. She inched herself toward him, weaving her way through the crowd and finally got near enough to quickly touch the edge of his cloak with her fingers. At once, her bleeding stopped and she was released from her suffering.

Jesus stopped in his tracks and turned around. "Who touched me?" he asked.

People shook their heads, denying it was them, and the disciples said, "Master, there are so many people crowding around you! How can you ask who touched you?" But Jesus kept turning his head and looking around to see who it was. Eventually, the woman bowed down before him, trembling with fear, and told him the truth.

"Daughter," said Jesus, "your faith has healed you. Go in peace and be freed from your suffering."

While he was speaking to the woman, some men came to Jairus with bad news. "Your daughter is dead," they said. "Why bother the teacher any more? There is no point in him coming with you now."

But Jesus ignored them. "Don't be afraid," he told Jairus. "Just believe and she will be healed." And he continued on his way to the house, taking only three of his disciples with him—Peter, James, and John. As they approached, they could see the flautists playing music for the dead, and the people outside, weeping and sobbing. "Why all this commotion and wailing?" Jesus asked. "The child is not dead but asleep!" But the mourners did not believe him.

He and the disciples went into the house with Jairus and his wife. Their daughter was lying on her bed, cold and still. Jesus bent over her and took her small hand in his. "Little girl," he said softly. "I say to you, get up!" Her eyelashes fluttered and opened and she smiled. Then she stretched and yawned and jumped off the bed and ran to her parents. Astonished, they clutched her tightly to them and looked at Jesus in amazement. He gave them strict instructions not to tell anyone what had happened. And he told them to give her something to eat.

A woman touches the corner of Jesus's robe so that she can be free of her suffering

The Sower

*J*esus went to the lake to preach and a large crowd
gathered to hear him. There were so many people that he
got into a little fishing boat and spoke to them from that.

They listened from the shoreline, where the wading birds wandered to and fro,
and from the bulrushes, where the waterfowl watched from their nests. Other
people perched on the rocks or sat quietly on the soft green grass. Jesus's voice
rang out across the water, clear as a bell, telling them a parable.

"A farmer went out to sow his seed. As he scattered it, some fell along the
path and the birds came and ate it up. Some fell on rocky places where there
was not much soil. It sprang up quickly, but when the Sun shone the plants
were scorched and they withered because they had no roots. Other seed fell
among thorns, which grew up and choked the plants. And the remaining seed
fell on good soil where it produced a fine crop and multiplied greatly—by thirty,
sixty, or even one hundred times." Jesus paused briefly
and then added, "He who has ears, let him hear."

*The seed that lands
on good soil produces
a bountiful crop*

At first, the crowd had listened quietly but, as Jesus went on, a few of them started to shuffle their feet and whisper to each other. They wondered why the preacher, who had such a growing reputation, was telling them a simple story about an ordinary farmer sowing his seeds. Others stayed silent, listening to every word that Jesus said.

Later, when everyone had gone home and the disciples were alone with Jesus, they asked him why he spoke in parables. Jesus replied, "You are my disciples and I explain to you the secrets of the Kingdom of Heaven, but to everybody else I speak in parables."

And, because even the disciples themselves did not always understand the details of every parable, he explained the meaning of the story he had just told.

> "The farmer sowing the seed is sowing the word of God."

"The farmer sowing the seed is sowing the word of God. Some people are like the seed along the path; no sooner is the word sown in them than Satan comes along and takes it away. Other people, like the seed sown on rocky places, hear the word with joy. But, because they have no roots, they quickly collapse and lose their faith when there is any trouble or opposition. Still others, like the seed sown among the thorns, hear the word but are choked by the worries and desires of this life. The remaining people, like the seed sown on good soil, hear the word and accept it. The seed can only grow in those people who live their lives according to the word of God."

Jesus told them that, although parables were not always easy, people must listen to them with an open heart and a receptive mind. Only then could the truth take root. They must search hard for the hidden meaning and take the message to heart.

The seed that lands on rocky ground quickly withers

The Death of John the Baptist

*H*erod Antipas, the ruler of Galilee, respected and feared John the Baptist. But his wife, Herodias, hated the holy man because he had spoken out against her marriage to Herod.

"It is not lawful for you to have your brother's wife," John had told Herod one day. Herodias wanted to have John put to death for his insolence, but Herod refused. He admired John and knew that many of his people held him in the highest esteem and thought that he was a great prophet. Herod did not want to risk an uprising. But, after much persuading, he did agree to have John arrested and put in prison.

Soon after, a huge banquet was to be held in the palace to celebrate Herod's birthday. It had taken months of planning. The guest list included all the highest officials and the most important men in the whole of Galilee. The leading lights of the Roman army would also be there, in full military dress. It would be a glittering occasion.

> "Whatever you ask, shall be yours."

When the great day came, all the guests sat down to a sumptuous feast. The finest wine flowed and musicians played on their harps and lyres. Then, Herodias's young daughter, Salome, appeared in front of her stepfather and his guests, a picture of beauty and grace. She smiled sweetly to the king and started to dance for him, her dress floating around her and flowers nodding in her long, dark hair. Effortlessly, she turned this way and that, holding her tambourine high in the air. Everyone watched, entranced by her. And Herod himself was spellbound, unable to take his eyes off her. When she had finished, he beckoned her over and kissed her fondly on both cheeks. "Whatever you ask, shall be yours," he promised. "Even half my kingdom!" And he swore this on oath in front of all his guests, raising his goblet of wine.

Salome ran over to her mother, Herodias, who had been watching her daughter dance. "What shall I ask for?" whispered Salome.

"The head of John the Baptist on a plate!" said her mother.

Salome went immediately back to Heriod and repeated her mother's words. "I would like you to give me the head of John the Baptist on a plate," she said.

Herod looked at her in horror, but he had sworn an oath in front of all his guests and he had to keep it. So he gave orders for his executioner to go to the prison to behead John the Baptist. He waited, sick at heart, while Herodias gloated.

At last the doors opened, and a servant entered carrying the bleeding head of John the Baptist on a large silver platter. A trail of blood stained the marble floor as he walked toward Salome, who reluctantly accepted her prize. She walked across the room, blood dripping around her feet, and offered the platter to her mother. Herodias gazed at the severed head of John the Baptist, and her dark eyes gleamed with satisfaction.

As soon as John's disciples heard the news, they went to the prison and took the body of John the Baptist and laid it in a tomb. When Jesus was told, he took a boat and went away to mourn and pray for his cousin.

John the Baptist's head is placed on a platter and taken to Salome

The Feeding of the Five Thousand

Jesus and his disciples tried to get away on their own for a little while, and they went to Bethsaida. But, as usual, the crowds followed them.

When Jesus saw the crowds, he smiled. He would never turn them away, whatever happened. They brought him their sick and he healed them.

By the time the Sun was low in the sky, everybody was tired and hungry. The disciples came to Jesus and said, "It has been a long day. And we are far from anywhere. Why don't you send the crowds away to find food for themselves?"

"They do not need to go away," Jesus replied. "You can give them something to eat here." The disciples laughed and said, "How can we do that? There must be at least five thousand of them!"

Then Andrew, the brother of Peter, spoke up, "There is a boy here who has five small barley loaves and two small fish. But how far will they go among so many?"

Jesus told the disciples to divide the people into groups of fifty or a hundred and make them sit down on the grass. The people sat patiently, waiting to see what would happen.

Meanwhile, Jesus took the loaves and the fish from the boy and, looking up to heaven, he gave thanks and started to break the first loaf into pieces. He gave them to the disciples to take around. The disciples could not believe it. There was more than enough for everyone. And then Jesus did the same with the fish—turning two small sardines into many thousands. Everyone ate gratefully—all five thousand of them. And, even after everyone had finished, there was still enough bread and fish left over to fill twelve baskets.

"There was more than enough for everybody."

When evening came, the boat was in the middle of the lake, and he was alone on land. He saw the disciples straining at the oars, because the wind was against them. About the fourth watch of the night he went out to them, walking on the lake. He was about to pass by them, but when they saw him walking on the lake, they thought he was a ghost. They cried out, because they all saw him and were terrified.

Mark 6:47–50

THE SEA OF GALILEE

Jesus found his first followers among the fishermen of the Sea of Galilee, a large freshwater lake. In the 1st century CE, several hundred fishing boats regularly worked the lake. It is still known for rich fishing and sudden storms.

Jesus Walks on the Water

*T*he crowds went away, talking of the miracle of the loaves and fish, and the disciples said goodbye to Jesus. They got back into their boat and started to row home.

Jesus stood on the shore, watching them go. Then he walked up the mountainside. When he got to the top, he could see the boat making its way across the calm water. He sat there, alone as night fell, praying to the Lord.

"Truly you are the Son of God!"

The disciples rowed on through the darkness toward the other side. They were far from the shore now and the inky water stretched around them, merging with the sky. The disciples were making good progress when, out of nowhere, the wind whistled in, whipping up the waves. The disciples gripped tight to their oars and battled on.

Then, in the distance, they saw a strange sight. It looked like a man walking over the water. The figure came nearer and nearer, gliding silently through the gloom and over the moonlit sea. The disciples rubbed their eyes and looked at each other in terror as the apparition approached. Now they could see that his sandalled feet were walking on the water as if it were solid ground. "It's a ghost!" they cried, shivering with fear.

But then the familiar voice of Jesus said, "Do not be afraid. It is only me." The disciples stared at him in amazement.

Then Peter said, "Lord, if it is you, tell me to come to you on the water."

"Come!" said Jesus, and he held out his hand.

Peter got up and climbed over the side of the boat, not taking his eyes off Jesus. He put his feet down on the surface of the water and walked slowly toward his master.

But when Peter looked down at the water and at the waves, his courage failed him, and he began to sink. "Lord! Save me!" he cried.

Jesus reached out his hand and caught him. "You of little faith," he said. "Why did you doubt?" He took Peter back to the boat and together they climbed in. Immediately, the wind died down, the waves vanished, and the sea lay calm and tranquil.

The disciples looked at Jesus in awe and said, "Truly, you are the Son of God!"

The Good Samaritan

*O*ne day, a lawyer asked Jesus a difficult question, trying to trick him. "What must I do to gain eternal life?"

"You know what the law says," replied Jesus. "What does it tell you?"

The lawyer thought for a while and then answered him. "Love the Lord your God with all your heart and with all your soul and with all your strength and with all your mind. And you must love your neighbor as you love yourself," he said finally.

"Good—that is absolutely right," answered Jesus. "Remember these words every day of your life."

The lawyer frowned. "But who is my neighbor?" he asked.

So Jesus told him a story. "A man was traveling along the lonely road from Jerusalem to Jericho through the desert land. Suddenly, he was ambushed and attacked by robbers. They stripped him of his clothes and everything he had, beat him savagely, and left him at the side of the road to die.

"Soon after, a priest walked along the road, through the heat and the dust. But when he saw the man lying there, covered in blood, he crossed over and hurried past on the other side of the road. Next, a Levite, who helped the priests in the Temple, appeared, but when he caught sight of his fellow Jew, bleeding and injured, he too crossed over quickly to the other side of the road and continued on his way. Then a Samaritan arrived and, when he saw the man lying there, he stopped and knelt down. And, although Jews and Samaritans were not the best of friends, he showed the poor man the utmost kindness, unlike the priest and the Levite. The Samaritan dressed his terrible wounds and bandaged them up. Then gently, he lifted the injured man onto his own donkey and took him to the nearest inn, where he looked after him.

The wounded man is left to die by the priest and the Levite

"The next day," Jesus continued, "when the Samaritan was getting ready to go, he gave the innkeeper two silver coins and asked him to look after the injured man. As he left, the Samaritan also asked the innkeeper to let him know next time he stayed if he owed any more money."

At the end of the story, Jesus paused and asked the lawyer, "Which of these three people do you think was a neighbor to the man who fell into the hands of the robbers?"

"The one who showed kindness," the lawyer said. "The Samaritan."

"Exactly," said Jesus. "Go and do likewise."

"And you must love your neighbor as you love yourself."

A Samaritan stops to help the injured man

The Transfiguration

When Jesus got to the region of Caesarea Philippi he asked his disciples, "Who do people say I am?"

"Some say you are John the Baptist, others say Elijah, Jeremiah, or one of the prophets," they said.

"But what about you?" Jesus asked the disciples. "Who do you say I am?"

"You are the Christ, the Son of God," Peter replied. No one else said anything.

Jesus smiled at Peter and said, "Blessed are you, Peter. God, my Father in heaven, revealed this to you. You are my rock and on you I will build my church. I will give you the keys to the Kingdom of Heaven." But he warned the disciples not to tell anyone that he was the Christ. He said that, in time, he would go to Jerusalem and suffer at the hands of the elders, the chief priests, and the teachers of the law. And he told them that he would die, but would rise again after three days.

"You are my rock and on you I will build my church."

Jesus tells Peter that he will give him the keys to God's Kingdom

Peter protested, "This cannot happen, Lord."

Jesus turned on him and said, "Get behind me, Satan! Do not speak like that. You are only thinking of yourself and not the will of God." Jesus went on to tell his disciples that, to follow him, they must give up all their worldly riches. "For whoever wants to save his life will lose it, but whoever loses his life for me will find it. What good will it be for a man if he gains the whole world yet forfeits his soul?"

A week later, Jesus took Peter, James, and John to the top of a nearby mountain to pray. It was a long and hard climb. As soon as they got to the highest peak, Jesus was transfigured in front of their very eyes, and a dazzling light radiated from deep within him. His face was illuminated, like the brightest sun.

Just then two men appeared from nowhere and began talking to Jesus. The disciples recognized them as Moses the law-giver and Elijah the great prophet. The three disciples watched in amazement.

Then, as Jesus, Moses, and Elijah were speaking, a bright cloud came down from the sky and enveloped them. And a great voice inside the cloud said, "This is my Son, whom I love. With him I am well pleased. Listen to him."

Jesus

Moses

Elijah

James

John

Peter

The disciples could not believe their ears and fell to the ground, hiding their eyes. But Jesus came and touched them. "Get up," he said. "Do not be afraid." They opened their eyes and looked around. Moses and Elijah had vanished and Jesus was by himself again, standing alone.

Then the three disciples came back down the mountain with Jesus, and he said, "Until I have risen from the dead, do not tell anyone about what you saw today."

Mary, Martha, and Lazarus

There was a man named Lazarus, who lived in Bethany with his sisters, Mary and Martha. Jesus had stayed in their house one day, and Mary had spent many hours sitting at his feet, listening to him.

Mary absorbed every word Jesus said. Her sister, Martha, on the other hand, bustled around, cleaning the house and preparing the food. Eventually, she moaned to Jesus, "Lord, it is not fair that my sister has left me to do the work."

"Martha," Jesus replied gently. "Mary is right. It is much more important to listen to my teaching than to worry about cooking and cleaning."

Weeks later, Lazarus was gravely ill. His sisters tried to make him better, but to no avail. They sent word to Jesus that their brother was on the brink of death.

When he got the message, Jesus said, "This sickness will not end in death. No, it is for God's Glory so that God's Son may be glorified through it." He did not rush to Bethany but stayed where he was for two more days. Then he said to his disciples, "Let us go back to Judea. Our friend Lazarus has fallen asleep. But I am going to wake him." The disciples looked at each other, puzzled, not realizing that Jesus was talking about death rather than sleep.

> "I am the resurrection and the life. He who believes in me will never die."

When they got to Bethany, they discovered that Lazarus had died four days earlier. He had been buried immediately, as was the custom, his body washed and wrapped in linen, scented with aloes and myrrh. Then it had been laid in a tomb in the hillside. As Jesus and the disciples approached, Martha ran out to meet them. Mary stayed in the house, mourning with her relatives.

Mary and Martha nurse Lazarus

"Lord," said Martha to Jesus, "If you had been here, my brother would not have died. But I know that even now God will give you anything you ask for."

"Your brother will rise again," replied Jesus. "I am the resurrection and the life. He who believes in me will never die. Do you believe this?"

"Yes, Lord," she answered. "I believe that you are the Christ, the Son of God, who has come into the world." Then she ran to the house and called Mary. "The teacher is here."

Mary went out to meet Jesus, accompanied by the other mourners. They had heard so much about the preacher who healed the sick that they wanted to see him for themselves.

Mary fell at his feet, sobbing, "Lord, if you had been here, my brother would not have died." Jesus was deeply moved by her sorrow and the tears of her family.

"Where have you laid him?" he asked.

"Come and see, Lord," she replied, tears running down her cheeks. Jesus wept.

One relative remarked, "See how he loved Lazarus, too."

But another replied, "If he can make a blind man see why did he not prevent Lazarus from dying?"

Together, they went to the tomb of Lazarus. It was a cave, and a huge rock had been rolled across the entrance to seal it. Jesus said, "Take away the stone."

Martha asked, "But Lord, are you sure? There will be a terrible smell."

He said, "Did I not tell you that if you believed you would see the Glory of God?"

The strongest men heaved the stone away from the entrance. Jesus looked to the heavens and said, "Father, I thank you that you have heard me. I know that you always hear me, but not everybody does."

Then, in a loud voice, Jesus shouted into the tomb, "Lazarus! Come out!" After a few moments, a shadowy figure appeared from the gloom. It was Lazarus, brought back to life from the dead. He was still wrapped in the linen strips of his shroud and a cloth was draped over his head.

Mary sobs at the feet of Jesus, surrounded by the other mourners

Lost and Found

*A*ll kinds of people had gathered around Jesus to hear him speak, including some tax collectors and criminals.

The Pharisees, who thought it essential to uphold the law at all times, were not happy with this. "Look at him! He makes sinners welcome!" they said to each other, stroking their long white beards. Jesus started to speak, telling the people a parable about a shepherd and his sheep.

"There was a shepherd who had a large flock of one hundred sheep. He looked after them carefully out in the fields, watching over them day and night. But one day, he was counting his sheep and one was missing. He counted again, just to be sure. There were only ninety-nine. So, leaving the ninety-nine behind to graze on their own, the shepherd went to look for the missing sheep. He searched high and low, never giving up hope.

> "He searched high and low, never giving up hope."

"Eventually, he found the sheep and, joyfully, he put it on his shoulders and carried it home. He called his neighbors and friends together and asked them to give thanks and celebrate with him because he had found his lost sheep."

And then, Jesus explained the story to them. "In the same way, there will be more rejoicing in heaven over one sinner who repents than over ninety-nine righteous people who do not need to repent." The crowd listened intently as he went on to tell another parable.

"There was a woman who had ten silver coins, but she lost one of them. She knew that it must be somewhere in the house. But she had no idea where. So she lit her lamp, took her broom, and swept the house thoroughly from top to bottom, searching for it. She looked in every corner, under each stick of furniture and rush mat and, at last, she found it hidden behind her stone water jar.

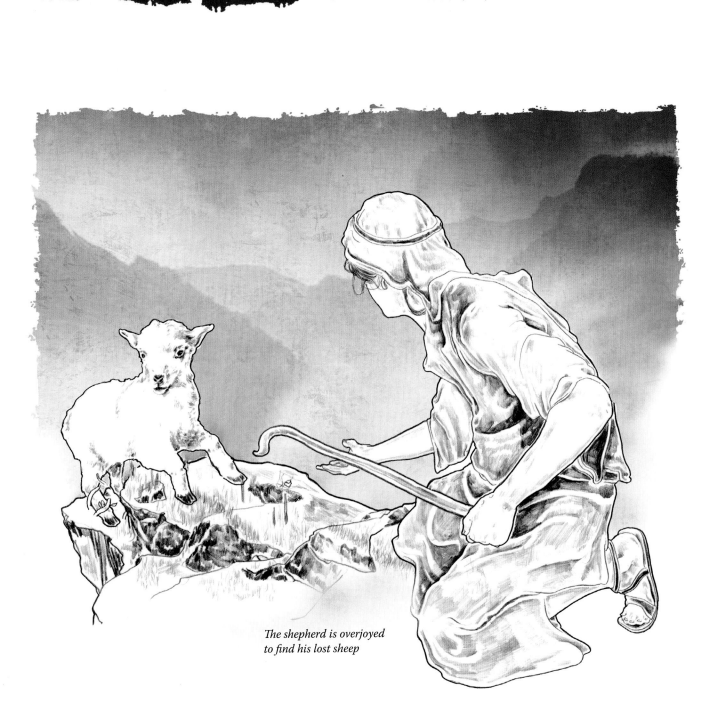

*The shepherd is overjoyed
to find his lost sheep*

She called her friends and neighbors together, asking them to rejoice with her. 'I am so happy that I have found my silver coin!' she told them."

And, when he had finished, he added, "In the same way, there is great rejoicing among the angels in heaven when even one sinner repents."

The Prodigal Son

Jesus told the crowd a parable about a rich farmer who had two sons and what happened when one of his sons left home.

"One day, the younger son came to him and said, 'Father, give me my share of your estate.' His father, who was a kind man, agreed, and divided his property equally between his two sons. Soon after, the younger son took his share of the inheritance, said goodbye to his father and brother, and left home. He went far away to a different country, settled there, and started a new life very unlike the one he had left behind.

> "We shall have a great feast to celebrate. For this son of mine was dead and is alive now. He was lost and he is found."

He lived it up day and night, drinking and dancing with his wild new friends and spending his money in the most extravagant way. It did not take him long to go through the whole of his fortune and soon nothing was left. Then, to add to his woes, there was a terrible famine in his adopted country and people began to die of hunger.

"The young man was desperate and did not know what to do. Eventually, he had to swallow his pride and work as a lowly farm laborer, tending pigs out in the fields. His own stomach was so empty that he eyed the pigs' food enviously and wondered about stealing some of it. Hunger gnawed at him day and night and his thoughts turned to home. Finally, he said to himself, 'Even my father's humblest servants will have something to eat and food to spare and here am I starving to death.' He knew that he had sinned against heaven and against his father, and that he must make amends.

"He set off on the long journey, and when he got close to his home, his father saw him and his eyes filled with tears. He ran to meet his son with his arms outstretched and hugged him warmly. And the son said to him, 'Father, I have sinned against heaven and against you. I am no longer worthy to be called your son.'

"But his father would not hear of it and told his servants to fetch the finest robe that could be found. He dressed his son in it, put a ring on his finger and sandals on his feet. 'Bring a fattened calf and kill it,' he ordered his servants. 'We shall have a great feast to celebrate. For this son of mine was dead and is alive now. He was lost and he is found.' The celebrations began.

"Meanwhile, the elder son had been working in the fields. When he came home at the end of the day, tired and hungry, he was amazed to hear music and dancing in the house. He asked one of the servants what was going on, who replied,

The younger son squanders all his inheritance

'Your brother has come home and your father has killed the fattened calf because he is back safe and sound.' The older brother could not believe it. Anger swelled within him and he could not bring himself to set foot in the house.

"His father went out to plead with him, but his son shouted at him, 'All these years that he has been gone, I have slaved away for you and never disobeyed you. And you have never given me so much as a miserable goat to say thank you. But when your precious young son comes home after squandering every last penny, you kill the fattened calf for him!'

"His father replied, 'My son, everything that I have is yours and I love you dearly. But we have to celebrate and give thanks because this brother of yours was dead and is alive again. He was lost and is found.' "

Jesus looked at the crowd and said, "Like the father in this parable, God will open his arms to all those who repent. He will rejoice when they return to Him!"

The father is overjoyed to see his younger son return home

The Unmerciful Servant

Peter came to Jesus one day and said, "Lord, how many times should I forgive my brother when he sins against me? Up to seven times?"

Jesus answered, "I tell you, not seven times but seventy times seven." And he told the disciples a parable. "There was a king who was very kind and often used to lend his servants money when they were in need. The time came for the accounts to be settled, so he called everybody to him, one at at time. A servant owed him ten thousand talents, which was an extremely large sum of money. The King asked for the debt to be settled, but the servant had nothing and could not pay him back. So the King ordered that the man and his wife and all his children should be sold as slaves in order to raise the money.

"Be patient with me, I beg you, my Lord! I will pay back everything!"

"Distraught, the servant fell down on his knees before the King. 'Be patient with me, I beg you, my Lord!' he pleaded. 'I will pay back everything!' The King was a merciful man and took pity on him. He decided to cancel the debt—all ten thousand talents of it—and let the man go.

"Not long after, the servant met one of his friends who worked at the palace and owed him one hundred denarii. It was not a large amount of money. As soon as the servant saw his friend, he shouted, 'I want that money you owe me! Pay me back now!' And he grabbed his friend around the throat and started to beat him.

"Gasping for breath, the man fell to his knees and begged for mercy. 'Be patient with me, please!' he cried. 'I will pay you back!' But his tormentor refused and had the man thrown in prison until he could pay his debt.

"When the other servants in the palace heard about this they could not believe it. They were so distressed that they went straight to the King and told him. He immediately summoned the servant to whom he had showed such kindness. 'You wicked man,' he said. 'I canceled all of your debt because you begged and pleaded with me. Should you not have had mercy on your fellow servant, just as I had on you?' And then, boiling with rage, he sent the man to prison to be punished, until he could pay back all of the money he owed."

At the end of the parable, Jesus said, "This is how my heavenly Father will treat each of you, unless you truly forgive your brother from the bottom of your heart."

The King gives orders for his servant to be jailed

Lazarus and the Rich Man

Jesus told the disciples a story about a rich man and a beggar, and what happened to them after they died.

"There was a rich man who dressed in purple and the most expensive linen. He lived in the lap of luxury in a splendid house, surrounded by every comfort and waited on hand and foot. The food he ate was the very finest, and the wine he drank was the best. But, at his gate, there lay a poor beggar, named Lazarus. He was a pitiful sight, and his body was covered in weeping sores. He was starving and longed to eat any scraps of food that might fall from the rich man's table.

"The time came when Lazarus died and the angels carried him up to heaven. Soon after, the rich man also died and his body was buried with all due ceremony. But he was taken straight down to hell, where he suffered the most terrible torment, roasting day and night in the flames. He looked up to heaven and saw Abraham, the father of his people, with Lazarus by his side. So he called up to him, 'Father Abraham!' he cried. 'Have pity on me and send Lazarus to dip his finger in water and come and cool my tongue! I am in agony!'

> "Remember, in your life you had everything, while Lazarus had nothing."

"Abraham looked down at him and shook his head slowly. 'My son,' he said. 'Remember, in your life you had everything, while Lazarus had nothing. He has now earned his comfort here in heaven, while you are being punished in hell. And besides, there is a great chasm between heaven and hell and no one can bridge it.'

" 'Then I beg you,' pleaded the rich man. 'Send Lazarus to my father's house, for I have five brothers. Let him warn them what has happened to me.'

" 'They have Moses and the prophets. Let them listen to them,' said Abraham.

" 'But they won't!' the rich man protested, as the flames licked around him. 'But, if someone from the dead goes to them, they will repent.'

"Again, Abraham shook his head. 'If they do not listen to Moses and the prophets, they will not listen if someone rises from the dead.' "

Lazarus begs for food by the rich man's gate

The Pharisee and the Tax Collector

Jesus told this parable about the dangers of being self-righteous and looking down on other people.

"Two people went to the temple to pray. One was a Pharisee and the other was a tax collector. The Pharisee stood up importantly, sure in the knowledge that he had observed all the Lord's commandments. Catching the priest's eye, he raised his head high in the air and started to pray to the Lord. 'God, I thank you that I am not like other men who commit crimes and sins, and I also thank you that I am not like that tax collector over there. I devote my life to you and am obedient in all things, fasting twice a week and giving a tenth of all I have to helping other people.'

> "For everyone who puffs themselves up and exalts themselves will be humbled."

"But the tax collector stood modestly some way away. Nobody took any notice of him. He did not think himself worthy enough even to raise his eyes toward heaven, so he bowed his head to the ground. 'God have mercy on me,' he prayed. 'I am a sinner.'"

Jesus concluded, "Now this was the man, rather than the Pharisee, who went home with God's blessing. For everyone who puffs themselves up and exalts themselves will be humbled. And those who are meek and humble will be exalted."

The Pharisee is full of self-importance, while the tax collector meekly bows his head

261

Jewish Sects

In Jesus's lifetime, there were several forms of Judaism, whose followers had different beliefs and who argued about how to live a holy life in a country ruled by the hated Romans. Many expected a messiah or savior, sent by God to restore Israel, but opinions differed over what kind of savior he would be.

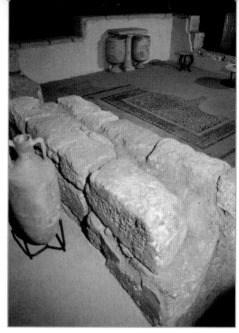

Pharisees

The Pharisees, whose name means "separate," believed in strict observance of Jewish law. They looked down on unholy people, such as tax collectors. Jesus said that the prayers of a humble tax collector had more value than those of a proud Pharisee.

Sadducees

The Sadducees were a class of wealthy priests who controlled Temple worship in Jerusalem. They were named after Zadok, King Solomon's high priest. This luxurious house belonged to a Sadducee family.

Essenes

The Essenes had an even stricter view of the law than the Pharisees. They separated themselves from other Jews and gentiles (non-Jews) by going to live in desert communities, such as this one at Qumran, by the Dead Sea.

Dead Sea Scrolls

In 1947, a shepherd found a library of scrolls hidden by the Essenes in caves near Qumran. The Dead Sea Scrolls show that the Essenes believed they were living in the last days. Jewish prophecies would be fulfilled and Israel would be restored.

DIFFERENT BELIEFS

Pharisees

Pharisees followed the oral, or spoken, law, based on their interpretations of Jewish scriptures. They believed that, one day, God would restore the dead to life and punish the wicked and reward the good.

Sadducees

Sadducees followed only the laws written down in the Torah, the first five books of the Bible. They did not believe in the resurrection of the dead, which is not mentioned in the Torah.

Samaritans

The Samaritans also used the Torah as their holy book. They rejected Jerusalem Temple worship and said that their own temple was holier. They expected a savior, called the "Taheb" (restorer), who would restore them to their rightful position as the true Israel.

Essenes

The Essenes believed that, while the Temple in Jerusalem was holy, the Sadducees had no right to be priests there. Like the Pharisees, they also believed in the resurrection of the dead. They expected not one but two messiahs—a priest and a king.

Samaritans

The Gospels record the hatred between Jews and Samaritans who lived between Judea and Galilee. They claimed to be descended from the same Israelite tribes as the Jews, and had their own temple on Mount Gerizim, where Samaritans still worship today.

Ritual bath

This bath was used by the Essenes for ritual washing. Most Jews believed that, following contact with anything unclean, they should purify themselves by washing. But Jesus said, "It is what comes out of a man that makes him unclean."

263

Jesus and the Children

*O*n their way back to Capernaum, the disciples had been arguing. Jesus asked them what they had been quarreling about.

They had, in fact, been arguing about which of them would be considered the most worthy in the eyes of God, but they did not want to tell him. They were ashamed of themselves and kept quiet. But Jesus knew exactly what was in their minds. Sitting down, he beckoned all twelve disciples to him. They gathered around to listen. "If anyone wants to be first," he said to them, "he must be the very last and the servant of all."

> "Whoever welcomes one of these little children in my name, welcomes me."

Then a group of women arrived and came up to Jesus. They asked him if he would bless the children that they had brought with them. They clustered around him expectantly, babies in their arms and little children at their feet. It was quite a crowd and the disciples started to push the mothers away, telling them to stop bothering Jesus. But Jesus, who never turned anyone away, said to the disciples, "Let the little children come to me. Do not stop them for the Kingdom of Heaven belongs to them."

He took one little boy and lifted him gently onto his lap. The child looked up at him, wide-eyed, "Whoever welcomes one of these little children in my name, welcomes me," said Jesus. "And whoever welcomes me, welcomes the one who sent me. I tell you the truth. Unless you change and become like little children, you will never enter the Kingdom of Heaven." And he stretched out his hand and blessed each baby and child in turn, as their smiling mothers watched. The disciples stood back, quietly listening.

Jesus tells the disciples to let the children come to him

The Rich Young Man

As Jesus went on his way, a young man ran up to him and fell down on his knees before him.

"Good teacher," he asked, "what must I do to gain eternal life?"

"You know the commandments. You must follow them," Jesus answered.

"Teacher," the young man said. "I have kept all the commandments since I was a boy."

"All things are possible with God."

Jesus smiled at him. "Now all you have to do is to sell everything you have and give it to the poor, then come and follow me. You will have treasure in heaven."

The young man was filled with sorrow when he heard this because he came from a very wealthy family. As he walked away, Jesus said to the disciples, "I promise that it is easier for a camel to go through the eye of a needle than for a rich man to enter the Kingdom of God."

Like most people, the disciples thought that wealth and prosperity were a sign of God's blessing. "Who then can be saved?" they asked.

Jesus replied, "All things are possible with God."

"Lord, we have left everything behind to follow you!" said Peter. "What will happen to us?" he asked.

"Anyone who has left their homes and their fields and their families behind to follow me will receive one hundred times as much and will recieve eternal life," Jesus answered.

The rich young man asks Jesus what he must do to gain eternal life

265

Zacchaeus the Tax Collector

*O*n his way to Jerusalem, Jesus passed through the city of Jericho. People had heard so much about the teacher from Galilee that they lined the streets to watch him go by.

Among them was a man named Zacchaeus, who was an extremely wealthy tax collector. But he was a short man and was stuck at the back of the crowd, unable to see anything. He stood on tiptoes and craned his neck, but could not even catch a glimpse of Jesus. Determined not to lose his chance, he darted ahead and spotted a shady sycamore tree growing nearby. He heaved himself slowly onto the lowest branch and climbed up through the dense, green leaves to get a bird's-eye view of Jesus as he came along. The rest of the crowd watched him, surprised to see a fully grown man, and a tax collector at that, sitting up a tree.

All the while, Jesus was walking slowly along the road, talking to the people. When he got to the sycamore tree he stopped in his tracks and looked up. "Zacchaeus, come down immediately," Jesus said. "Please would you take me to your house? I would like to stay there."

"Today salvation has come to this house."

The people look on as Jesus asks Zacchaeus to come down from the tree

266

Zacchaeus climbs a tree to getter a better view of Jesus

The tax collector could not believe his ears and slithered down the tree, landing at Jesus's feet. He dusted himself and, bowing low, he said that he would be honored and glad to welcome Jesus to his house. They continued along the road as the crowd watched, surprised to see the two deep in conversation together. They did not like Zacchaeus because he worked for the Romans and they did not trust him. "Can you believe it?" they muttered to one another. "Jesus is going home with that sinner!"

But, when they got to the house, Zacchaeus said to Jesus, "Look, Lord. Here and now I promise to give half of my possessions to the poor. And, if I have ever cheated anybody out of anything, I will pay back four times that amount."

Jesus smiled and said to him, "Today salvation has come to this house. This man is, indeed, a son of Abraham. What was lost has been saved."

Workers in the Vineyard

Jesus told a parable about a man who owned a big vineyard. "It was harvesttime, and the man needed to hire some men to help with the grape picking.

"Early one morning he went down to the marketplace and chose some men who were standing there, looking for work. He agreed to pay them one denarius a day and they went to his vineyard to start a full day's work.

"Three hours later, he went back to the marketplace and found some more men. 'There is work in my vineyard for you,' he said to them. 'I will pay you the going rate!' They agreed and set off for the vineyard. After another three hours, the man went down to the marketplace yet again and hired some more men. And three hours after that, he did the same again.

> "I want to give the men who were hired last the same as you."

"Then, after eleven hours, he went down to the marketplace again and found some men who were still hanging around with nothing to do. He told them that they could go and work in his vineyard.

"When evening came, he summoned his foreman and said, 'Call the workers together and pay them their wages, beginning with the ones I hired last. Go through them in groups, finishing with the ones I hired first.' So the workers lined up and were paid one denarius each, in turn. They all got exactly the same amount, no matter how long they had worked.

"The men who had been hired first, and had worked hard all day in the heat of the Sun, were angry and grumbled, 'Those men only worked for one hour, but you are paying them the same as us!'

"The vineyard owner answered, 'Friend, I am not being unfair to you. Did you not happily agree to work for one denarius? I want to give the men who were hired last the same as you. I have the right to do as I like with my own money. Or are you annoyed because I am generous?'

"So, like the workers who were hired toward the end of the day, those who come late to God are loved just as much as those who have always been with Him."

The laborers who were hired first grumble to the vineyard owner

The Wedding Feast

One of the leading Pharisees had invited Jesus and the disciples to eat at his house. There were many other guests and, as they were sitting at the table, Jesus told them a parable.

"The Kingdom of Heaven is like the King who prepared a magnificent wedding banquet for his son. All the guests had been invited and everything had been prepared. He sent his servants out to summon the guests, telling them that the celebrations were about to begin. But, although, they had all accepted their invitations quite some time ago, the guests began to make excuses.

" 'I have just bought a field and I have to go and inspect it now!' said one, looking the other way. 'Please send my apologies!'

" 'I have just bought five teams of oxen and I'm on my way to try them out now!' said another. 'I am so sorry!'

" 'I have just gotten married myself so I am afraid I can't come!' said still another. 'Please excuse me!'

> "Many are invited in, but only those with the right spirit are chosen."

"The servants went back to tell their master the bad news. Not one of the guests was coming. The King was furious. 'They did not deserve to come to the banquet anyway!' he stormed. 'Go into town and pick up anyone you can find. It doesn't matter who they are! The more the merrier! Invite them all!' The servants did as they were told and brought back dozens of people, glad to be invited so unexpectedly to the wedding feast.

"The king came in and was pleased to see all the guests. But he noticed one disrespectful man sitting at the table who was not wearing wedding clothes. Going up to him, he said, 'Friend, how did you get in here without wearing wedding clothes?' The man looked at him and said nothing.

"Immediately, the King ordered his servants to seize the man. 'Tie him up, hand and foot, and throw him out into the darkness,' he said."

And, after he had finished telling the parable, Jesus looked around the table and said, "So it is with the Kingdom of Heaven. Many are invited in, but only those with the right spirit are chosen."

The King throws out the disrespectful guest

The Wise and Foolish Maidens

Jesus told another parable to explain the Kingdom of Heaven. It was about ten bridesmaids at a wedding.

"They had helped the bride to get ready and were waiting excitedly for the groom to arrive at her house. Then they would escort the couple back to the groom's house for the wedding ceremony. When evening came, it seemed unlikely that the groom would come that day, so they settled down for the night. But five of them—the wise ones—decided that they would keep enough oil for their lamps to light the wedding procession, if the groom should arrive during the night. The other five—the foolish ones—let their lamps burn out.

The five wise bridesmaids have saved enough oil to light their lamps

"At midnight there was a shout, 'Quick, wake up, he's here!' The wise bridesmaids hurriedly lit their lamps, but the foolish ones had no oil.

" 'Lend us some,' they said, 'Please!'

"But the others replied, 'No, we can't. There may not be enough for all of us!'

"And so, always be prepared."

"So the foolish young women hurried away to try to buy some oil, while the wise ones greeted the groom and proceeded with him and the bride to the groom's home, where the wedding ceremony started.

"Later, the five foolish bridemaids arrived and knocked at the door. But the groom refused to let them in. 'It's too late,' he said. 'You've missed your chance.' "

Jesus paused for a moment and then he said, "And so, always be prepared. You do not know the day or the hour when I will return."

The five foolish bridesmaids have no oil left for their lamps

The Parable of the Talents

Jesus told another parable about the Kingdom of Heaven. It was about a master and his three servants.

"The master called his three servants together and asked them to look after his money for him while he went on a journey. He gave them different amounts of money, according to their ability. To the first servant he gave five talents, to the second servant he gave two talents, and to the last servant he gave one talent.

"The first two men cleverly put the money to work for them and soon doubled the amount that they had been given. But the third man went and dug a hole in the ground and hid his money there.

"After a long time away, their master returned and wanted to know what had happened to his money. The first servant came to him and said, 'Master, you gave me five talents and I have turned them into ten.'

"The second servant said, 'I have doubled your money, as well. You gave me two talents and I have since made two more.'

The third servant digs a hole to bury his talent

"Their master was very pleased with them and said, 'Well done. You are good and faithful servants. You have both worked hard with what I gave you. I will put you in charge of all sorts of things now.'

"Then the servant who had been given one talent came and said, 'Master, I have always known that you are a hard man, harvesting where you have not sown and gathering where you have not scattered seed. So I was afraid and hid your talent in the ground. See, here is what belongs to you.' And he held out the talent.

"His master was furious and replied, 'You worthless and lazy man! Why didn't you put my money on deposit in the bank? Then, at least, when I returned I would have got the interest. Take the talent from him and give it to my servant who has ten talents.' And, with that, he gave orders for the man to be thrown out of the house."

> "So we must all make the most of what God gives us and then we will be ready to enter the Kingdom of Heaven."

Explaining the parable, Jesus went on, "The two servants who used their abilities to the full to benefit their master are rewarded, but the other man loses everything. So, we must all make the most of what God gives us and then we will be ready to enter the Kingdom of Heaven."

The master is furious with the servant who buried his talent

Jesus Enters Jerusalem

*I*t was the week before Passover, and Jesus and the disciples were on their way to Jerusalem. They came to Bethphage on the Mount of Olives and stopped for a little while.

Jesus sent two of the disciples into the village. "You will find a donkey tied up there, with her young colt. Untie them both and bring them to me. If anyone asks you what you are doing, tell them that the Lord needs them." And so the words of the prophet Zechariah would now come true. Many years before, he had said, "See, your king comes to you, gentle and riding on a donkey, on a colt, the foal of a donkey."

The disciples fetched the two animals and spread one of their cloaks over the colt. Then Jesus climbed on the colt, and they set off down the hill. The olive trees cast a dappled light, protecting them from the sun. Although the little donkey had never been ridden before, he was good-tempered, and plodded down the path, taking Jesus to Jerusalem. The disciples walked by his side.

Soon, they were joined by other pilgrims, also going to celebrate Passover. Word spread that the teacher who could heal the sick had traveled all the way from Galilee and was on his way to Jerusalem.

Crowds of people welcome Jesus as he rides into Jerusalem

People stared in wonder and whispered that he was the Messiah. They clustered around him and gradually the crowd swelled. Some people took off their cloaks and laid them on the ground in front of him as he passed. Others climbed up the tall trunks of the date palm trees and cut branches to scatter beneath the donkey's feet. They praised Jesus and called his name, shouting, "Hosanna to the son of David! Blessed is he who comes in the name of the Lord!"

Some of the Pharisees were shocked to hear the people calling Jesus "son of David," since this was the special name for the expected Messiah. "Teacher! Can't you control your disciples?" they said.

> "Blessed is he who comes in the name of the Lord!"

"I tell you," replied Jesus, "If they keep quiet, the stones will cry out." And he rode on.

At last, the procession approached the city walls. But as he drew near, Jesus wept, knowing that before long Jerusalem would be destroyed again. "The day will come when your enemies will surround you on every side," he said, as if talking to the holy city itself. "They will destroy everything because you did not recognize God's coming."

Many pilgrims had gathered in the city already. They watched in astonishment as Jesus and his followers streamed through the gate, making their way toward the Temple.

Many people have come to Jerusalem for the Feast of Passover

Jesus and the Temple Traders

Jesus walked up the great steps and into the courtyard that led into the Temple. He looked around sadly. It was like a bustling marketplace, full of people buying and selling their wares as fast as they could.

Cattle and sheep stood lined up in the sun, waiting to be sold for sacrifice, flicking their tails to keep the flies away. Doves and pigeons cooed pitifully in their baskets beside them. The traders haggled loudly, all determined to get the very best price. The money exchangers sat at their tables, competing with each other furiously. They raked in the foreign coins with greedy fingers, changing them into shekels at the worst possible rate. The pilgrims waited for their money to be handed back so that they could go into the Temple.

> "It is written that my house will be a house of prayer."

Overwhelmed with sorrow and filled with rage, Jesus walked right up to the nearest money exchanger, grabbed his table, and turned it over. The man sat there, unable to believe his eyes, as his money cascaded to the ground. Jesus went to the next table and did the same. One by one, he turned over all the tables, the coins bouncing and rolling into every corner of the courtyard. Everyone watched in utter amazement.

Then, Jesus went up to the traders, who had by this time stopped their haggling and were watching open-mouthed. "It is written that my house will be a house of prayer," he thundered. "But you have turned it into a den of thieves." And he began to drive them out of the Temple. Filled with fear they ran, taking their animals with them. The money exchangers followed, hot on their heels. Before long, the courtyard had been cleared completely.

The pilgrims walked quietly into the Temple to pray, and Jesus started to heal the sick. They crowded around, waiting to be cured by him, but the chief priests and the teachers of the law watched with pursed lips. And, when they heard the children singing "Hosanna to the son of David," they marched up to Jesus. "Do you hear what these children are saying?" they demanded indignantly.

"Yes," replied Jesus. "Have you never read the psalm that says it is the lips of children that praise God most sweetly?"

As the sun set, Jesus left Jerusalem and went back to Bethany for the night. The next morning, he returned with the disciples to begin teaching in the Temple. The chief priests and the elders came up to him in front of everybody and asked, "Who gave you the authority to come and teach here?"

"I will ask you one question," Jesus replied. "If you answer me I will tell you by what authority I am here. Was my cousin John given the right to baptize by God or by men?"

The chief priests and elders scratched their heads and could not make up their minds. "If we say that God gave him the right, then Jesus will ask us why we did not believe John the Baptist. But if we say that men gave him the right, then the people will stone us because they believed that John was a prophet."

So, reluctantly, they turned to Jesus and said, "We don't know."

"In that case," replied Jesus, "neither will I tell you by what authority I am here."

Jesus challenges the religious leaders

THE TEMPLE OF JERUSALEM
Around 19 BCE King Herod began to rebuild
the temple in Jerusalem on a huge scale, but
it was completely destroyed by the Romans in
70 CE. Only this western wall of its platform
survives. It is still a holy place for Jews.

As he was leaving the temple, one of his disciples said to him, "Look, Teacher! What massive stones! What magnificent buildings!"
"Do you see all these great buildings?" replied Jesus. "Not one stone here will be left on another; every one will be thrown down."

Mark 13:1–2

Judas Plots to Betray Jesus

*T*he priests and the elders had seen Jesus ride into Jerusalem and they had watched him teaching the people and healing the sick.

They had also witnessed him driving the traders and the money exchangers out of the Temple. They knew that his following was growing by the day and that people were calling him the Messiah, the king who had been promised to the Jewish people for so long. The teacher from Galilee was a thorn in their flesh, challenging their authority and putting their livelihoods at risk. Something had to be done.

What are you willing to give me if I hand him over to you?"

In the evening, they gathered secretly at the house of Caiaphas the high priest to try to find a solution. They racked their brains and talked long into the night, discussing how they could get rid of Jesus once and for all. They must find some way of arresting him that would not attract too much attention, and then find grounds to have him executed. "But let's wait till after Passover, shall we? We do not want to cause a riot." They all agreed.

Jesus and the disciples had gone to Bethany, a short distance away, and were staying in the house of Lazarus and his sisters Mary and Martha. There was to be a great feast and Martha had spent all day preparing and cooking. Jesus sat down at the table, in the place of honor, with the disciples and Lazarus around him, while Martha started to serve the food.

As she was doing this, her sister Mary went up to Jesus, carrying a beautiful alabaster jar. It was filled with nard, which was an expensive and aromatic ointment, made with the oil of the spikenard plant. Kneeling at his feet, she broke the jar open and carefully poured the nard over his feet. Then she bent down and wiped his feet clean with her hair. The exotic perfume wafted through the air, filling the whole house.

But one of the disciples, named Judas Iscariot, objected. "What a waste!" he said. "That nard must be worth at least a year's wages! Why did you not sell it and give the money to the poor?"

"Leave her alone," Jesus replied. "She has done a beautiful thing. The poor you will always have with you and you can help them any time you want. But you will not always have me. When Mary poured perfume on my body, she did it to prepare me for burial. What she just did will be remembered always."

Soon after, Judas left the other disciples and went to the chief priests and the elders and told them that he was willing to betray Jesus. "What are you willing to give me if I hand him over to you?" he asked.

The priests and the elders were delighted and immediately counted out thirty pieces of silver and put them into his hand. From that moment on, Judas did not leave Jesus's side, waiting for an opportunity to hand him over.

Judas agrees to betray Jesus for thirty pieces of silver

Preparing for the Passover

It was just before Passover and Jesus knew that the time had come for him to leave this Earth and go to his Father in heaven.

Jesus's disciples, wanting to make sure that everything would be ready for the Passover Feast, came to him and asked, "Where do you want us to prepare the meal?"

Jesus told two of them, Peter and John, to go into Jerusalem. "As you enter the city," he said, "you will meet a man carrying a jar of water. Follow him to a house and go in with him. Ask the owner of the house to show you the room where your teacher will celebrate Passover with his disciples. He will take you upstairs to a large room where you will find everything you need. Stay there and start to prepare the Passover meal."

> "You are all equal. No master is greater than his servant. You should do as I have done for you."

Peter and John did exactly as Jesus had said, making all the preparations and laying out the food for the Feast. In the evening, Jesus and the other disciples arrived at the house, went upstairs, and sat down.

But, before they started to eat, Jesus got up from the table and knotted a towel around his waist. He fetched a basin, which he filled with clean water. He bent down and started to wash the feet of the disciple sitting next to him. Then he dried them carefully with the towel wrapped around his waist. When he had finished, he moved to the next disciple and did the same. Slowly, Jesus worked his way around the table, washing the feet of each of his disciples. Peter watched, unhappy, and when it came to his turn, he objected.

"Lord, why are you kneeling down to wash my feet?" he asked.

"You do not realize what I am doing now," said Jesus. "But later, you will understand."

"No," replied Peter. "You will never wash my feet!"

"Unless I wash your feet, you are not part of me," answered Jesus.

"Then, Lord," said Peter, "not just my feet, but my hands and my head as well."

Jesus shook his head. "A person who has had a bath needs only to wash his feet. His whole body is clean. And you are clean, though not every one of you is," he replied, looking around the table at the twelve disciples. He knew exactly who was going to betray him.

When Jesus had finished, he sat down at the table. "Do you understand what I have just done?" he asked them. "Now that I, your Lord and teacher, have washed your feet, you should also wash one another's feet. I have set you an example. You are all equal. No master is greater than his servant. You should do as I have done for you."

Jesus washes the feet of his disciples

The Last Supper

Jesus and the twelve disciples sat quietly, eating their Passover Feast together. "I have been looking forward to this last meal with you," Jesus said. "Next time, it will be in the Kingdom of Heaven."

He took a loaf of unleavened bread, blessed it, and broke off a large piece. He gave it to the disciples and said, "Take it and eat. This is my body given to you. Do this in remembrance of me." At the end of the meal, he took his cup of wine, gave thanks, and offered it to them. "Drink from it, all of you. This is my blood, the blood of the the covenant, which is poured out for many for the forgiveness of sins. I tell you, I will not drink of the fruit of the vine from now on until that day when I drink it again with you in my Father's kingdom."

And then he looked at the disciples and said, "I tell you the truth, one of you is going to betray me."

The disciples shook their heads in dismay and disbelief. "Surely not me, Lord? Surely not me?" they all said.

"It is one of the twelve," replied Jesus. "One who is eating with me. The Son of Man will go just as it is written about him. But woe to the man who betrays me. It would be better for him if he had not been born."

> "one of you is going to betray me."

Peter turned to the disciple who was sitting next to Jesus and whispered, "Ask him which one he means."

Leaning toward Jesus, the disciple said, "Lord, who is it?"

"I will give this bread to him," Jesus answered. He tore a piece off the loaf. The disciples watched his every move. He dipped the bread into a dish in front of him, carefully removed it, and gave it to Judas Iscariot.

"Surely, not me, Rabbi?" gasped Judas, taking the bread. The color drained from his face.

"Yes, it is you," said Jesus. "What you are going to do, do it quickly." Judas looked at him in dismay, then rushed out of the room. He fled into the night. No one tried to stop him.

Later, Jesus and the other disciples prayed together and then left the house to go to the Mount of Olives.

THE GARDEN OF GETHSEMANE
Since the 4th century CE, this olive grove in east
Jerusalem has been identified as the Garden of
Gethsemane, where Jesus prayed on the night
before his death. Gethsemane means "oil press"
and ancient olive trees still grow here.

*They went to a place called Gethsemane,
and Jesus said to his disciples, "Sit here while I pray."
He took Peter, James, and John along with him, and
he began to be deeply distressed and troubled. "My soul
is overwhelmed with sorrow to the point of death,"
he said to them. "Stay here and keep watch."*

Mark 14:32–34

The Garden of Gethsemane

Jesus and his twelve disciples crossed the valley and walked slowly up the stony path to the garden of Gethsemane.

It was a quiet and tranquil spot, just outside the city walls, where the wild flowers and figs flourished and the ancient trees shook their silver leaves in the gentle breeze. Jesus and his disciples often came here to be alone, far from the hustle and bustle of the Temple.

"Stay here while I go and pray," Jesus told his disciples. And he chose three of them to take with him—Peter, James, and John. He was deeply distressed and knew that, come what may, death was drawing near. "My soul is overwhelmed with sorrow," he told them. "Stay here and keep watch while I pray." He went farther through the darkness before kneeling on the ground. "Father, if it is possible, please take this cup of suffering from me. But let your will, not mine, be done," he prayed.

An angel appeared silently before him, a sign from God, helping to give him strength in his anguish. He went on praying. When he had finished, he returned to the three disciples and found them asleep. He woke them up and asked, "Could you not even stay awake for one single hour? Please keep watch and pray that you will not fall into temptation. The spirit is willing but the flesh is weak." For the second time, he went away and prayed. And again, when he came back, he found them sleeping. They did not know what to say. For a third time, Jesus went and prayed and came back to find the three disciples asleep.

"Are you still sleeping?" he asked. "Enough! The hour has come. The Son of Man is betrayed into the hands of sinners. Get up. Let's go. Here comes my betrayer."

While Jesus was still speaking, Judas arrived with the elders, the chief priests, and the soldiers. Their flaming torches lit up the dark hillside. Judas had told his group, "The one I kiss is the man you are after. Arrest him." Then, Judas went right up to Jesus and greeted him with a kiss on the cheek.

Jesus looked at him and asked him sadly, "Judas, are you betraying the Son of Man with a kiss?" Immediately, the soldiers seized Jesus and arrested him. But, before they could take him away the disciple Peter, who had a sword, drew it from his side and lunged at one of the guards, slicing off his right ear. And Jesus reproached him, "Put it away. All those who live by the sword will die by the sword." And he gently touched the guard's bleeding head and healed it, making his ear whole again.

Jesus looked at the elders and the chief priests and the soldiers and said to them, "Do you think that I am leading a rebellion? Is that why you have come out with swords and clubs to capture me? I have sat in the Temple teaching, day after day. You could have arrested me there, but you did not." Then he added, "This is all taking place so that the scripture and the writings of the prophets will be fulfilled."

And, as the soldiers bound his wrists, the disciples were overwhelmed with terror and fled into the night, deserting Jesus.

◄◊►

"Judas, are you betraying
the Son of Man with a kiss?"

◄◊►

*Judas betrays
Jesus with a kiss*

Peter's Denial

*O*n the Mount of Olives, before his arrest, Jesus had said to his disciples, "This very night, you will desert and betray me."

Peter looked at him in disbelief. "I will never leave you!" he protested.

"I tell you the truth," Jesus replied. "This very night, before the cock crows, you will disown me three times."

"Even if I have to die with you, I will never disown you!" Peter declared. The other disciples all said the same.

But now, Jesus had been arrested and

> "This very night, before the cock crows, you will disown me three times."

taken from the Garden of Gethsemane to the house of Caiaphas, the high priest, to be tried by the Sanhedrin, the powerful council of elders and chief priests. The other disciples had disappeared, fleeing into the night, and it was Peter, alone, who followed Jesus. He kept a safe distance and watched as Jesus was taken inside. He went into the courtyard and sat down with the guards around the fire to warm his hands, waiting to see what would happen.

The night was dark, but the flames leaped and jumped in the air, lighting up their faces. A young servant girl came up behind Peter and peered at him. "You were with Jesus of Nazareth, weren't you?" she said.

"I don't know what you are talking about," replied Peter nervously, glancing at the guards around the fire. He got up quickly and went toward the gate of the courtyard. Another girl came up, pointing at him. "This fellow was with Jesus of Nazareth," she said to the people with her.

Again, Peter denied it. "No, I swear I do not know that man!" he cried.

After a while, another man who had been watching came up and said, "But surely, you must be one of the disciples? I can tell from your accent. You are from Galilee."

Enraged, Peter swore, for the third time, that he did not know Jesus.

Immediately, he heard an unearthly cry piercing the night air. It was a cock crowing. And, as if a dagger had been plunged deep into his heart, Peter remembered Jesus's words— "Before the cock crows, you will disown me three times." He staggered out of the courtyard into the night, far from the high priest's house, weeping silently.

Peter weeps when he remembers Jesus's words

Roman Judea

In 6 CE, Judea became a Roman province, under the direct rule of a governor. Its most famous governor was Pontius Pilate, who crucified Jesus. The Gospels present a sympathetic portrait of Pilate, who is reluctant to condemn Christ. Yet Jewish writers of the time describe him as a harsh and cruel man, insensitive to their religious beliefs.

Crucifixion

In Roman Judea, crucifixion was a common punishment used for rebels and criminals. In 1968, archeologists found a crucifixion victim's heelbone with a nail still driven through it. Death by crucifixion took a long time, and was agonizing.

Prefect Pilate

Pilate spent most of his time in his headquarters, on the coast at Caesarea. In 1961, archeologists found an inscription set up by Pilate in Caesarea. The second line gives his name, "Pontius Pilatus," and his title, "prefect," which means officer.

Standards

Pilate offended Jews by bringing standards with portraits of the emperor into Jerusalem, breaking the Jewish ban on images. A crowd of protestors lay on the ground outside his house, refusing to move for five days. Pilate backed down.

TIMELINE

4 BCE
On the death of Herod the Great, Emperor Augustus divides his kingdom among three of his sons: Herod Antipas, Philip, and Archelaus, who receives Judea.

6 CE
Following Jewish complaints against Archelaus's misrule, Augustus banishes him to Gaul (France). He appoints Coponius as the first Roman governor.

9 CE
Coponius appoints Caiaphas as high priest.

10–26 CE
Judea is ruled by three governors: Marcus Ambivulus (10–13 CE), Annius Rufus (13–15 CE), and Valerius Gratus (15–26 CE)

14 CE
Augustus dies and is succeeded by Tiberius as emperor.

26 CE
Tiberius appoints Pontius Pilate as governor of Judea.

c. 30 CE
Jesus is crucified by Pilate.

36 CE
Pilate's troops attack a Samaritan religious procession. The Samaritans complain to his superior, Vitellius, governor of Syria, who removes Pilate from office.

c. 36 CE
Vitellius deposes Caiaphas and appoints a new high priest, Jonathan, son of Annas.

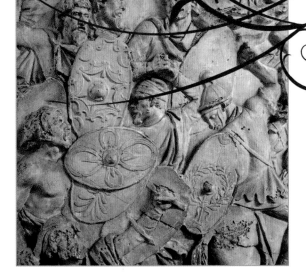

Auxiliaries

Pilate had a force of just 3,000 men to control Judea. The soldiers, called auxiliaries, were not Romans but locally recruited gentiles (non-Jews). Jews could not serve, for they refused to fight on the Sabbath. Auxiliaries (above) carried oval shields.

High priest

Like most Romans, Pilate found Jewish religion baffling. He left religious law cases to Caiaphas, the high priest. Caiaphas, shown here with Pilate, had been appointed by an earlier Roman governor. He was expected to be loyal to Rome.

Festival time

During great festivals, such as Passover, Jerusalem was crowded with pilgrims. To keep order, Pilate came up to the city from Caesarea with 500 soldiers. Here his troops stand guard on the walls, looking down on the pilgrims in the Temple courtyard.

Jesus Before the Sanhedrin

Jesus was brought before the Sanhedrin, the Jewish council made up of all the chief priests, elders, and teachers of the law.

The high priest, Caiaphas, presided over them all. A string of witnesses had been bribed to appear with trumped-up evidence against Jesus. One by one, they stepped forward and told their stories, and one by one they were dismissed.

Finally, two men came forward and said, "This fellow, Jesus, said that he could destroy the Temple of God and rebuild it single-handedly in three days."

"Are you, then, the Son of God?"

The high priest looked at Jesus. "Are you not going to answer? What is this testimony that these men are bringing against you?" he asked. Jesus said nothing.

"I charge you, under oath by the living God, to tell us if you are Christ, the Son of God," the high priest ordered.

"If I tell you, you will not believe me," Jesus replied.

"Are you, then, the Son of God?" asked the men who made up the Sanhedrin.

"You are right in saying I am," Jesus answered.

"What blasphemy!" said the high priest, tearing at his clothes. "Why do we need any more testimony or witnesses? We have heard it from his own lips!" And he turned to the assembled Sanhedrin. "What do you think?"

"He should be put to death!" replied the holy men. They surrounded Jesus, spitting at him and slapping him.

When Judas heard what had happened, he was overwhelmed with remorse. He went to the Temple and tried to give back the thirty silver coins that he had accepted in return for betraying Jesus. "I have sinned," he said bitterly. "I have betrayed innocent blood."

The high priest accuses Jesus of insulting God

Then Judas flung the coins down on the Temple floor and went away and hanged himself. The holy men picked up the money from the floor and counted it. They decided that they would use it to buy a field that belonged to a potter, which they would use as a burial place for foreigners. It became known as the Field of Blood.

Jesus Before Pilate

*V*ery early the next morning, the Sanhedrin had reached a unanimous verdict—Jesus should be put to death.

They bound his hands and took him to appear before Pontius Pilate, the Roman governor of Judea. The chief priests and the elders began to accuse him again, in front of Pilate. Jesus stood in front of them, saying nothing. "They are accusing you of so many terrible things. Why don't you reply?" asked Pilate from his judge's seat. But Jesus said nothing.

"Are you the king of the Jews?" he asked.

"Yes," replied Jesus. "It is as you say."

Pilate turned to the priests and elders and said, "I see no reason to charge this man." But the Sanhedrin would not give up. "He has incited people all over Judea with his teaching," they insisted. "Where will it end?" So Pilate agreed to punish Jesus and put him in prison.

Each year, at the Feast of Passover, the people were allowed to choose a prisoner who would be released from jail. Pilate went out and asked the crowd, "Which of the two do you want me to set free—Barabbas the murderer, or Jesus?"

But the chief priests and the elders had already told the crowd what to do and there was a great roar as the crowd shouted "Barabbas!"

> "They are accusing you of so many terrible things. Why don't you reply?"

"And what do you want me to do with Jesus?" Pilate asked.

"Crucify him!" they shouted.

Pilate called for a bowl of water and washed his hands in front of everyone. "I am innocent of this man's blood," he said. And, with that, he gave the order for Jesus to be flogged and crucified.

The soldiers took Jesus away, stripped and beat him. They put him in a robe and made a crown of thorns for his head. Then they made him hold a wooden staff and knelt down mockingly in front of him. "Hail, king of the Jews!" they jeered. When they had tired of their fun, they put his own clothes back on before taking him away to be crucified.

Jesus is brought before Pilate

Jesus is Crucified

The soldiers led Jesus away to be crucified outside Jerusalem. He was made to carry the wooden cross.

Jesus's followers gathered behind him. He stumbled on the stony path, and the soldiers beat him on. Then they seized a man named Simon from Cyrene and made him help Jesus carry the cross the rest of the way.

At last, they arrived at Golgotha, a rocky, skull-like hill. At nine o'clock in the morning, they crucified Jesus, nailing him to the cross and hoisting it high in the air. Above him, they put a mocking sign saying "This is Jesus, the king of the Jews." Two common criminals were crucified with him—one to the right and one to the left. And the soldiers had already begun to share out his clothes between them, drawing straws to see who would get what.

Looking down from his cross, Jesus said, "Father, forgive them, for they know not what they do."

Mary Magdalene, Mary the mother of the disciple James, and Jesus's mother sat not far away. The crowds had begun to gather and started to taunt Jesus. The chief priests and the elders and the teachers of the law also made fun of him. Even one of the criminals by his side joined in. But the other rebuked him, saying, "We are punished justly, but this man has done no wrong! Jesus, remember me when you are in heaven!"

Jesus replied, "I tell you the truth. Today you will be with me in paradise."

At noon, the sky suddenly darkened and night fell. It lasted for three long hours. Then, as the first rays of light appeared again, Jesus cried out in a loud voice, "My God, my God, why have you forsaken me?" Soon after, he took his last breath. At that exact moment, the curtain in the Temple in Jerusalem was torn in two from top to bottom. At the same time, the earth trembled and shook and rocks split in two.

The soldiers guarding Jesus looked up, terrified. "Surely, he was the Son of God!" they whispered to each other.

In the evening, a man named Joseph of Arimathea went to Pontius Pilate. He was an important member of the Jewish council, but also a follower of Jesus. He asked Pilate if he might be allowed to bury Jesus's body. Pilate agreed, and so Joseph went to Golgotha. With the help of a man named Nicodemus, Joseph took the body down from the cross. He anointed it with myrrh and aloes, as was the custom, and wrapped it in a clean linen cloth. Then Joseph and Nicodemus carried the body to a tomb that had been cut out of the rock. They rolled a big stone across the entrance to keep the body safe.

"Father, forgive them, for they know not what they do."

The Resurrection

It was the day after the Sabbath and, just as dawn was breaking, Mary Magdalene and her friend, who was also called Mary, went to the tomb where Jesus had been buried.

It was two days since he had died. The entrance had been sealed tightly with a huge stone, and Pontius Pilate had sent two soldiers to guard it around the clock. The chief priests and the Pharisees had warned him that the disciples might try to steal the body to make it look as though Jesus had risen from the dead. Pilate wanted to avoid this at all costs. They all remembered Jesus saying that he would rise again after three days.

"Go and tell my brothers to go to Galilee. There they will see me."

The two Marys were just approaching the tomb when the earth beneath them started to shake violently. At the same time, an angel of the Lord appeared, shining in glory. He went over to the tomb and slowly rolled away the great stone from the entrance. The women watched, amazed, and peered into the gloom. The tomb was empty. There was no sign of Jesus.

The angel sat on the stone, as dazzling as lightning, his clothes white as snow.

Outside Jesus's tomb, an angel appears and tells the women that Jesus has risen

Doubting Thomas

*A*s the disciples were talking in a house, Jesus suddenly appeared among them. *"Peace be with you!" he said.*

They looked at him in terror and did not know where he had come from. They thought that he was a ghost. "Why are you so worried?" Jesus asked. "Look at my hands and feet. Feel them. They are mine. Touch me and see— I am flesh and blood, like you. I am no ghost."

Tentatively, they went to him, looking him up and down with fearful eyes. They touched him quickly, their hands darting out uncertainly, to see if he was real. And then they smiled with relief at each other, knowing that it was Jesus standing there with them. He asked them if they had any food and they gave him a plate of grilled fish. He ate it while they all watched.

But one of the disciples, Thomas, who was known as Didymus, had not been with them at the time. Later, when they told him that they had seen Jesus, he did not believe them. "Unless I see the wounds in his hands and in his side with my own eyes and feel them with my own fingers, I will not believe it!" Thomas said.

A week later, all the disciples had gathered together, including Thomas. The doors of the house were closed and locked so that no one could get in. But, all at once, Jesus was standing there with them. "Peace be with you!" he said. And he turned to Thomas and said, "See my hands. Feel the holes where the nails went in. Look at my side. Feel the wounds. Stop doubting, Thomas, and believe."

> "Touch me and see— I am flesh and blood, like you. I am no ghost."

Thomas looks at Jesus's wounds

Cautiously, Thomas stretched out his hand and looked at Jesus's wounds. Then he drew back, ashen-faced and said, "My Lord, my God!"

Jesus replied, "Because you have seen me with your own eyes, you now believe. But blessed are those who have not seen but still believe!"

301

Breakfast by the Lake

O ne evening, some of the disciples were together by the Sea of Galilee when Peter decided that he wanted to go fishing. His companions said that they would like to go, too.

So they all got in the boat and set off, rowing far out to sea where the waters were usually teeming with fish. They cast their net over the side again and again, but each time they hauled it back up, it was empty. They fished all night, but caught nothing.

Early the next morning, just as dawn was breaking, they gave up and headed back to shore. As they approached, they saw a man standing there, watching them.

"Friends," he called to them, across the water. "Have you caught any fish?"

"No!" they shouted back. "Not one."

"Throw your net over the right-hand side of your boat and you will find some."

They did as he said, letting the net down from the boat into the water. Immediately, it swelled, full of fish. They tried to haul the net in, but it was so heavy that they could not lift it out of the water. The disciples were amazed.

The disciples cast their net and it fills with fish

Then John looked at the man standing on the shore again, and suddenly he recognized him. His face lit up with joy. "It is the Lord!" he said to Peter. At this, Peter jumped over the side of the boat and swam as fast he could through the water to Jesus, his robe billowing around him. The other disciples followed in the boat, towing the bulging net behind them.

"Peter, do you truly love me?"

When they had landed, they saw that a fire had been lit and a row of fish was grilling in the flames. Loaves of bread were laid out by the side.

"Bring some of the fish that you have caught," said Jesus. Peter dragged the huge net ashore. It was bursting with large fish—one hundred and fifty-three altogether—but the net was not torn or broken. "Come and have breakfast," said Jesus.

All the disciples had recognized him by now. It was the third time that he had appeared to them after he had been raised from the dead. He offered them the fish and the bread, and they all enjoyed the food together.

When they had eaten their fill, Jesus said, "Peter, do you truly love me?"

"Yes, Lord," replied Peter. "You know that I love you."

"Feed my lambs," said Jesus. And he asked again, "Peter, do you truly love me?"

"Yes, Lord," answered Peter again. "You know that I love you."

"Take care of my sheep," said Jesus. "Peter, do you truly love me?"

Peter was hurt because Jesus had repeated the same question three times. "Lord, you know all things. You know that I love you," he replied.

Again, Jesus said, "Feed my sheep." Then Jesus foretold how Peter would be martyred and crucified. "I tell you the truth. When you were younger you dressed yourself and went wherever you wanted. But when you are old, you will stretch out your hands and someone will dress you and lead you where you do not want to go." Then Jesus said to Peter, "Follow me."

Jesus is Taken Up to Heaven

Jesus told the eleven disciples to go to a mountain in Galilee. He met them there and they prayed with him.

Then he told them, "With my authority in heaven and on earth, go and spread the word. Make disciples of all nations, baptizing them in the name of the Father and of the Son and of the Holy Spirit. Teach them to obey everything I have commanded you. And surely, I am with you always and forever, to the very end of time."

For the last forty days, since he had risen from the dead, Jesus had appeared to the disciples, talking about the Kingdom of God. On one occasion, when he had been eating with them, he had told them, "Do not leave Jerusalem, but wait for the gift my Father promised, which you have heard me speak about. For John baptized with water, but in a few days, you will be baptized with the Holy Spirit."

> "This same Jesus, who has been taken from you into heaven, will come back in the same way you have just seen him disappear."

The disciples asked him, "Lord, are you then going to restore the kingdom to Israel?"

"It is not for you to know the times or the dates the Father has set. But you will receive power when the Holy Spirit comes on you. And you will be my witnesses in Jerusalem and in Judea and Samaria and to the ends of the earth."

As he finished speaking, he was taken up in the air in front of their eyes, and a cloud enveloped him, hiding him completely. The disciples were looking up into the sky when, suddenly, two men dressed in white appeared, standing beside them.

"Men of Galilee," they said. "Why do you stand there looking at the sky? This same Jesus, who has been taken from you into heaven, will come back in the same way you have just seen him disappear."

Then the disciples returned to Jerusalem. When they got there they went upstairs to the room where they were staying. They knelt down in prayer together with some women and Mary the mother of Jesus, and his brothers. And they knew that they must choose someone to replace Judas, the disciple who had betrayed Jesus. Two names were put forward—Joseph, known as Barsabbas, and Matthias.

They appealed to the Lord for help. "Lord, you know everyone's heart," they prayed. "Show us which of these two you have chosen to replace Judas." Then they drew straws and Matthias was chosen to become the twelfth disciple.

*The disciples look up in amazement
as Jesus is taken to heaven*

Tongues of Fire

*I*t was Pentecost and Jerusalem was crowded with people celebrating the Jewish harvest festival.

Jesus's disciples and the wider group of Jesus's followers met quietly in Jerusalem, encouraging each other and waiting for the fulfilment of Jesus's promise about the gift of the Holy Spirit. They did not have to wait for long.

On the day of Pentecost, the disciples were sitting together when suddenly, a violent wind howled through the house, whistling around every corner and rattling every door. Then, shining tongues of fire appeared from nowhere, darting brightly through the air. They hovered for a moment before coming silently down, one little flame settling over the head of each person like a flickering crown. It was the Holy Spirit, filling them all, as Jesus had promised. When they started talking to each other, they found that they were speaking many different languages from strange and exotic countries. And they could all understand every word.

When they went out into the streets to teach, the people listened to them in astonishment. "Aren't these men from Galilee? How are they able to speak so many languages? We can all understand them, no matter where we come from—Parthia, Egypt, Crete, Mesopotamia. It is incredible! We can all hear them spreading the word of God."

"God has made this Jesus, whom you crucified, both Lord and Christ."

Then Peter stood up and addressed the crowd, describing the miracles that Jesus had performed in God's name. "God raised Jesus to life and we are all witnesses of the fact. Exalted to the right hand of God, he has received from the Father, the Holy Spirit, and has poured out what you see and hear. Let all Israel be assured of this: God has made this Jesus, whom you crucified, both Lord and Christ."

Their hearts touched, the people asked, "Brothers, what shall we do?"

"Repent and be baptized, every one of you, in the name of Jesus Christ, for the forgiveness of your sins," said Peter. "And you will receive the gift of the Holy Spirit. This is a promise to you and your children and to all whom our Lord God will call. Save yourselves."

The crowds flocked to hear the disciples speak that day and at least three thousand people were baptized. They became devoted followers of Jesus.

Peter the Healer

*O*ne day, Peter and John were going to the Temple to pray. They went through the Court of the Gentiles and approached the magnificent gate called Beautiful.

As they drew near they saw a man, who had been crippled since birth, being carried there by his friends. This was where he sat, day after day, begging for alms. As soon as he saw the disciples, he asked them for some money.

"Look us in the eye," said Peter. The beggar fixed him with a sad gaze.

"Silver or gold I do not have," Peter continued. "But what I have, I will give you. In the name of Jesus Christ, walk!" And, taking him by the right hand, he gently helped him up. The beggar got to his feet, shook his legs, wriggled his toes, and took a few cautious steps.

Peter tells the crippled man to walk

Then he took a few more, his face lighting up with joy. Praising the Lord, he walked with Peter and John into the Temple itself to pray. People stopped to stare, hardly able to believe their eyes. When the prayers were over, Peter and John came out and made their way through the outer courtyard to Solomon's Colonnade. They started to teach, and the crowds thronged around them. The beggar who had been cured stood beside them for all to see.

"Why does this amaze you?" asked Peter. "Do not think that we made this man walk. We did nothing, but faith in the name of Jesus cured him. The God of Abraham, Isaac, and Jacob, the God of our fathers, has glorified his servant Jesus." And he went on, teaching and preaching to the people, telling them to repent their sins in the name of Jesus.

The priests, the Sadducees, and the Temple guard had all been watching and listening from the shadows. They were angry that the disciples were teaching

> "Do not think that we made this man walk. We did nothing, but faith in the name of Jesus cured him."

in the Temple and proclaiming that Jesus had risen from the dead. They seized Peter and John and put them in prison for the night. But, despite this, the people who had listened to them had been convinced by their teaching and wanted to be baptized. By now, there were more than five thousand followers of Jesus.

The next morning, Peter and John were brought before the Sanhedrin—the Jewish council. The chief priests, the elders, and the teachers of the law had all assembled, with the high priest presiding. "By whose authority were you teaching in the Temple?" they demanded.

Peter, filled with the Holy Spirit, replied, "Rulers and elders of the people. If we are being called to account for an act of kindness shown to a cripple and are asked how he was cured, know this: It is by the name of Jesus Christ of Nazareth, whom you crucified but whom God raised from the dead, that the man stands before you, healed."

The council listened and were astounded by the courage of Peter and John. They were surprised that the disciples were ordinary, uneducated men and took note that these were the kinds of men who had been Jesus's companions. They were not sure what to do and ordered them to leave for a few moments.

"Everybody knows that they have performed a miracle and we certainly cannot deny it. But we must stop word spreading," they said to each other. They called Peter and John back in and ordered them to stop teaching in the name of Jesus.

"Judge for yourselves whether it is right in God's sight to obey you rather than God. For we cannot help speaking about what we have seen and heard," Peter replied. The Sanhedrin did not think it would be safe to punish them, seeing as so many people had seen the miracle. So they cautioned Peter and John, and let them go.

Crowds watch the miracle of the crippled man walking for the first time

The Death of Stephen

One of the early leaders in the Church was Stephen. He performed so many miracles and spoke with such wisdom and strength that people flocked to his side.

Some of the priests and elders in the Temple were worried and threatened by the size of Stephen's following. They wanted to find a way of stopping him spreading the word of Jesus.

So, they had him brought before the Sanhedrin, and witnesses were summoned to give false evidence against him. "We have heard him say that Jesus of Nazareth will destroy the Temple and change the laws that Moses handed down to us," they lied.

As the charges were brought against him, Stephen stood quietly in front of the council. The assembled priests, elders, and teachers of the law were consumed with rage at the sight of him. When the witnesses had finished, the high priest got up. "Are these charges true?" he asked.

Stephen replied, reminding the Sanhedrin that true worship did not depend on ritual or the trappings of the Temple. And he quoted the prophet Isaiah: "Heaven is my throne, and the earth is my footstool. What kind of house will you build for me? says the Lord. Or where will my resting place be? Has not my hand made all these things?"

> "Lord, do not hold this sin against them!"

Stephen tried to explain that Jesus was the Savior, promised by prophets through the generations, all the way back to Abraham. Finally, Stephen attacked the Sanhedrin's narrow-mindedness. "You stiff-necked people, you are just like your fathers," he said. "You always resist the Holy Spirit. Was there ever a prophet your fathers did not persecute? They even killed those who predicted the coming of the Righteous One. And now you have betrayed and murdered him."

The council listened and their faces darkened. They ground their teeth in fury, appalled that he dared to speak to them like this. But Stephen carried on calmly, "Look, I can see heaven opening and the Son of Man standing at the right hand of God." At this, the holy men were furious. They rushed toward him, seized him, and dragged him out of the court. He put up no resistance. They took him out of the city, through the Lions' Gate, to be stoned to death. The witnesses who had accused Stephen left their cloaks with a young man named Saul, and then they threw the first stones.

Stephen is stoned to death

Stephen prayed as the rocks and stones rained down on him, "Lord Jesus, receive my spirit." He fell to his knees, bleeding, and cried out, "Lord, do not hold this sin against them!"

Then, Stephen collapsed on the ground and died. His persecutors left him there, but later, his followers came to get him and bury him with all due ceremony. Stephen was the first Christian martyr, and they mourned him deeply. After Stephen's death, there was a persecution of all the Christians in Jerusalem. For their own safety, many of them had to flee far away to other countries.

Saul's Journey to Damascus

*S*aul *was a strict Pharisee, who observed all the Jewish laws and customs. He persecuted Jesus's disciples and their followers zealously, and was one of the great enemies of the early Church.*

One day, he went to the high priest in Jerusalem asking for letters to the synagogues in Damascus, giving him authority to arrest any Christians he found there and bring them back to Jerusalem. He set off on the long journey with his companions. As they were drawing near to Damascus, a blinding light suddenly streaked down from the heavens. Saul fell to the ground in terror, hiding his face, and he heard a loud voice, saying, "Saul, Saul, why do you persecute me?"

"Who are you, Lord?" asked Saul, fearfully.

"I am Jesus, whom you are persecuting," the voice replied. "Now get up and go into the city and you will be told what you must do." Saul's companions stood, speechless and rooted to the spot. They had heard the voice, but had not seen the light.

Slowly, Saul lifted his head and opened his eyes to look around. But he could see nothing. He was totally blind. His companions helped him up, amazed and astonished by what had happened, and together they slowly made their way along the road to Damascus. For three long days Saul stayed in the city, blind and unable to eat or drink.

> "This man is my chosen instrument to spread my word to the gentiles and their kings—and to the people of Israel."

There was a man named Ananias, who lived in Damascus and was a follower of Jesus. One day, the Lord appeared to him in a vision and said, "Ananias! You must go to the house in Straight Street and ask for a man named Saul. Lay your hands on him and restore his sight."

"Lord," answered Ananias, "I have heard so much about this man and all the terrible harm he has done to your followers in Jerusalem. He has come here to Damascus with authority from the chief priests to arrest your people."

"Go!" said the Lord. "This man is my chosen instrument to spread my word to the gentiles and their kings—and to the people of Israel. I will show him how much he must suffer for my name."

Ananias did as the Lord had commanded. He found Saul and laid his hands on him and said, "Brother Saul, the Lord—Jesus who appeared to you on the road as you were coming here—has sent me so that you may see again and be filled with the Holy Spirit." Saul opened his eyes and his sight was restored. After three days, he could see properly again. He looked around, seeing the world with fresh eyes. Then, weak with hunger, he asked for some food to regain his strength.

For the next few days, Saul stayed with Jesus's followers and preached the word with them. He went into the synagogues to teach, telling the Jews that Jesus was the Son of God. Everyone was astonished. But, day after day, Saul preached the word of Jesus and more and more people came to hear him.

Some of the Jewish people thought that he was becoming a threat, however, and plotted to kill him. But Saul heard of the plan and, with the help of some of his followers, was lowered over the city walls in a basket and escaped.

At first, when he got back to Jerusalem, the disciples were afraid and could not believe the change in him. They did not trust him. But one of them, called Barnabas, explained that Saul had seen and heard the Lord on the road to Damascus. He also told them that Saul had preached fearlessly in the name of Jesus. When they heard this, the disciples welcomed Saul into their fold and told him to stay with them.

On the way to Damascus, Saul is blinded by a white light

The Christians

Soon after Jesus's crucifixion, his followers in Jerusalem preached that he had risen from the dead and was the Messiah foretold in the scriptures. The first Christians were Jews, who did not see themselves as followers of a new religion. As time passed there was a growing conflict between the followers of Jesus and other Jews. Christianity was then given a new start by Paul, who preached the faith to gentiles (non-Jews).

Stephen

This medieval illustration shows the death of Stephen, the first believer to die for his faith. In about 34 CE, he was stoned to death in Jerusalem by the Sanhedrin (Jewish authorities). The Sanhedrin wanted to stamp out the new movement.

Paul

Paul, a Jew from Tarsus (in present-day Turkey), had a dramatic conversion to Christianity when he felt that Christ appeared to him in a vision. Paul believed that he had been chosen to be the "apostle (teacher) to the gentiles."

Paul's letters

Paul spread the faith by preaching, founding new churches across the eastern Mediterranean. When he could not appear in person, he sent letters to his churches. These are the oldest writings in the New Testament.

This map shows the rapid spread of Christian churches across the eastern Mediterranean. This was the work of Paul and other missionaries influenced by him.

Gospel of Thomas
Early Christians had many gospels alongside the four later included in the Bible. The Gospel of Thomas, named after Jesus's disciple (above), taught that believers would be saved through self-knowledge, for "the Kingdom of God is inside you."

Mithras
Christianity was one of several eastern religions spreading around the Roman Empire at the same time. Unlike traditional Roman gods, new gods, such as Mithras, promised believers a glorious afterlife. This is a Mithraeum, a sanctuary for Mithras worship.

Christ as a fish
Christians decorated their homes and places of worship with religious symbols, such as the fish in this mosaic. The letters of the Greek word *icthys* (fish) stood for "Jesus Christ, God's Son, Savior" in Greek. The anchor recalls Christ's cross.

TIMELINE

c. 30 CE
Crucifixion of Jesus Christ. His followers in Jerusalem found the first church, headed by James the Just, the brother of Christ.

c. 34 CE
The Sanhedrin orders the stoning of Stephen, beginning a wider persecution of the Jerusalem Church.

c. 47–60 CE
Paul makes three missionary journeys, establishing churches among the gentiles.

c. 50 CE
Church leaders, including Paul, Peter, and James the Just, hold their first council in Jerusalem. They agree that gentile converts do not have to be circumcised or follow most Jewish laws.

64 CE
Following a great fire in Rome, Emperor Nero blames the Christians. Peter and Paul are both executed in the persecution.

66–73 CE
The Jews rebel against Rome. The Romans crush the rebellion, destroying the Jerusalem Temple in 70 CE.

c. 70 CE
Mark's gospel is written.

c. 85–100 CE
Matthew and Luke's gospels and the Acts of the Apostles are written.

c. 100 CE
John's gospel is written.

Peter and Cornelius

*C*ornelius lived in Caesarea. He was a centurion with the Italian regiment and, like the rest of his family, was God-fearing and devout, praying regularly and giving to the poor. He was a gentile.

One day, at about three o'clock in the afternoon, he had a vision. An angel appeared to him saying, "Cornelius!"

"What is it, Lord?" he asked fearfully.

"You must send some of your men to Joppa to get Peter. He is staying with Simon, the tanner, who has a house by the sea," replied the angel. Cornelius summoned two of his servants, as well as one of his most trusted soldiers. He told them to go to Joppa to get Peter immediately.

At about noon the next day, Peter went up on the roof to pray. He was hungry, and while the meal was being prepared for him, he fell into a trance. He saw heaven opening above him and something that looked like a large sheet being lowered to earth by its four corners. Inside, were all kinds of animals and reptiles and birds. Then a voice told him, "Get up, Peter! Kill and eat!"

"Surely not?" he said, knowing that Jews were forbidden from eating such creatures. "I have never eaten anything impure or unclean."

"Do not call anything impure that God has made clean," the voice answered. This happened three times and then the sheet was taken back up to heaven. Peter sat there puzzling about what it all meant. Meanwhile, the men who had been sent by Cornelius had found the house and stopped by the gate to ask for Peter. The Holy Spirit told Peter that three men were looking for him. "Get up and go downstairs. Go with them for I have sent them," it said.

So, the next day, Peter and some of his companions set off with the men to Caesarea. Cornelius was waiting for him and, as Peter came into the house, Cornelius fell at his feet.

Cornelius falls down on his knees before Peter

Peter looked down at him, smiling, and made him get up again. "Stand up," he said. "I am only a man myself." He went on inside the house and was surprised to find a large gathering of people there. "You know it is really against our law for a Jew to associate with gentiles," he said. "But God has shown me that I should not call any man impure or unclean. So when I was sent for, I came without any objection. May I ask why you sent for me?"

Cornelius told him about his vision a few days earlier. "So I sent for you immediately and it was good of you to come," he said politely. "Now we are all here in the presence of God to listen to everything the Lord has commanded you to tell us."

> "God has shown me that I should not call any man impure or unclean."

Peter began to speak. "I now know that God does not have any favorites but accepts anyone, from any nation, who fears him and does what is right." And he went on to tell them about Jesus's ministry in Galilee and Judea and the miracles that he had performed in God's name. The crowd listened, hanging on his every word. They were filled with the Holy Spirit and began to praise God, much to the amazement of Peter's companions. But Peter reproached them, saying, "Can anyone keep these people from being baptized? They have received the Holy Spirit, just as we have."

After this, Peter left to go back to Jerusalem, where the other disciples and followers of Christ criticized him for mixing with gentiles. In reply, Peter told them about his vision and described how the Holy Spirit had come down on Cornelius and his friends and family. "So, if God gave them the same gift as he gave us, who was I to think that I could oppose God?"

When they heard this, the disciples had no more objections and praised God, saying, "So then, He has even allowed the gentiles to be saved."

Peter in Prison

King Herod Agrippa was the grandson of Herod the Great. He had recently been made king of Judea by his friend, Emperor Claudius.

Herod persecuted the Christians relentlessly and had James, the brother of John, put to death. Then, during the Feast of Passover, Peter was arrested and thrown into prison. He was closely guarded, day and night, by four different teams of soldiers. Herod was planning to bring him out to stand trial once Passover was over. The other disciples and followers of Christ prayed constantly for Peter.

The night before he was due to stand trial, Peter was sleeping in his cell between two soldiers, his wrists bound in chains. Sentries stood guard at the door. Suddenly, an angel of the Lord appeared and a bright light filled the cell. The angel touched Peter gently on his side. Peter woke up with a start and could not believe his eyes.

"Quick! Get up!" said the angel urgently, and the chains fell off Peter's wrist. Then the angel continued, telling him what to do. "Put on your clothes and your sandals. Wrap your cloak around you and follow me."

An angel comes to rescue Peter from prison

318

Peter looked at him uncertainly and followed him out of the cell, as if he were in a dream. They passed one group of guards and then another, and came to the great iron gate that led out of the prison and into the city. It opened obediently for them, swinging back on its hinges of its own accord.

> "Now I know, without a doubt, that the Lord sent his angel and rescued me from Herod's clutches."

Silently, Peter and the angel swept through it, out into the night air. They walked together down the deserted street right to the very end, and then the angel disappeared into thin air. Peter pinched himself and realized what had happened. "Now I know, without a doubt, that the Lord sent his angel and rescued me from Herod's clutches," he said. "He also saved me from my fate at the hands of the Jewish people."

Peter went straight to the house of Mary, the mother of Mark, where people had gathered to pray. He knocked at the door and a servant girl, named Rhoda, came to answer it. But when she recognized Peter's voice, she was so overjoyed that she forgot to open the door and rushed back, crying, "Peter is at the door!"

"You are out of your mind!" they all said, knowing that Peter was in prison. But when she insisted that it was Peter at the door, they laughed at her, saying, "It must be his ghost!"

All the time, Peter kept knocking at the door and finally, when Mary and all her friends opened it, they were astonished. Peter gestured with his hand for them to be quiet and then told them exactly how the Lord had rescued him.

In the morning, when the soldiers discovered that Peter had escaped, there was pandemonium. They searched the prison from top to bottom, but there was no sign of him. When he heard the news, Herod was furious and cross-examined all the guards. He then gave orders that they should be executed.

The Adventures of Paul

Saul was a Roman citizen and was now known by his Roman name, Paul. He was worshipping at the church in Antioch with Barnabas when the Holy Spirit told them that they had been chosen to spread the word of Jesus further afield.

So, sixteen years after the crucifixion, Paul set off on his first mission to convert people of all beliefs—both Jews and non-Jews—to Christianity. Over the next twenty years, he would make three long missionary journeys around the Mediterranean and Middle East and into Europe. He followed the main trade routes, going from city to city, by sea or road.

On this first journey with Barnabas, Paul traveled first to Cyprus in the Mediterranean. They landed in the capital, Salamis, and preached in the synagogue there before going all over the island, teaching and talking to the people. Then they crossed the sea to Perga in Asia Minor and traveled on inland to Antioch in Pisidia.

> "We are bringing you good news, telling you to turn from these worthless things to the living God"

On the Sabbath, they were preaching in the synagogue there, and Paul was telling the Jews about Jesus's death and resurrection. He explained that the only way to God was through Christ. They were invited back to speak again the next week and a huge crowd gathered to hear them. Seeing that they were attracting such an enormous following of different people, some Jews felt jealous and threatened. They started to attack the two disciples.

"We had to speak the word of God to you first," said Paul and Barnabas. "But since you reject it and do not consider yourselves worthy of eternal life, we now turn to the gentiles." And they told them what the Lord had said: "I have made you a light for the gentiles, that you may bring salvation to the ends of the earth." And, despite the opposition, Paul and Barnabas continued to spread the word of Jesus. But their Jewish opponents were determined to get rid of them and, with backing from the most prominent people in Antioch, managed to get them expelled from the city.

The disciples carried on with their travels. They went to Lystra, a city in the remote Roman province of Galatia. One day, as Paul was preaching, he saw a crippled man in the crowd. His legs were bent helplessly beneath him and he was sitting on the ground. He was listening to every word.

Paul looked at him and could see that he had the faith to be healed. He called to him, "Stand up on your feet!" At once, the man jumped up and began to walk, a look of amazement on his face.

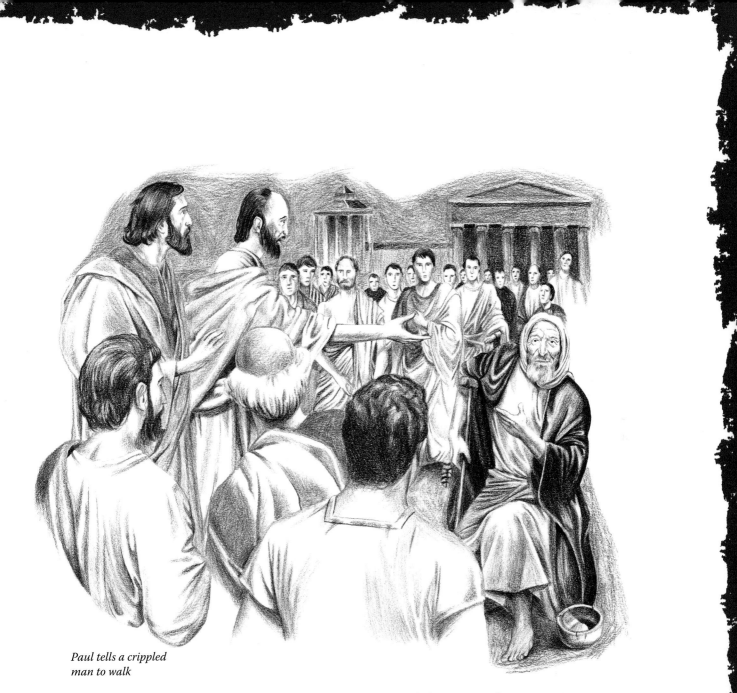

*Paul tells a crippled
man to walk*

The crowd watched, astonished by the miracle. "The gods have come down to us in human form!" they cried joyfully—and they insisted that Barnabas was Zeus and that Paul was Hermes. The priest at Zeus's temple, just outside the city, brought a bull to be sacrificed and wreaths to honor them. Paul and Barnabas were horrified. "What are you doing?" they asked. "We are only human like you. We are bringing you good news, telling you to turn from these worthless things to the living God, who made heaven and earth and sea and everything in them."

Some Jews, who had followed them from Antioch, had joined the crowd and started to stir up trouble. In a flash, the mood changed and the mob started to hurl stones at the disciples. They drove them out of the city and left them, for dead, outside the walls. The disciples had been badly injured, but were still breathing. Their followers went to them and took care of them, taking them back into Lystra.

On Paul's next journey, a few years later, his companion was Silas. They traveled through Syria and Cilicia, and across Asia Minor to Macedonia. When they arrived in Philippi, they went down to the river to find a place to pray, and to speak to the women who were gathered there. One of them was called Lydia. She was a wealthy Roman business woman, and was a believer. She and all her household were baptized, and she invited Paul and his companions to stay with her.

One day, as they went down to the river to pray, Paul and Silas met a slave girl, who could predict the future. She made a lot of money for her owners by telling fortunes. She followed Paul wherever he went, screaming like a mad woman. At last, at the end of his tether, Paul turned around and said to the spirit who was possessing her, "In the name of Jesus Christ, I command you to come out of her!" Immediately, the spirit left and the girl stood by his side, wondering what had happened. But, when her owners discovered that their slave girl had lost her magic powers, they were furious and dragged Paul and Silas off to appear before the magistrates. Paul and Silas were thrown into prison, and, after a flogging, they were put under close guard in an inner cell.

At about midnight, Paul and Silas were praying and singing hymns to God. The other prisoners were listening to them. Suddenly, there was a violent earthquake and the foundations of the prison shook. At the same time, the doors to the cells opened and all the chains binding the prisoners fell to the floor. The jailer awoke with a start and saw, to his horror, the doors swinging back and forth. He assumed that all the prisoners had escaped and drew his sword, ready to kill himself. But he heard Paul, saying, "Don't harm yourself! We are all here!" Calling for the lights, the jailer rushed into the cell and fell at Paul's feet, trembling. "What must I do to be saved?" he asked.

"Just believe in the Lord," answered Paul. The jailer washed the men's wounds and dressed them. He took them to his house and gave them food to eat. Then he and his family were baptized, and they were filled with joy because they had found God. The next morning, the magistrates gave the order for Paul and Silas to be released.

On his third missionary journey, Paul spent a long time in Ephesus—a wealthy seaport and trading center in the Roman province of Asia. A craftsman named Demetrius worked there, producing silver shrines to the goddess Artemis. He had always done very well for himself, but now, when he saw how many people were being converted by Paul, he was worried. He called all his fellow craftsmen together to discuss the problem. Soon an angry mob had gathered and they seized two of Paul's companions. Paul, himself, wanted to talk to the crowd, but his disciples stopped him, worried for his safety. Eventually, the city clerk arrived and managed to quieten things down. Soon afterward, Paul left Ephesus and set off for Macedonia.

In the city of Troas, Paul and his followers gathered in a room on the third floor of a house. Paul talked to them long into the night. One young man named Eutychus was sitting on a window sill, listening. His eyes began to grow heavy and he fell fast asleep. His body leaned toward the open window. Finally, he fell through it.

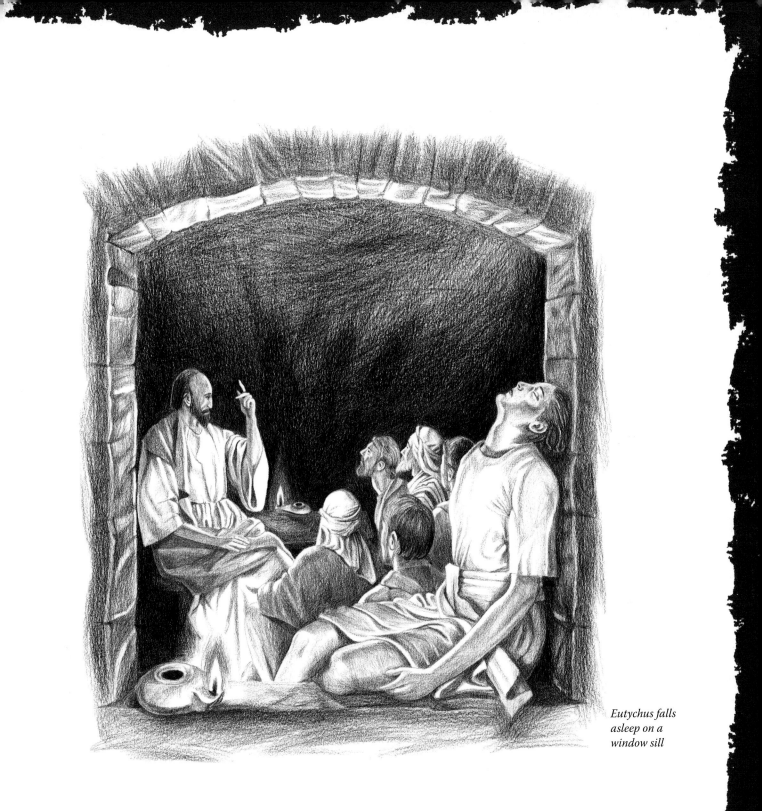

Eutychus falls asleep on a window sill

His friends rushed down and picked up his lifeless body. Paul joined them and put his arms around Eutychus. "Don't be alarmed," he said. "He is alive!" Immediately, Eutychus started breathing again. His friends looked at each other in astonishment and then took him home.

Paul is Arrested

A long with his companions, Paul arrived in Caesarea and stayed with a disciple named Philip. Days later, a prophet named Agabus arrived from Judea.

Agabus took Paul's belt from him and tied his own hands and feet with it saying, "The Holy Spirit says that this is the way you will be treated by the Jews in Jerusalem. They will hand you over to the Romans."

When they heard this, Paul's followers begged him not to go back to Jerusalem. But he said, "Why are you weeping? I am ready not only to be bound, but also to die in Jerusalem for the name of the Lord Jesus."

> "I am ready not only to be bound, but also to die in Jerusalem for the name of the Lord Jesus."

When Paul got to Jerusalem he went to the Temple, where a group of Jews accosted him, shouting, "This is the man who teaches people to turn against us and our Temple! He has even brought Greeks into the Temple, where foreigners should never go! He has defiled this holy place!"

More people came running to join them, from all parts of the city, and soon there was an angry mob, baying for Paul's blood. They seized him and dragged him out of the Temple. When news of the disturbance reached Claudius Lysias, the commander of the Roman troops in Jerusalem, he rushed down with his soldiers. As they approached, the rioters stopped beating Paul and a hush descended on the crowd.

The crowd react angrily to Paul

Claudius Lysias arrested Paul. Then he tried to find out what he had done, but the crowd started shouting. The commander could not make sense of it at all. He ordered that Paul should be taken and imprisoned in Fort Antonia, where the Roman troops were garrisoned. As the soldiers led him away, the crowd followed, chanting, "Away with him!" Paul had to be carried by the soldiers for his own safety.

Before he went into the fort, Paul asked to address the people. The commander agreed, so Paul stood on the steps, protected by the guards, and spoke in Aramaic. "I am a Jew, born in Tarsus in Cilicia, but brought up here in Jerusalem. I was trained in the law of our fathers and was just as zealous as any of you. I persecuted many Christians here in Jerusalem and was about to do the same in Damascus. But on the way there, I saw a brilliant light and I heard the voice of Jesus, and then I was baptized. From that moment on, I have spread the word to Jews and gentiles alike."

The angry crowd listened, then started shouting, "Rid the earth of him! He's not fit to live!" The commander told the soldiers to take Paul to prison to be flogged. As they prepared him, Paul said to the soldiers, "Are you sure that it is legal for you to flog a Roman citizen who hasn't even been found guilty?" Claudius Lysias was filled with alarm because he knew that he had no right to treat a Roman citizen like this. He agreed to release him, but insisted that Paul was brought before the Sanhedrin.

Paul stood before the council of elders, priests, and teachers of the law, and said, "My brothers, I have fulfilled my duty to God in all good conscience this day." The high priest's face darkened with fury. He ordered his men to hit Paul in the mouth.

"God will strike you!" said Paul, still reeling from the blow. "You sit there to judge me according to the law, yet you yourself violate the law by commanding that I be struck." At this, there was uproar in the Sanhedrin as the Pharisees and the Sadducees started quarreling among themselves. It became so violent that Claudius Lysias ordered his men to take Paul back to the fortress.

There, the Lord appeared to Paul and said, "Take courage! As you have testified about me in Jerusalem, so you must also testify in Rome."

Meanwhile, more than forty Jews had gathered together to hatch a plot to kill Paul. They swore an oath not to eat or drink anything until he was dead. They asked the chief priests and the elders to persuade the commander to bring Paul out again to appear before the council. They would be waiting to ambush him and take him away to be killed. But Paul's nephew heard about the conspiracy and went to the prison to warn him. Paul asked him to tell the commander, which the young man duly did. Claudius Lysias listened, and then made arrangements for Paul to be taken to Caesarea so that the Roman governor there could hear his case. That very night, Paul was escorted out of Jerusalem, flanked by an armed guard of two hundred soldiers, seventy horsemen, and two hundred spearmen.

THE THEATER OF EPHESUS
Around 57 CE, Paul's preaching led to a riot in the theater of Ephesus, in what is now Turkey. Seeing Christianity as a threat to Artemis, their mother goddess, the people shouted, "Great is Artemis of the Ephesians!"

Soon the whole city was in an uproar. The people seized Gaius and Aristarchus, Paul's traveling companions from Macedonia, and rushed as one man into the theater. Paul wanted to appear before the crowd, but the disciples would not let him. Even some of the officials of the province, friends of Paul, sent him a message begging him not to venture into the theater.

Acts 19:29–31

Paul's Journey to Rome

At last, after so many accusations had been made against him, Paul set off to stand trial before Caesar in Rome.

He was handed over to a centurion named Julius, and together they boarded a ship for Italy. They sailed along the island of Crete, making slow progress. Conditions grew worse, and the waves grew bigger and bigger. Paul warned the sailors, "Men, I can see that our voyage is going to be disastrous and will bring great loss to ship and cargo." But no one would listen and they sailed on.

The winds grew stronger and the waves towered above them, threatening to smash the ship to pieces. Even the sailors were terrified now and began to throw the cargo overboard. The storm raged on for days, the sun and the stars disappeared, and everyone gave up hope.

Paul stood up, as the waves crashed over the deck, and said to them all, "You should have taken my advice. But keep up your courage because not one of you will be lost. Only the ship will be destroyed. Last night an angel of the Lord stood beside me and told me that I would stand trial before Caesar and that God will protect us."

The ship in which Paul sets sail for Rome is caught in a violent storm

For two long weeks, the ship was driven across the Adriatic Sea from Crete. At last, to their great joy, the sailors saw a bay with a sandy beach and headed for it as fast as they could. But, as they approached, the ship ran aground and began to break up, pounded by the waves. The centurion ordered everybody to jump overboard and to swim for shore or to float in on planks of wood. Against the odds, they all reached land safely.

> "You should have taken my advice. But keep up your courage because not one of you will be lost."

They discovered that they had arrived on the island of Malta, where the people gave them a warm welcome. They lit a big fire and Paul helped them gather brushwood. But, as he put it on the flames, a viper slithered out and wound itself tightly around his fingers. When the islanders saw the poisonous snake hanging from his hand, they looked at each other and said, "This man must be a villain. He has escaped from the sea, but justice has caught up with him now." But Paul just shook the snake from his hand and into the fire, where it sizzled and shrank to nothing. Paul was completely unharmed. The people watched in amazement and changed their opinion about him. Now they thought that he must be a god.

Publius, the chief official of Malta, welcomed Paul and his companions to his house and for three days, he entertained them. Paul found out that Publius's father lay dangerously ill in bed and so he went to see him. Paul prayed and laid his hands on him and healed him. When word of the miracle got around the island, people flocked to Paul to be cured.

After three months in Malta, it was time to set off on the last leg of the journey to Rome. Once they had arrived there, Paul was allowed to live in a house on his own, with a soldier to guard him. He called together all the leaders of the Jews and talked to them about his arrest and why he had come to Rome to appear before Caesar. He stayed in the house, under guard, for two years and welcomed all those who came to see him, preaching the Kingdom of God and teaching about the Lord Jesus Christ.

Paul's Letters

DuYou uring his missionary journeys, teaching the word of Jesus, Paul helped to establish churches around the Mediterranean countries. He kept in touch by writing letters.

The letters were taken, over land and sea, by envoys to be read at church. Even his opponents admitted that the letters were "weighty and strong." Thirteen letters in the Bible bear Paul's name. Most were for Christian communities.

The earliest letter was probably to the Galatians and was written in about 49 CE, after his first missionary journey. The letters to the Thessalonians were written from Corinth on his second journey. Two letters to the Corinthians and one to the Romans followed on his last missionary journey. In 61 CE, he was in prison for two years. During this time he wrote to the Colossians, Philemon, the Ephesians, and the Philippians. His final letter, the second one he wrote to Timothy, was probably written in Rome when he was imprisoned again and was awaiting execution.

Some letters dealt with problems, such as in 1 Corinthians, when Paul warns members of the newly established Church about the dangers of division. He compared the Church to a human body. "The body is a unit, though it has many parts. So it is with Christ. We are all baptized by one spirit into one body and we were all given the one Spirit to drink. Now, the body is not made up of one part, but of many. If the ear should say, 'Because I am not an eye, I do not belong to the body,' it would not, for that reason, cease to be part of the body. If the whole body were an eye, where would the sense of hearing be? If the whole body were an ear, where would the sense of smell be? In fact, God has arranged the parts in the body just as he wanted them to be."

"We are all baptized by one spirit into one body"

Paul also wrote to the Corinthians about Love. "If I speak in the tongues of men and of angels but have not love, I am only a resounding gong or a clanging cymbal. If I have the gift of prophecy and can fathom all mysteries and all knowledge, and if I have a faith that can move mountains but have not love, I am nothing."

Then he described love in words, "Love is patient, love is kind. It does not envy, it does not boast, it is not proud. It is not rude, it is not self-seeking, it is not easily angered, it keeps no record of wrongs. Love does not delight in evil but rejoices in truth. It always protects, always trusts, always hopes, always perseveres. When I was a child, I talked like a child, I thought like a child, I reasoned like a child. When I became a man, I put childish things behind me. Now these three remain: faith, hope, and love. But the greatest of these is love."

Paul wanted to establish relations with the Church in Rome, and use it to spread the word of Jesus. In a letter to the Romans, he writes this important passage: "For I am convinced that neither death nor life, neither angels nor demons, neither the present nor the future, nor any powers, neither height nor depth, nor anything in all creation, will be able to separate us from the love of God that is in Jesus Christ our Lord."

While under arrest, Paul dictates his letters

The Jewish Revolt

The 1st century CE saw a growing Jewish resistance movement against Rome. In 66 CE, after years of Roman misrule, the Jews finally broke out in open rebellion. They seized control of Jerusalem and Herod's fortified palaces, and defeated a Roman army sent from Syria. Yet, despite their early successes, the rebels could not defeat the mighty Roman Empire.

Freedom coin
After the rebellion, the Jewish leaders issued coins celebrating their new freedom. This coin has a wine jar, with the Hebrew inscription "Year Two" of the rising (67–68 CE). The reverse proclaims the freedom of Israel.

Vespasian
Emperor Nero sent Vespasian, an experienced general, to crush the rebellion. In 67 CE, Vespasian arrived in Judea with an army of 80,000 men. By 69 CE, he had conquered all of Judea except for Jerusalem and three fortresses.

TIMELINE

64 CE
Gessius Florus made Roman procurator (governor) of Judea

66 CE
Florus causes outrage in Jerusalem by taking money from the Temple treasury. Rioting breaks out, and Florus withdraws to Caesarea with most of his troops. Zealots seize Masada and massacre the Roman garrison. Cestius Gallus, governor of Syria, leads his army into Judea, but is defeated by the rebels.

67 CE
Vespasian, an experienced Roman general, arrives with a large army and regains control of Galilee.

68 CE
Vespasian retakes most of Judea except for Jerusalem and the strongholds of Masada, Machaerus, and Herodium.

69 CE
Fighting breaks out in Jerusalem between three rival Jewish groups, led by Simon Bar Giora, Eleazer ben Simon, and John of Gischala. In Italy, Vespasian becomes emperor after winning a civil war against his rival, Vitellius.

70 CE
The Roman army, now commanded by Titus, son of Vespasian, captures Jerusalem after a six-month siege.

71 CE
Vespasian and Titus celebrate their capture of Jerusalem with a great triumphal procession in Rome. In Judea, the Romans retake Herodium.

72 CE
The Romans capture the Jewish fortress Machaerus.

73 CE
Masada, the last Jewish stronghold, falls to the Romans.

Masada

The last fortress to be captured, in 73 CE, was Herod's palace at Masada. According to the Jewish historian Josephus the rebels chose to die by their own hands rather than be captured. The Romans found more than 900 dead bodies in Masada.

Jerusalem

In 70 CE, Vespasian's son Titus captured Jerusalem, which his army sacked and burned. The Temple was destroyed. This is part of a Jewish house burned down by the Romans. The rooms of the house were covered in soot.

Triumph

In 71 CE, Titus and Vespasian, who was now emperor, celebrated the capture of Jerusalem with a great triumphal procession in Rome. The rebel leaders and the treasures of the Jewish Temple were paraded through the streets of the city.

Victory coin

Titus issued a coin showing a captive Jewish rebel, with hands tied behind his back. He has been stripped of his armor, which is displayed above him. Such coins spread the news of Titus's victory around the Roman Empire.

The Book of Revelation

About thirty years after Paul's last journey, the Christians were still suffering terrible persecution at the hands of the Romans.

They had been tortured and burned and crucified for their faith. Now, the Roman Emperor Domitian had proclaimed himself a god and ordered all his subjects to worship him. The disciple John refused and was exiled—with many others—to the island of Patmos.

One day, he had an extraordinary vision of Judgment Day, with God triumphing gloriously over evil. From out of nowhere, he heard a voice, loud and clear, like a trumpet, saying, "I am Alpha and Omega, the first and the last. Write down what you see." And the voice told him to send what he wrote to seven churches in the province of Asia, as a message of hope and encouragement to his fellow Christians.

> They will be His people, and God Himself will be with them and be their God."

Immediately, John turned to see who had spoken to him. He saw seven golden candlesticks and, standing among them, someone who looked like Jesus. When John saw him, he fell flat at his feet, but Jesus said, "Do not be afraid! I am the first and the last. I am the living one. I was dead, and behold I am alive forever and ever! And I hold the keys of death and Hades."

John looked up and saw a door opening to heaven above him. God was sitting on a magnificent throne, which flashed with lightning and rumbled with thunder. A beautiful rainbow arched above it. Twenty-four elders sat around in a circle on their thrones. Seven torches blazed by God's throne, and a sea of glass stretched away into the distance. And John could see four astonishing creatures that looked like a lion, an ox, a man, and an eagle. But they each had six wings and their bodies were covered with dozens and dozens of eyes staring in different directions. In unison, the four of them chanted, "Holy, holy, holy is the Lord God Almighty who was, and is, and is to come."

In His right hand, God held a large scroll, and all seven of its seals were intact. John wept bitterly because he knew that there was no one worthy enough to break the seals. But then he saw what looked like a lamb, except that it had seven horns and seven eyes. It went up to God and took the scroll from Him. Immediately, the elders fell off their thrones and threw themselves down in front of the lamb. They knew it was the Son of God. After a moment, the many-eyed creatures joined them, bowing low on the ground and folding their wings neatly behind their backs to worship.

Hearing a choir of heavenly voices, John looked up and saw a host of angels. "Worthy is the lamb, who was slain, to receive power and wealth and wisdom and strength and honor and glory and praise!" they chorused.

The lamb started to break open the seals. His seven eyes stood out on stalks as the scroll slowly unrolled to reveal the suffering that was in store. Disaster upon disaster was shown being unleashed on the world and on mankind—war, earthquake, famine, pestilence, plague. And afterward, came Judgment Day, with God sitting on His throne, as it thundered and flashed beneath Him. The great Book of Life lay open on His lap, while everybody, great and small, lined up before Him to be judged.

But, at the very end of his vision, John saw a new heaven on earth. It was the Holy City, the new Jerusalem. The walls were made of solid jasper and the gates were carved out of pearl. The foundations were encrusted with precious jewels on every side. Water from the river of life flowed down the middle of the great street. On each side of it stood the tree of life, rustling with healing leaves and heavy with fruit.

John heard a loud voice coming from the throne above, saying, "Now the dwelling of God is with men, and He will live with them. They will be His people, and God Himself will be with them and be their God. He will wipe away every tear from their eyes. There will be no more death or mourning or crying or pain, for the old order of things has passed away!"

John hears a voice speak to him

335

The Church and Rome

Roman rulers were alarmed by the spread of Christianity. They saw Christians as traitors who hated the Roman gods. Christians also refused to sacrifice to the emperor, which was the main way of showing loyalty to Rome. In the third century CE, Roman emperors made a serious attempt to crush Christianity, executing those who refused to worship their gods. Everything changed in 312 CE, when Constantine, Rome's first Christian emperor, came to power.

Donkey on a cross
To many Romans, the idea of worshiping a crucified criminal was ridiculous. This mocking cartoon, scratched on a wall in Rome, shows a Christian beside a donkey-headed Christ on a cross. The writing says "Alexamenos worships (his) god."

Persecution
Many Christians were killed by wild animals in Roman amphitheaters. This did not stop their faith from spreading. The victims were often eager to become martyrs, certain they would go straight to heaven. Roman audiences were impressed by their bravery.

Constantine
Constantine ruled the West from 312 CE after defeating a rival, Maxentius, in battle. He believed that his victory had been due to Christ's protection. After becoming ruler of the whole empire, in 324 CE, Constantine made Christianity the state religion.

Sol Invictus

Before becoming a Christian, Constantine worshiped the Sun god Sol Invictus, shown with him here. He decided that the birthday of the Sun, on December 25, should be Christ's birthday. Sunday, sacred to the Sun, became the Christian day of rest.

Council of Nicea

Constantine was horrified to discover that Christians disagreed about what they believed. In 325 CE, he summoned 220 church leaders to Nicea, in present-day Turkey, where he persuaded them to agree on a common creed, or statement of belief.

TIMELINE

285 CE
Emperor Diocletian divides the Roman Empire in two. He rules the East while his co-emperor, Maximian, rules the West.

303 CE
Emperor Diocletian begins the worst persecution of Christians.

312 CE
Constantine defeats his rival, Maxentius, becoming emperor of the West.

313 CE
Constantine and the eastern emperor, Licinius, issue the Edict of Milan, proclaiming freedom of worship for Christians.

324 CE
Constantine defeats Licinius, becoming sole emperor.

325 CE
The Council of Nicea agrees on a shared set of Christian beliefs, called the "Nicene Creed."

326 CE
Constantine founds Constantinople as his new Christian capital.

337 CE
Constantine is baptized a Christian, on his deathbed.

A Roman Christ

The Romans' idea of Christ was far removed from the original Galilean Jew. This mosaic shows him as a clean-shaven Roman soldier, wearing the halo of the Sun god. He tramples on a lion and serpent, the forces of evil.

337

People of the Old Testament

AARON
The first high priest of Israel and older brother of Moses. Along with Moses, he tried to persuade Pharaoh to free the Israelites.

ABEDNEGO
Babylonian name given to one of Daniel's three Judean friends, who were thrown into the furnace by King Nebuchadnezzar.

ABEL
Adam and Eve's second son, who was a shepherd. He was murdered by his jealous brother, Cain.

ABIGAIL
King David's beautiful wife, who had first been married to the wealthy Nabal.

ABRAHAM
Chosen by God to be the forefather of the Israelite nation. Abraham was married to Sarah, but through her maidservant Hagar, he had a son named Ishmael. Sarah later bore him a second son, Isaac, whose grandsons were the ancestors of the twelve tribes of Israel.

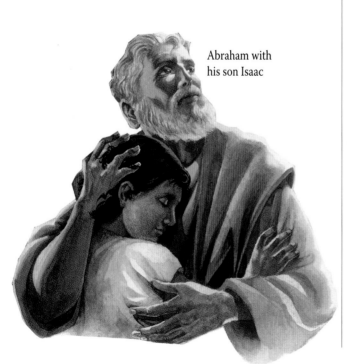

Abraham with his son Isaac

ABSALOM
King David's son, who rebelled against his father in an attempt to seize the throne. He was killed by David's army chief, Joab.

ADAM
The first man created by God and husband of Eve. In Hebrew, Adam means "man" and also humankind.

AHAB
A king of Israel who lived in the time of Elijah. Ahab was married to Jezebel, a Phoenician princess, and allowed her to promote the worship of Baal, a pagan god.

AMNON
King David's first son, who loved his half-sister Tamar. He was killed by his half-brother Absalom.

ARTAXERXES
King Artaxerxes of Persia allowed his cupbearer Nehemiah to go back to Jerusalem and help in the rebuilding of the city.

ASHER
Jacob's eighth son, the second of two boys born to him by Zilpah, who was his wife Leah's maid. Asher was the founder of one of the twelve tribes of Israel, which settled in northwest Canaan.

BALAAM
A soothsayer from Mesopotamia, Balaam was summoned by Balak to curse the Israelites. Instead, having seen the angel of the Lord, he blessed them.

BALAK
King of Moab at the time when Israel entered Canaan. He had asked Balaam to curse the Israelites.

BATHSHEBA
First married to the soldier Uriah the Hittite, she later became the wife of King David, who had plotted the murder of Uriah so that he could marry her. She was the mother of Solomon.

BELSHAZZAR
A Babylonian ruler who had asked Daniel to help interpret the mysterious writing on the wall.

BENJAMIN
Jacob's twelfth and youngest son, and his wife Rachel's second and last child. He was the only full brother of Joseph and founder of the smallest but very important tribe of Israel.

BILHAH
A maidservant to Jacob's wife, Rachel. She gave birth to two of Jacob's sons—Dan and Napthali.

BOAZ
A Bethlehem farmer, who married Ruth. He was the great-grandfather of King David.

CAIN
First son of Adam and Eve, who killed his younger brother, Abel. Cain was a farmer.

Cain

CALEB
One of twelve spies sent ahead by Moses to check out Canaan, the Promised Land.

CYRUS
Founder of the Persian Empire. Under his rule (c. 549–530 BCE), the Israelites were allowed to return to Judah from Babylon.

DAN
Jacob's fifth son and founder of one of the tribes of Israel. His mother was Bilhah, the maidservant of Jacob's favorite wife, Rachel.

DANIEL
An Israelite from the tribe of Judah, who was exiled to Babylon. Daniel was favored by King Nebuchadnezzar because he had a gift for interpreting dreams. He was also thrown into the lions' den by King Darius, but miraculously survived.

DARIUS
In the Book of Daniel, Darius the Mede is described as ruler of Babylon after its conquest in 539 BCE by the Persians. He threw Daniel into the lions' den.

DAVID
The Bethlehem shepherd boy who became the greatest king of Israel. He is also attributed with being the author of many psalms.

DELILAH
The beautiful Philistine woman who betrayed Samson to the Philistines—she tricked him into revealing the secret of his strength, which was his hair.

DINAH
The daughter of Jacob and his first wife Leah.

EBED-MELECH
A palace official who rescued the prophet Jeremiah from the pit.

ELI
The high priest who took care of Samuel when he was a boy and trained him. Eli's own two sons were wicked, and were eventually killed in battle. Samuel took over from Eli as the next high priest.

ELIJAH
One of the greatest prophets of Israel. He confronted Ahab when Ahab tried to encourage his people to worship the pagan god Baal. According to the Bible, he was taken up to heaven in a whirlwind.

ELIMELECH
Husband of Naomi. He was from Bethlehem, but died in Moab.

ELISHA
Disciple and successor to the prophet Elijah. He was an important prophet in Israel during the 9th century BCE.

Daniel

ELKANAH
The husband of Hannah and father of Samuel.

ESAU
Son of Isaac and Rebekah and twin brother of Jacob. He gave his birthright to Jacob for a bowl of stew. He was then tricked out of his father's blessing by Rebekah and Jacob.

ESTHER
Jewish wife of the Persian King Xerxes. She prevented the massacre of the Jewish people.

EVE
In Genesis, Eve was the first woman created by God. She was deceived by a serpent in the garden of Eden. She ate from the forbidden tree, and persuaded Adam (her husband) to eat the fruit. God banished them from Eden because they had disobeyed Him.

GAD
Jacob's seventh son and the founder of one of the tribes of Israel. His mother was Zilpah, who was the maidservant of Jacob's wife Leah.

GIDEON
A judge (an Israelite tribal leader) during the 12th century BCE, who defeated the Midianites and Amalekites.

Moses

GOLIATH
At the time of King David, Goliath was the leading warrior of the Philistine army. He challenged the Israelites to fight with him. David took up the challenge and killed him with a single stone.

HAGAR
The maidservant of Sarah, who was married to Abraham. She was the mother of Abraham's son Ishmael.

HAM
One of Noah's three sons.

HAMAN
An Amalekite who was made chief minister by the Persian King Xerxes. He plotted to massacre the Jews. Haman was sentenced to death when his plans were discovered.

HANNAH
The wife of Elkanah and mother of the prophet Samuel. She was blessed by the high priest Eli as she prayed for a child. Her prayers were answered, and she bore a son named Samuel.

HEZEKIAH
A wise king of Judah, who obeyed God's laws.

ISAAC
The son of Abraham and his wife Sarah, who was born to them late in life. He was the father of Jacob and Esau, and the grandfather of the founders of the twelve tribes of Israel.

ISAIAH
An important 8th-century-BCE prophet, who warned the people of Israel what would happen if they did not obey God's commandments.

ISHMAEL
Abraham's son and half-brother of Isaac. His mother was Hagar, the maidservant of Abraham's wife, Sarah.

ISRAEL
The name God gave to Jacob, meaning "He strives with God." He was the grandson of Abraham and the son of Isaac.

ISSACHAR
Jacob's ninth son, who founded one of the tribes of Israel. His mother was Jacob's wife Leah and he was her fifth son.

JACOB
Son of Isaac and Rebekah, Jacob became known as Israel. He cheated his twin brother, Esau, out of his inheritance. He had twelve sons who became the founders of the tribes of Israel.

JAPHETH
One of Noah's three sons.

JEPHTHAH
An Israelite commander. He sacrificed his only daughter because of a vow he had made to God.

JEREMIAH
A prophet who warned the people of Judah that they would be destroyed if they did not listen to God's word.

JESSE
A farmer in Bethlehem. Jesse had eight sons. The youngest, David, was chosen by God to be the second king of Israel, after Saul.

JETHRO
A priest in the land of Midian and the father-in-law of Moses.

JEZEBEL
A Phoenician princess and King Ahab's scheming wife.

JOAB
The commander of King David's army.

JONAH
A prophet who tried to escape God's calling to save the city of Nineveh. He was swallowed by a big fish, but survived.

JONATHAN
The eldest son of King Saul and a close friend of David.

JOSEPH
Jacob's eleventh son—but the first with his favorite wife, Rachel. Joseph founded one of the tribes of Israel but, as a boy, was sold into slavery in Egypt. He later rose to a position of great power and was the savior of his own people.

JOSHUA
Successor of Moses. Joshua led the people of Israel across the Jordan River into Canaan.

JOSIAH
Became king of Judah when he was only eight years old. He repaired the Temple in Jerusalem.

JUDAH
Jacob's fourth son, who founded one of the twelve tribes of Israel. His mother was Jacob's first wife, Leah.

LABAN
The brother of Rebekah, uncle of Jacob, and father of Leah and Rachel.

Laban

Jacob

LEAH
Daughter of Laban, sister of Rachel, and first wife of Jacob. Mother of Reuben, Simeon, Levi, Judah, Issachar, Zebulon—and one daughter, Dinah.

LEVI
The third son of Jacob and Leah and founder of the Levite tribe of Israel, which was set aside for the service of God.

LOT
Abraham's nephew who lived in Sodom. His wife was turned into a pillar of salt as she fled from Sodom and Gomorrah.

MESHACH
One of Daniel's three Judean friends, who were thrown into the furnace by King Nebuchadnezzar.

MICHAL
Saul's daughter who became David's first wife.

MIRIAM
The sister of Moses and Aaron. Miriam danced and sang with the Israelite women after they had crossed the Red Sea.

Rachel

MORDECAI
The cousin of Esther and her foster father.
Mordecai saved King Xerxes's life.

MOSES
A Levite by birth, but brought up at Pharaoh's
court. He led the Israelites out of slavery and
received the Law from God on Mount Sinai.

NAAMAN
The commander of the Syrian army whose skin
disease was healed by Elisha.

NABAL
A wealthy but mean Calebite, married to
Abigail—who later became the wife of David.

NABOTH
A vineyard owner in Samaria whose death was
engineered by King Ahab's wife, Jezebel.

NAOMI
A widow who was the mother-in-law of Ruth.

NAPHTALI
Jacob's sixth son. He founded one of the
tribes of Israel. His mother was Bilhah,
the maidservant of Jacob's wife, Rachel.

NATHAN
A prophet who rebuked King David for
committing adultery with Bathsheba and
arranging the death of her husband, Uriah.

NEBUCHADNEZZAR
The king of Babylon who captured Jerusalem
and took the people of Jerusalem into exile.

NEHEMIAH
A cupbearer to King Artaxerxes. He was
allowed to go back to Jerusalem and help in
the rebuilding of the city.

NOAH
Built an ark as instructed by God so that he
and his family, along with the animals he took,
would survive the flood. Noah was the father
of Shem, Ham, and Japheth.

ORPAH
The daughter-in-law of Naomi and sister of Ruth.

POTIPHAR
Pharaoh's captain of the guard, who bought
the young Joseph as a slave in Egypt.

RACHEL
Jacob's favorite wife and the mother of
Joseph and Benjamin.

RAHAB
The woman who hid two Israelite spies in her
house in Jericho and helped them to escape.

REBEKAH
The wife of Isaac and the mother of Jacob and Esau.

REHOBOAM
Inherited the throne of Israel from his father,
Solomon, but the nation divided under his rule.

REUBEN
Eldest son of Jacob and his wife, Leah, and
ancestral head of one of the tribes of Israel.

RUTH
The Moabite daughter-in-law of Naomi.
She married a farmer named Boaz.

SAMSON
He possessed super-human strength because of
his long hair. A sworn enemy of the Philistines,
Samson was betrayed by Delilah.

SAMUEL
Son of Elkanah and Hannah. He was the prophet who anointed Saul and David as kings of Israel.

SARAH
Abraham's wife and the mother of Isaac.

SAUL
A Benjamite, Saul was chosen by God to be the first king of Israel. He was the father of Jonathan.

SENNACHERIB
The ruler of Assyria whose army besieged Jerusalem in the reign of King Hezekiah.

SHADRACH
One of Daniel's three Judean friends.

SHEBA
The queen who visited King Solomon to see for herself if he was as wise as everybody said.

SHEM
Eldest of Noah's three sons.

SIMEON
Jacob's second son with his wife Leah. He was the founder of one of the twelve tribes of Israel.

Simeon

Solomon

SOLOMON
Son of David and Bathsheba. He was the third king of Israel. Solomon built the Temple in Jerusalem and was renowned for his wisdom.

URIAH
Married to Bathsheba, Uriah was a loyal soldier. He was sent to his death by King David.

VASHTI
Xerxes's first wife, who refused to obey her husband and was thus banished.

XERXES
The Persian ruler who divorced his wife Vashti to marry Esther.

ZEBULON
Jacob's tenth son, who founded one of the twelve tribes of Israel. His mother was Leah, Jacob's first wife.

ZEDEKIAH
The puppet king chosen by Nebuchadnezzar to rule Judah after Jerusalem had been conquered by the Babylonians.

People of the New Testament

AGABUS
A prophet who predicted that Paul would be imprisoned.

ANANIAS
A follower of Jesus, who restored Saul's sight after he had been left blinded on the road to Damascus.

ANDREW
A fisherman from Galilee and one of Jesus's twelve disciples. He was the brother of Peter.

ANNA
A prophetess who recognized the baby Jesus as the Messiah when he was presented in the Temple.

AUGUSTUS
First emperor of Rome (c. 31–14 CE). Born Octavius, but took the name Augustus, which means "lofty." Jesus was born during his reign.

BARABBAS
The criminal who was chosen by the crowd to be set free instead of Jesus.

Cornelius

BARNABAS
Paul's companion on his first missionary journey.

BARTHOLOMEW
One of Jesus's twelve disciples who was, reputedly, flayed alive, and the patron saint of tanners.

CAIAPHAS
The high priest at the Temple in Jerusalem when Jesus was arrested and crucified.

CLEOPAS
One of two men who met Jesus on the road to Emmaus after Jesus had risen from the dead.

CORNELIUS
A Roman centurion in Caesarea. Together with his family, he was converted to Christianity by Peter.

DEMETRIUS
A silversmith in Ephesus. Demetrius made shrines to the goddess Artemis. When Paul's teaching threatened his livelihood, he started a riot against Paul.

ELIZABETH
The cousin of Jesus's mother Mary, and mother of John the Baptist. She was married to Zechariah, and had been childless for many years. According to the Gospel of Luke, an angel told Elizabeth she would have a son.

EUTYCHUS
The young man who fell out of the window while Paul was preaching. According to Acts 20, Eutychus was brought back to life by Paul.

GABRIEL
Name of an angel, or heavenly messenger, who appears four times in the Bible.

Jesus

HEROD AGRIPPA
Grandson of
Herod the Great.
As king of Judah
(c. 37–44 CE), he
persecuted the
Christians to gain
favor with the
influential Jews.

HEROD ANTIPAS
Herod the Great's
son, who ordered the
beheading of John the
Baptist at the request of his niece,
Salome. Antipas was tetrarch (ruler) of
Galilee and Perea (4 BCE–39 CE).

HEROD THE GREAT
King of Judea (c. 37–4 BCE) at the time
of Christ's birth, and responsible for
rebuilding the Temple.

HERODIAS
Herod Antipas's wife and granddaughter
of Herod the Great. She told her daughter,
Salome, to ask for John the Baptist's head
because he proclaimed her marriage to
Herod as being immoral.

JAIRUS
The head of the synagogue whose daughter
was healed by Jesus.

JAMES
Son of Zebedee, brother of John, and one
of the twelve disciples.

JAMES
Son of Alphaeus and brother of John.
James was one of the twelve disciples.

JESUS
Thought by Christians to be the Son of
God and the Messiah. He was born in
Bethlehem to Mary and Joseph.

JOHN
Son of Zebedee, brother of James,
and one of the twelve disciples. John
was very close to Jesus and is thought
to be the author of the fourth Gospel.
He was present at the transfiguration
and in the garden of Gethsemane

JOHN THE BAPTIST
Son of Elizabeth and Zechariah and cousin
of Jesus. John was a Jewish holy man and
prophet, who called on people to repent,
and offered to baptize them.

JOSEPH
A carpenter who lived in Nazareth. He was
married to Mary, the mother of Jesus. Joseph
was descended from the house of David.

JOSEPH
Also known as Barsabbas, he was one
of the two men whose names were put
forward to replace the disciple Judas,
who had betrayed Jesus.

JOSEPH OF ARIMATHEA
A wealthy follower of
Jesus and member of
the Sanhedrin. He took
Jesus's body down from
the cross and buried it
in a tomb.

Joseph

Mary

JUDAS ISCARIOT
Son of Simon Iscariot and one of the twelve disciples. Judas betrayed Jesus for thirty pieces of silver. He later killed himself.

JULIUS
The Roman centurion who escorted Paul to Rome.

LAZARUS
The brother of Martha and Mary, who lived in Bethany. According to John's Gospel, Jesus raised him from the dead.

LUKE
A physician and thought to be the author of Acts and the Gospel of Luke. He accompanied Paul on his missionary journeys.

LYDIA
A rich business woman. Lydia lived in Philippi. She was a gentile who was attracted to the Jewish way of life and was baptized by Paul. She became Paul's first European convert.

MARK
Accompanied Paul and Barnabas on their first missionary journey, and is thought to be the author of the Gospel of Mark.

MARTHA
The elder sister of Lazarus and Mary, and friend of Jesus. Martha lived in Bethany.

MARY
Married to the carpenter Joseph, Mary was the mother of Jesus.

MARY
The sister of Martha and Lazarus, who lived in Bethany. She was a very close friend of Jesus and anointed his feet with perfume before his death.

MARY
The mother of the disciple James. Along with Jesus's mother Mary and Mary Magdalene, she was present at Jesus's crucifixion.

MARY MAGDALENE
A follower of Jesus. Mary Magdalene was present when Jesus was crucified, and was the first witness of his resurrection. In the Bible, Jesus appeared to her first and told her of his coming ascension into heaven.

MATTHEW
Also known as Levi, Matthew was a tax collector from Capernaum. He was one of the twelve disciples, and is also thought to be the author of the first Gospel.

MATTHIAS
The man who was chosen to replace Judas Iscariot as one of the twelve disciples.

NICODEMUS
Along with Joseph of Arimathea, Nicodemus helped to take Christ's body down from the cross and prepare it for burial.

PAUL
Born a Pharisee in Tarsus, Paul was at first a persecutor of the Christians. But he was converted after he saw a vision of Jesus, changing his Hebrew name of Saul to Paul. He spread the word on his missionary journeys and helped to build up the early Church.

Paul

PETER
A fisherman and brother of Andrew,
Peter was one of the twelve disciples.
During the trial of Jesus, he denied knowing
him three times. He was the first disciple
chosen by Jesus Christ. His original name
was Simon, but Jesus renamed him Cephas,
meaning "rock" in Aramaic. He is better
known by the Greek version of his name,
Peter, which also means rock.

PHILIP
One of the twelve disciples. He came
from the town of Bethsaida.

PONTIUS PILATE
The Roman governor—or procurator—
of Judea from c. 26–36 CE. Pilate
condemned Jesus to death although
he knew Jesus was innocent.

PUBLIUS
The governor of Malta when Paul
and his companions were shipwrecked.
Paul helped to heal Publius's father.

RHODA
The servant girl who answered the
door to Peter after he had escaped
from prison.

SALOME
The daughter of Herodias, who danced for
her stepfather, Herod Antipas. As a reward
for pleasing him, she asked for the head of
John the Baptist on a plate.

SAUL (see Paul)
Hebrew name for Paul.

SILAS
Paul's companion on some of his
missionary journeys.

SIMON
One of the twelve disciples, sometimes
known as Simon the Zealot.

SIMON
A tanner from Joppa. Peter was staying
at Simon's house when he had a vision.

SIMON OF CYRENE
The man from Cyrene who helped Jesus
to carry the cross.

STEPHEN
The first Christian martyr, who was stoned
to death by some Jews.

ZECHARIAH
Married to Elizabeth, who was the cousin
of Jesus's mother, Mary. Zechariah was
the father of John the Baptist. According
to Luke's Gospel, he doubted the angel's
prophecy that he would have a son. As a
result of his disbelief, he was struck dumb.

Zechariah

Index

Note: page references in **bold** indicate background information on the subject.

H

Hadassah *see* Esther
Hagar 32, 34
Haggai 183
hailstones 73
Ham 23, 26
Haman 178–**81**
Hammurabi, king of Babylon 28, 29
Hannah 110
Haran 30, 44, 45, 46, 50
Harod, Spring of 96
Hasmonean dynasty 190, 211
healings
    by Elisha 160–1
    by Jesus 223, 230–1, 236–7, 243, 276
    by Paul 320, 322–3, 329
    by Peter 308
    see also dead, raising the
heaven
    beggar in 260
    creation of 18
    Jesus taken up to 304–5
    see also Kingdom of Heaven
Hebron 88, 132, 136
hell 260
Hellenism 190–**1**
Herod Agrippa, king of Judea 318–19
Herod Antipas, governor of Galilee
    218, **224**, 292
    and John the Baptist 240–1
Herod Antipater 211
Herod the Great, king of Judea **210–11**
    alarm at birth of Jesus 208–9, 212
    massacre of the innocents 213
    death of 213, 292
Herodias 240–1
Herodium 210–11, 332
Hezekiah, king of Judah 153, 163
"high places" 91
Hilkiah 164–5
Hiram, king of Tyre 140
Holy Spirit
    disciples and 304, 306–7, 309, 316
    gentiles and 317
    Paul (Saul) and 312, 320
    Stephen and 310
honey 102, 104
Hophni 112
Horeb, rock at 79
Huldah 165

I

Idumea 210, 211
iron 101
Isaac 33, 34, 38–9
    marries Rebekah 40–1, 42
    sons of 42–4
Isaiah 162, 163, 202, 310
Ish-Bosheth 132
Ishmael 32, 33, 34

Ishmaelites 53
Ishtar Gate 168–9, 182
Israel
    Jacob given name of 51
    earliest mention of 57
    separated from Judah 148
    Assyrians and **152–3**, 163
Israelites
    as Egyptian slaves 66–7, 68, 70
    escape from Egypt 56, 69, 70–9
    and Passover feast 74, 165
    journey to Canaan 76–87
    and pagan gods 82–3, 96, 102, 150–1,
        163, 165, 166
    defeat Amorites 84, 92
    in the wilderness 88–9
    grief for Moses 89
    win Battle of Jericho 95
    defeat Midianites 96–7
    defeat Ammonites 98–9, 116–17, 134
    defeated by Philistines 112–13
    decide to choose a king 114
    forbidden to sell ancestral lands 154
    see also Jews
Issachar 49

J

Jabbok River 51, 98
Jabesh 116–17, 131
Jacob
    and Esau 42–4, 51
    ladder of 45
    and Rachel 46–9
    sons of 49, 52–3, 62–5
    new name 51
Jairus's daughter 236–7
James, son of Alphaeus 223
James, son of Zebedee 223, 236, 250,
    287, 288, 318
James the Just, brother of Christ 315
Japheth 23, 26
Jason 191
jealousy 22
Jebusites **128**, 132
Jehoiachin, king of Judah 166
Jehu, king of Israel 152, 153
Jephthah 98–9
    daughter of 99
Jeremiah 11, 166–7, 170–1,
    183, 213
Jericho 84, 87, 89
    Israelite spies in 92–3
    Battle of 94–5
    prophets in 156
Jerome, St 8
Jerusalem
    as City of David 11, **128–9**, 132, 134
    Queen of Sheba in 145
    attacks on 11, 153, 163, 166, 170–1,
        182, 183
    rebuilding of 184–5
    religious pilgrimages to 189
    Jesus enters 8, 274–5
    Jesus predicts destruction of 275

at Passover 293
    disciples instructed to stay in 304
    harvest festival celebrations 306
    Lions' Gate 310
    Saul (Paul) joins disciples in 313
    Paul returns to 324–5
    sacked by Romans 332–3
    John's vision of the new Jerusalem 335
    see also Temple in Jerusalem
Jesse 118–19
Jesus Christ
    new covenant of 11
    birth of 192–3, 198–9, 202–5, 208–9
    circumcision and presentation 206–7
    childhood 207, 212–13, 214–15
    John baptizes 216–17, 218–19
    Devil tempts in the wilderness 220–1
    chooses his disciples 222–3
    in Galilee 222–3, **224–5**, 226–7,
        230–3, 236–7
    healings by 223, 230–3, 236–7,
        243, 276
    first miracle at wedding in Cana 226–7
    Sermon on the Mount 228–9
    calms the storm 234
    casts out evil spirits 235
    and death of John the Baptist 241
    feeding of the five thousand 242–3
    walks on water 244–5, 246–7
    the transfiguration 250–1
    raises Lazarus from the dead 252–3
    and the children 264
    and the rich young man 265
    and Zacchaeus the tax collector 266–7
    enters Jerusalem 8, 274–5
    called the Messiah 195, 275, 280
    weeps 275
    anger with the Temple traders 276
    teaches in the Temple 277
    predicts destruction of Temple 279
    anointed by Mary 280
    prepares for Passover 282
    Judas decides to betray 280–1, 282,
        285, 288–9
    washes feet of disciples 282–3
    at Last Supper 11, 284–5
    arrested in Gethsemane 286–7,
        288–9, 290
    denied by Peter 290–1
    brought before the Sanhedrin 294
    believed to be the Son of God 294,
        296, 313, 337
    brought before Pilate 295
    asked if he is king of the Jews 295
    flogged and mocked 295
    crucified 292, 296–7, 315
    moved to tomb 296
    resurrection 298–9, 314
    appears to Cleopas and companion 300
    appears to disciples 301
    ascends into heaven 304–5
    Peter heals in the name of 308–9
    Stephen speaks to Sanhedrin about 310
    appears to Saul and Ananias 312
    fish as emblem of 315
    appears to John 334
    see also parables
Jethro 68, 70

ACKNOWLEDGMENTS

The publisher would like to thank the following for their kind permission to reproduce their photographs:

(Key: a–above; b–below/bottom; c–center; l–left; r–right; t–top)

8 akg-images: Erich Lessing (bc); Rabatti—Domingie (br). **The Art Archive**: Alfredo Dagli Orti/Scrovegni Chapel Padua (tr). **Corbis**: West Semitic Research/Dead Sea Scrolls Foundation/Bruce E. Zuckerman (bl). **The Schøyen Collection Oslo & London**: (c). **9 akg-images**: British Library (tr) (bl); CDA/Guillemot (tl). **The Bridgeman Art Library**: Bildarchiv Steffens/Universitatsbibliothek, Gottingen, Germany (br). **10 Alamy Images**: Mary Evans Picture Library (l). **Corbis**: Godong/P. Deliss (br); David H. Wells (tr). **11 akg-images**: Erich Lessing (cl) (b). **Alamy Images**: Visual Arts Library (London) (r). **Private Collection**: (t). **14–15 akg-images**: Erich Lessing. **16 akg-images**: Erich Lessing (r). **The Bridgeman Art Library**: Victoria & Albert Museum, London, UK (c). **Corbis**: Richard T. Nowitz (tl). **17 Alamy Images**: Rough Guides (br). **Getty Images**: The Bridgeman Art Library (cl). **The Egypt Exploration Society/The Imaging Papyri Project, Oxford**: (t). **28 Photolibrary**: Nico Tondini (b). **US Department of Defense**: D. Wilkerson/US Army Corps of Engineers (c). **29 Alamy Images**: Visual Arts Library (London) (b). **The Art Archive**: British Museum (r); Gianni Dagli Orti/Musée du Louvre Paris (tl). **56 akg-images**: Erich Lessing (br). **Werner Forman Archive**: (l). **57 akg-images**: Kunsthistorisches Museum, Vienna (r). **Photolibrary**: Stephanie Lamberti (tl). **Zev Radovan/www.biblelandpictures.com**: (bl). **60–61 akg-images**: Erich Lessing. **86–87 Alamy Images**: Jon Arnold Images Ltd. **90 akg-images**: Erich Lessing (b). **90–91 Photolibrary**: Hanan Isachar. **91 akg-images**: Erich Lessing (br). **DK Images**: Alan Hills & Barbara Winter (c) The British Museum (tr) (bl). **100 Zev Radovan/www.biblelandpictures.com**: (l). **100–101 Werner Forman Archive. 101 akg-images**: Erich Lessing (c). **Zev Radovan/www.biblelandpictures.com**: (tl). **128–129 Todd Bolen/bibleplaces.com. 146–147 Alamy Images**: Ilan Rosen. **152 akg-images**: Erich Lessing (tl) (bl). **Professir David Ussishkin and the Institute of Archaeology of Tel Aviv University**: (r). **153 akg-images**: Erich Lessing (t) (c). **The Bridgeman Art Library**: Boltin Picture Library (b). **168–169 Alamy Images**: The Print Collector. **182 Alamy Images**: Robert Harding Picture Library Ltd (b). **DK Images**: Alan Hills & Barbara Winter (c) The British Museum (tr). **182–183 Alamy Images**: Images&Stories (c). **183 akg-images**: National Museum, Teheran (tr). **Alamy Images**: Robert Preston (tl). **Corbis**: Paul Almasy (tc). **Zev Radovan/www.biblelandpictures.com**: (clb). **190 akg-images**: Erich Lessing (l) (br). **191 akg-images**: Erich Lessing (tr). **Zev Radovan/www.biblelandpictures.com**: (tl). **The Schøyen Collection Oslo & London**: (br). **192–193 akg-images**: Erich Lessing. **194 akg-images**: (br).

The Bridgeman Art Library: British Library Board (tr). **topfoto.co.uk**: Ann Ronan Picture Library (tl). **195 akg-images**: British Library (c); Cameraphoto (tr); Erich Lessing (tl). **Private Collection**: (bl). David Towersey: (br). **210 Alamy Images**: Israel images (br). **Zev Radovan/www.biblelandpictures.com**: (bl). **210–211 Corbis**: Charles & Josette Lenars (c). **211 Alamy Images**: Israel images (tr). **216–217 Photolibrary**: Jon Arnold Travel. **224 Zev Radovan/www.biblelandpictures.com**: (tl). **225 akg-images**: Erich Lessing (b). **Art Directors & TRIP**: Hanan Isachar (t). **244–245 Photolibrary**: Jon Arnold Travel. **262 Israel Ministry of Tourism**: (tr). **Zev Radovan/www.biblelandpictures.com**: (bl). **262–263 Corbis**: Richard T. Nowitz. **263 Alamy Images**: Israel images (br). **Corbis**: Yonathan Weitzman (tr). **278–279 Corbis**: Benjamin Rondel. **286–287 Rex Features**: Francis Dean. **292 akg-images**: Museo della Civiltà Romana (l). **Zev Radovan/www.biblelandpictures.com**: (c) (r). **293 akg-images**: Peter Connolly (b); Museo della Civiltà Romana (tl). **314 akg-images**: Bibliotheque Nationale (cl). **The Art Archive**: Alfredo Dagli Orti/Museo Civico Pisa (r). **V&A Images**: Photo Catalogue (tl); Gianni Dagli Orti/Archaeological Museum Sousse, Tunisia (tr). **315 The Art Archive**: Alfredo Dagli Orti/Galleria degli Uffizi Florence (tl). **326–327 Corbis**: K. & H. Benser. **332 DK Images**: Courtesy of the Vatican Museum (tr). **Zev Radovan/www.biblelandpictures.com**: (tl). **332–333 akg-images**: Peter Connolly (b). **333 Alamy Images**: Israel images (tr). **Israel Ministry of Tourism**: (tl). **Zev Radovan/www.biblelandpictures.com**: (c). **336 akg-images**: (tl). **Alamy Images**: The Print Collector (r). **Corbis**: Christie's Images (bl). **337 akg-images**: Erich Lessing (br). **The Art Archive**: Gianni Dagli Orti/Roger Cabal Collection (tr). **Photo12.com**: ARJ (tl).

Jacket images: *Front*: Steve Noon (illustration); *Back*: Nilesh Mistry (illustration); *Front, Back, and Spine*: Roman Dekan (swirls), Pamela Cowart-Rickman (stars), Kathy Konkle (doves).

US Editor: Margaret Parrish
Indexer: Jackie Brind
Proofreader: Niki Foreman

All other images © Dorling Kindersley
For further information see: www.dkimages.com